D0464878

75992   D
                           727
Gafencu   G313
                           1970
Last days of Europe

Date Due

APR 23 '83			
MAY 7 '83			

CHABOT
COLLEGE
LIBRARY

25555 Hesperian Boulevard
Hayward, California 94545

 PRINTED IN U.S.A.

LAST DAYS OF EUROPE

LAST DAYS
OF EUROPE

A
DIPLOMATIC JOURNEY
IN 1939

BY
GRIGORE GAFENCU
FORMER RUMANIAN MINISTER FOR FOREIGN AFFAIRS
AND AMBASSADOR TO RUSSIA

TRANSLATED BY
E. FLETCHER-ALLEN

ARCHON BOOKS
1970

Copyright, 1948, by Grigore Gafencu
Reprinted 1970 by arrangement with Yale University Press
in an unaltered and unabridged edition

ISBN: 0-208-00955-8
[Reproduced from a copy in the Yale University Library]
Library of Congress Catalog Card Number: 73-120373
Printed in the United States of America

CONTENTS

ILLUSTRATIONS

Facing page

PREFACE

IN this book I write of things seen in 1939. They were seen with prewar eyes, and it is as they then engraved themselves on my mind that I have endeavored to describe them.

I know with what caution this method should be followed, how easily the "diplomatic" presentation of a world so changed by events may leave a false impression. What seemed true before the war is no longer truth today. Between that period, already so distant, when the drama was beginning to take shape among the calculations of politicians and the formulas of diplomats, and today when the survivors are groping in the ruins for something on which to pin their hopes, havoc unimaginable has raged. War, with massacre and destruction in its train, tore the peoples asunder, while vile passions ravaged individual men, racked their bodies, and killed their spirit. Catastrophe filled the whole world, crushing everything and leaving its imprint on every mind. It was the only *reality* that counted—the reality which determined the "responsibilities" and, according to their moral worth or their infamy, fixed the places of each of the protagonists in the great drama.

Nothing can more definitely illustrate the extent of the catastrophe than the fate that, in a brief six years, has befallen the principal characters in the action described in this book. Colonel Beck is dead, after having known the bitterness of defeat and the misery of exile. Von Ribbentrop and Göring died as war criminals. The devastating storm has shaken kings and princes. King Boris is dead; and Prince Paul, driven from the regency by an uprising of the Serb people, has taken refuge in South Africa. King Carol is in Brazil, King Leopold is in Geneva. Mr. Chamberlain and General Metaxas are dead. President Hacha also is dead. Ciano has been shot by order of Mussolini and the Germans.

Mussolini, slain by Italian partisans, has been exhibited in a square in Milan, along with Starace and others. Finally, Hitler, the evil genius, protected by the Furies until the tragedy was utterly fulfilled, has disappeared last of all, "dissolved" in the ruins of the Reich Chancellery.

These modest recollections are not published merely to distract attention from the profound upheaval caused by such events. How could they hope to lighten the grim picture which war has painted? Yet, inversely, by balancing the ruin and desolation of today's scene with the course diplomatic action took in 1939, they may serve some useful purpose. Seen after the event, the early efforts to preserve peace reveal an astounding weakness and futility, while the agency which consciously drove on to disaster becomes an unleashing of demoniacal forces. In such a study as this, the reader who has suffered and has understood will color and stress the picture for himself—which the author has refrained from doing. Thus he will join that countless jury which, on the evidence of painful experience, is called upon to play an active part in deciding the verdict of history.

The study of the last diplomatic moves of the former Europe raises two equally dramatic problems. The first relates to Hitlerian Germany and its action on neighboring peoples.

Was there any *necessity* which made for war? On the eve of the conflict, it was impossible to believe this to be so.

The Reich did not find itself in an economic situation which made peace insupportable. The closed economy to which it had restricted itself had not prevented it from extending its outlets or from conquering one market after another toward the east. Of all the great continental states, the German Reich appeared most capable of profiting by a long period of peace. It was developing its machinery, expanding its production, and perfecting its technique at a rate with which neither its neighbors to the west nor Soviet Russia could keep pace. Certainly, thanks to its prodigious advance, it was better equipped for war than any other country; but it had the greatest interest in maintaining peace. For it was to be foreseen that war, like a far-reaching revolution, would everywhere arouse latent energies, and would transform certain empires, with vastly greater resources than those at Germany's disposal, into formidable military powers. In provoking a war, the Reich would force its own rhythm of technical development on the world, and risk being left behind by richer and better situated adversaries. How could anyone credit Germany with such intentions?

On the political plane, war was no less hazardous an undertaking for the German Empire. By putting the accent on the need of the German "mass" for expansion and power, the Reich risked raising the claims of masses infinitely more numerous, capable of breaking its forward urge and reducing still further its "vital" living space.

For such realities to be disregarded, there must have been an element of madness in the German people's mentality, and in that of its leaders, also, a madness whose force and influence it was difficult to forecast. Yet such a madness was not foreign to Europe. It was that "spirit of invasion," of which a political writer of the last century, Emile Montaigu, has said (in terms which are worth recalling) that "it exists, and will exist, until Europe has again found its lost unity, or, shall I say, until it has found its new unity.

"The spirit of invasion is the aspiration to world dominion." And the moralist added: "This desire, which seems like the dream of a lunatic, has nevertheless been the determining motive behind more than one action which has upset the world. . . . Unity through world dominion means the triumph of external forms, the hypocrisy of appearances; it means tyranny and the constraint of men's souls, the artificial reign of a system or a mechanical force substituted throughout the civilized world for the free development of life and the spontaneous expression of the intimate forms of being."

It is astonishing to reread these lines written in 1858: "A just chastisement has never failed to overtake these paroxysms of pride. Moral breakdown, or furious dementia, has seized the countries where this idea reigns, and the peoples which sought to impose it. Thereby they have lost the virtues which these furious desires roused in them, and they have not regained others. On the other hand, they have learned to know the exact nature of a certain vice, what utility it has, and the profit to be drawn from it. . . . Yet this conception of pride, which is always fatal to the people concerned, and is always followed by prompt chastisement, has not disappeared from the world. . . ." [1]

It was, indeed, to this "spirit of invasion" and its deep unrest which periodically upsets our continent that Europe was delivered. Few statesmen were capable of foreseeing the nature and gravity of the danger. Most of them calculated the chances of conflict while trying to discover the "interest" and the "motives" of the presumed aggressor. They thought to find political solutions, first of all by paying due regard to his self-love, and then by erecting a slender barrier of security formulas in his way. They did not seem to understand that the evil they had to face constituted—as Professor Jung was to call it—"the greatest mental epidemic since the Middle Ages."

The Hitlerian invasion was to stand out from all the other conquests which sought to enslave Europe in modern times, by reason of its fierce will to create "unity," not only on the plane of brute force but also, and above all, by debasing and perverting men's minds. European unity was to be brought about by the negation of Europe and the renunciation of all faith in the essential values of civilization. This "lunatic's dream" could not, of course, be realized. It carried within

1. Emile Montaigu, *Libres opinions morales et historiques* (Paris, 1858).

itself the vacuum wherein it was condemned to collapse after a thousand disasters. But its influence was to exert itself far beyond the frontiers of Germany, and was to shake those consciences and wills which were necessary for the defense of society. Well before the German armies had embarked on war, contagious ideas had already broken down strong positions of resistance on the Continent. The spiritual capitulation of certain individuals and certain political circles had weakened both the popular instinct for conservation and the will to fight. Events might have taken another course, and Europe might have avoided humiliation and dishonor, if the revolt against Nazi thought had been more spontaneous, more violent, and more general.

It appears today more clearly than anyone could have seen it in 1939 that the insufficiency of prewar diplomatic efforts (efforts, however, which were devoid of neither good will nor persistence) was largely due to the absence of a deep moral reaction against the absurd and sacrilegious Hitlerism.

Through not having developed such a resistance in time, Europe was destined to see the personal action of the German dictator become ever more imperious and decisive. Never was history more exclusively subjected to the will of one man. Diplomacy was henceforth impotent to check Hitler's will, loudly proclaiming his dream as he did, not masking his ambitions or his designs. Because he was fifty years old, because he believed that he could no longer wait, because he felt himself ripe for attempting the impossible adventure, the old Europe was destined to live its last days and the world to slip into the most frightful of wars.

But the man whom men could no longer halt was himself to lose control of events. His action, which no longer had anything human about it in spite of its precisely calculated external manifestations, was to liberate forces not subject to his will. Like the sorcerer's apprentice, he was to lose the formula which conjured up the elements. And fate, set in movement by the aberrations of a man possessed, was to strike with powerful, blind force before the final scene which was to take on the significance of a judgment of God.

The most striking reflection of supernatural forces was shown in Hitler's mind. He had gone to war without God or Providence. His first speech as a belligerent, delivered on September 1, 1939, was a hymn to his triumphant "I": "*I* have made a last effort, *I* have worked things out, *I* have declared; *I* have noted; *I* have decided to speak to Poland; *I* have decided to resolve the Danzig problem, the question of the Corridor, the question of peace . . . ; *I* shall conduct this struggle against all comers. . . ." Then came the foolish, fatal words: "Once more *I* have taken the position most dear and sacred to me. *I* shall depart from it only after victory is won, or else—*I shall not see the end.*" This was a pledge with death, but above all it was a challenge; for on that day there was no question of defeat. "*I* have said that, if our will is strong enough, our will and German steel will break and vanquish distress itself." Having set out to vanquish distress and death, Hitler acknowledged no external aid. No appeal to divine protection diminished his paean of pride.

Only much later, on the occasion of the first reverses suffered in Russia, did Providence appear in the Führer's speeches. At first he only addressed to it a recall to order: how did Providence intend to justify to the German people the painful defeats? Then, as victory increasingly went to the other side, the allusions became more frequent, the appeals more pressing. Hitler could scarcely hide the bitterness that the ways of Providence caused him. He nevertheless persisted in believing that he was in intimate association with Providence. Therefore he was not yet willing to cancel his trust in it. Providence would certainly end by saving him.

It needed the great reverses of 1944, the invasion of German territory by the Russians, and the Allied landing in

Europe to persuade Hitler to fall back on a still higher authority. The Almighty was hastily called upon to come to the rescue, when the German will and German steel were yielding on all fronts. Hitler overwhelmed the Almighty with favors, going so far as to concede to him a position equal to his own in the National Socialist hierarchy. His last speech, delivered on January 30, 1945, was heavy with the sense of terror in face of the implacable march of doom. In it the name of the Almighty is invoked ten times with gloomy fervor. "The Almighty has created our people; always He has protected me; on the day of the attempt against my life He saved me; He will never abandon me, I know it . . . ; when we appear before the Almighty, we shall seek His grace and His blessing."

But it was too late. No longer could anything stay the fulfillment of a somber destiny. The ephemeral Greater Reich was crumbling everywhere. Death was already at the door, demanding its own. Of all the agreements, of all the treaties contracted in anticipation of war in a panic-stricken continent, when the storm had spent itself there remained only the pact which Hitler had made with Death. The day dawned which Hitler had pledged himself never to see. Would he keep his word for once; or would he try to trick Death also?

The Führer disappeared and the mistrust associated with him was not dissipated. Contrary to all probability, since it is he who is in question, the world still fears another piece of deceit.

The second problem concerns the relations between the western powers and Soviet Union.

The attempts made in 1939 to save the peace led to the Moscow negotiations between England, France, and Russia. Discussions ceased on August 21. On September 1 Hitler attacked Poland.

Today, new negotiations are taking place between the

U.S.S.R. and the western world. Once again peace and the fate of the world depend upon their outcome.

It is tempting to compare these two diplomatic actions, and to search the still recent past for the causes of a failure which, should it be renewed, would provoke disaster anew.

The present situation is certainly not identical with that before the war. At that time there was an ambitious empire in the center of Europe which disturbed relations between the states in order to safeguard its liberty of action and to impose its will to power. This element of dissociation is no longer to be feared today. From west to east the road seems to be open. Russians and westerners have drawn closer together after the terrible trials which they have overcome in common.

Unfortunately the Hitlerian Reich did not go down alone. The senseless battle it waged against Europe prostrated and ruined the whole Continent. Smitten in its prestige, deprived of its radiance, fallen in the scale of political values diminished, divided, humiliated and almost emptied of its substance, Europe must be a great vacuum for some time to come. In this vacuum it is more difficult to negotiate than it would have been in 1939. All the status acquired in the former Europe, all the material and spiritual possessions for which the nations had struggled for centuries, the established order which assured to each state its rights, and finally the general equilibrium, today seem again in doubt. The powers which have retained the privilege of negotiation possess a disturbing freedom of movement. Nothing any longer limits the sphere of their negotiations. This renders their task singularly difficult. The same difficulties arise which the west and the Soviet east have previously had to face; time has only increased certain fundamental divergencies. Today, as in 1939, mutual mistrust clouds the debates. One single, identical formula expresses contradictory thoughts. Men ceaselessly retrace their steps without finding a way out. Every point of right raises a problem of force; and, under cover of the idea of a large "union," each country seems to pursue its own ends.[1] So the efforts of the great powers fail to establish the idea of peace, one and indivisible. The proclaimed goal, the establishment of a rule of general law, is lost in the mists of never-ending discussions; and *the principle of the partition of the world into zones of influence*, the same principle which Hitler caused to triumph at Munich in 1938 and at Moscow in 1939, the same principle which provoked the war, presents itself anew as a calamitous makeshift. Partition is compromise at the cost of third parties. It is security guaranteed in reverse, protecting the strong against aggression by the weak. It is the right of the strongest to override Europe's liberties. But it is also the consecration of a rivalry among the "great" exercising itself outside all established order and rule of law. This means an open road to ambitions and dreams of hegemony. Partition into zones of influence means war.

There is no peace possible, nor is there any means of reaching that agreement between the west and the Soviet which is indispensable, unless the experiences of these last terrible years are taken into account. The causes underlying the conflict and the elements constituting the victory must be recalled. Because liberty was in danger, war broke out in 1939. The desperate struggle of the nations consecrated the triumph of the principle of union over that of partition, of the principle of equilibrium over that of hegemony, the triumph of liberty over Hitlerian fascism. Peace must be directed in the same way as the struggle and the victory; it cannot be otherwise. After the disaster which has ravaged the world, peacemaking means putting an end to the abuse of force, assuring the liberty of nations, letting equilibrium re-establish itself in diversity. In a word, it means the restoration of Europe. For the very great powers whose will is the

1. Some of them endeavor to establish a stable order of things; others overflow on to their neighbors and tend to assure to themselves a complete liberty of movement.

determining factor today, it also means that they will set
bounds to themselves, in order to save a principle of right
which alone can assure them the just and tranquil enjoyment
of the fruits of common victory.[1]

But peacemaking today implies making a still further
effort, for peace can never again be regarded in the light of
the past. General security is no longer conceivable under
conditions which used to be considered *normal*. Modern
armaments cause the danger of death to hover over the
whole of humanity; and, so long as fully sovereign states
confront one another, no treaty, no diplomatic arrangement,
can avert from them the menace of sudden and total anni-
hilation. Only a *higher authority*, placed above the states,
above the great as well as the small powers, can be capable
of guaranteeing the peace. The entire attention of the world
should therefore be concentrated on the creation of this
higher authority, which is indispensable for real pacification
and the salvation of humanity. The responsibility for bringing such a thing to pass would lie, above all, with the very
great empires. They, having preserved the full exercise of
their sovereignty, would have to be willing to make the
heaviest sacrifices of all so as to attain a common world order.
To put an end to the profound trouble of our age and avoid
the terrible fate which menaces mankind, it would be necessary for the trend of policy having as its ideal a world feder-
ation to gain precision and force, and triumph over the contrary wills which tend to oppose a partition of influences to
the hegemony of a single ideology or a single power.

All the states, large and small, will in any case have to pronounce their judgment on the principles which will determine the new peace, whose task will be to guarantee the
rights and liberties of each within the framework of general
security. The "great" have already put the accent on "democracy." Popular suffrage is the method by which the

1. Cf. Appendix II, p. 226.

states must manifest their individual wills and preferences. This would apply particularly to the countries of eastern Europe.

But democracy is subject to interpretations which have varied in the course of history and still vary at the behest of political passions. Not only do London and Moscow define democracy in different fashion. The European Continent is full of contradictions on this subject—not that reference to the peoples of Europe can ever turn to Europe's disadvantage, if the elections are rigorously supervised. There is no people which would not vote for liberty. But, in the manner of acknowledging each people's right to democracy there are so many different nuances that the most lively arguments on the formulae are already raging among the powers, and "democracy," far from being a means of unification, risks becoming the cause of even graver dissensions.

Yet what really is at stake is not democracy itself, which is, and can only be, the manner (albeit the wisest and most equitable) in which the will of a nation is expressed. The problem is more complex and profound. It is a question of the very existence of nations in so far as they are attached to, and incorporated in, the body of traditions, beliefs, and aspirations which make up European civilization. To this civilization the European peoples are bound (whatever be the character and degree of their development). In this civilization they rediscover themselves, and wish to abide. This civilization means, for them, the protection of rights, the assurance of individual liberties, the very reason for being. Its absence is something they apprehend with unspeakable anguish, as they sense the shadow spreading over them, and the enveloping silence. Never did the peoples of Europe, above all the so-called "border peoples," feel themselves part of this common civilization more profoundly than after their liberation from the fascist nightmare. At that moment, rising from the ruins of war, they believed that they saw a

Europe which was to them not only a political ideal but the vision of renascent life whose spirit animated individuals and nations.

Their profound attachment to a common civilization (an attachment which is shown poignantly today, when every hope and every fear is possible) does not set these peoples in opposition to the great neighboring empires. From the east as well as from the west, it is possible for Europe to receive great impulses toward renewal, able to create new bonds and new values within the human community. Never have the nations been as receptive to the ideas of social justice and technical perfection as now in their moment of weakness. But the ideal of a civilization cannot be made the object of negotiations or compromise; this ideal creates a solidarity among nations, which cannot be sacrificed without provoking upheavals, much more of a moral than of a political order, which no peaceful arrangement could withstand.

The ultimate problem, which intelligence and courage demand should be thought through to the very end, is a problem of life.

Upon the will to participate in common in a work of life itself hangs the possibility of accord among the great powers—and the peace of the world.

Geneva   G. G.

INTRODUCTION

THE second World War was destined to break out on October 1, 1938.

This was the day Hitler had chosen to send his troops into the region inhabited by the Sudeten Germans. The Führer had made up his mind to change the status of Europe by force. On September 26 he had declared: ". . . And now we come to the last problem, which must be solved and which will be solved. *This is the last territorial claim I have to make in Europe;* but it is a claim from which I shall not depart, and which I shall realize, God willing." Thus Hitler burned his boats. Göring hastened to announce general mobilization. The German armies were on the point of taking the field.

It seemed that the western powers, having reached the end of their concessions, had resigned themselves to accepting war. A witness who followed events closely related on October 4: "During the two days, September 27 and 28, one felt disaster drawing hourly nearer. . . . It was in this atmosphere that, toward ten o'clock of the evening of September 28, news began to spread of a four-power conference at Munich the next day. It immediately gave rise to a feeling of immense satisfaction. Nobody doubted for a moment that it would dispel the threat of war. The unhoped-for miracle had happened." [1]

This "miracle" was to be accomplished in a flash: by the next day, September 29, 1938, the Munich Agreement was concluded. The day afterward, Mr. Neville Chamberlain signed with the Reich Government an engagement for "mutual consultation." Landing from the air in London on October 1, amid an enthusiastic crowd, the British Prime Minister declared that peace was henceforth assured for a

1. Report of M. François-Poncet, French Ambassador in Berlin, October 4, 1938.

generation. The same day the German armies entered the Sudeten regions, just as Hitler had intended. But occupation was not now carried out by force; conquest was effected "in execution of an arrangement concluded under the guarantee of the four powers."

The entire press, in Germany and elsewhere, celebrated this miraculous agreement, "the starting point for the creation of a new Europe, free from prejudices and mutual hatreds, dominated by respect for the vital rights of all peoples, and directed toward harmonious collaboration among the nations."

Better-placed observers, however, drew attention to those among the German leaders "who insist that it is still necessary to push forward and make as much capital as possible out of the military superiority which the Reich believes it possesses. . . . While the German Army is occupying the mountains of Bohemia, they scan the horizon in search of new claims to be made, new battles to wage, and new objectives to attain." [1]

In the midst of the joy which had followed the general anguish, the world was little disposed to listen to Cassandras. Winston Churchill found only a feeble echo when he announced that the *total defeat* suffered by the western powers at Munich was but the "beginning of the great settling of accounts."

The world wanted peace, wanted it desperately, for it felt that, apart from Hitler, no one was really prepared to face the trials and bear the misfortunes of war.[2] Chamberlain

1. Report of M. François-Poncet, cited above.
2. The French Government had made inquiries of the governments of friendly countries concerning the state of their military preparations and their corresponding political arrangements. The result of these investigations had been most discouraging.

On September 17, 1938, England had made known its resolve to give France all possible aid "in case it itself should be attacked"; but it stated that it was "impossible" for it to undertake engagements in advance, in the event of France's making war in execution of its treaty with Czechoslovakia. Two weeks earlier (September 2), the French Government had was approved of because he had taken the German dictator at his word; had compounded with him in regard to his "last territorial claim"; and had forced him to incorporate this claim in an international treaty. If Hitler was telling the truth, this was the only means of saving the peace. It had to be tried.

In the last resort, the "Munich Peace" rested on Hitler's word. Even though this word might be doubtful, the agreement still seemed to offer certain advantages. It allowed time to be gained—precious time, which could profitably be used the better to prepare armaments and alliances. It bound England more closely to the fate of the Continent. England joined with France (in the Annex to the agreement) to "stand by the offer, contained in paragraph 6 of the Anglo-French proposals of the 19th September, relating to an international guarantee of the new boundaries of the Czechoslovak State against unprovoked aggression." So the British Government took a step forward into Europe. After having recognized "the Rhine frontier" as its own, it was preparing to guarantee the far-distant territory of Czechoslovakia and to assume definite responsibilities in Central Europe. This was an obvious contribution to the strengthening of French policy. In addition, since Germany and Italy had equally undertaken (by the same article) to guarantee Czechoslovakia "when the question of the Polish and Hungarian minorities has been settled," hope might be entertained that the policy of sudden and violent moves so far practiced by Hit-

---

been informed that England's aid on land and in the air during the first six months of war would probably amount to two divisions, not equipped with modern material, and 100 to 150 planes.

The American Government had definitely stated from the beginning of the crisis that it was not in a position to furnish any aid.

Soviet Russia, which was twice approached (in March and June, 1938), had made it known through M. Litvinov that it would not refuse to aid Czechoslovakia in case of German aggression if Poland and Rumania first undertook to allow the Soviet armies to pass through their territory. As neither Poland nor Rumania intended to make such an anticipatory engagement, it could not be expected that Russia would intervene.

ler would be replaced by a policy of European collaboration.

Everything depended on the interpretation which the four signatory powers intended to place on the Munich Agreement. At the beginning, it seemed that Germany had accepted the thesis of the French Government, according to which it was not a question "of an armistice concluded in consequence of victorious German military operations," but of an agreement having "the character of an amicable arrangement, its execution being necessarily submitted to the control, and in numerous cases to the actual decision, of an international commission." In point of fact, why should the Reich have undertaken to guarantee the Czech frontiers, and how could it have contracted a pact of "mutual consultation" with England (and two months later with France) in order to settle "international difficulties," had it not accepted the principle of collaboration among the four powers, with a view to "controlling" the affairs of Europe in common?

Evidently this principle no longer corresponded with the doctrine of collective security as defended by the League of Nations; and yet it did not inaugurate a really new policy. In a sense, it was a continuation of the Locarno Agreements and the famous project of the "Four-Power Pact" (intended to place European peace under the aegis of the united action of England, France, Germany, and Italy). It gave satisfaction to many Europeans who, discouraged by the procrastination of the League of Nations, considered that it was necessary to create a higher authority on the Continent to save peace. The grave defects of such a policy were that it legalized violence, and that it excluded the European east, principally Soviet Russia, from the joint action of the directing nations. It might be thought, however, that England and France would succeed in overcoming the existing enmity between Berlin and Moscow, and so change the initial agreement into a five-power pact.

There remained a worse defect, one more difficult to correct—namely, Hitler's bad faith. The Third Reich put *its* doctrine and *its* principles higher than diplomacy of any sort. National Socialism was to determine the nature and meaning of international engagements entered into by the Nazi leaders. The conquest of the Sudeten lands was only a stage on the road toward the complete realization of the National Socialist "program." The Nazis were to regard the Munich Agreement as an acknowledgment by the western powers of Germany's right to its *Lebensraum*. Hitler was to claim that, from Munich onward, he had assured himself of a free hand in the east. This interpretation, which was manifestly false, was to be used by Nazi propaganda to defend, with vehemence and increasing insistence, first the "aspirations" of the German people, and later Germany's "sacred right" to decide alone the fate of eastern Europe as it saw fit.

Immediately it was concluded, the Munich Agreement was thus subject to two different and contradictory interpretations. The western powers hoped that they had settled Hitler's "last territorial claim," and believed that they had made Germany a partner in "a general work of peace." The German Government, however, was certain that it had won the right to impose on eastern Europe the peace which suited its pleasure.

There was the breach, which was to grow wider in the course of the winter and, from the spring of 1939 onward, was to provoke the final and decisive crisis prior to the great conflict.

The French and English leaders tried to show that no *misunderstanding* was possible and that France and England, as great powers, had not renounced the right to take part in everything concerning Europe. Had they not guaranteed the new frontiers of Czechoslovakia? Had they not obtained from Germany the undertaking to give an identical guarantee? Were they not ceaselessly to insist that this promise should be kept? In addition, had not France affirmed its will to maintain the ties of alliance, assistance, and friendship which bound it to Poland, the Soviet Union, and Rumania?

The Hitlerian Reich responded by acts. A few weeks after Munich it settled by itself the frontier conflict between Hungary and Czechoslovakia. "We did so in order to render Europe a service," declared Hitler to M. François-Poncet. "A larger conference would have provoked a new crisis." But to the eastern states the Führer explained that the western powers had nothing further to say in Central Europe; these powers were foreign to that region (*Raumfremd*). The Little Entente had had its day, and therefore Germany adjusted its policy in regard to Rumania, Yugoslavia, and the Balkans.

So the principle of *partition* penetrated into European politics. Hitlerian Germany profited by the Munich Agreement to impose its "European doctrine" by way of interpretation. Unified security systems had had their day. Henceforth the Continent was to be divided into two zones: to the west, the western democracies: to the center and east, the guardian power of the Greater Reich. This partition was not expressed in any diplomatic text; it resulted from the facts of the situation, from the steady, systematic pressure with which the Reich was expelling the western powers from its Lebensraum, from the new economic and political situation which was being established between the Rhine and Black Sea. To win over the western powers to its policy, the Reich was ready to assure them the security of their frontiers in every conceivable manner. It was with this intention that it concluded the pacts of consultation with England (September 30) and France (December 6), while reserving to itself the possibility of interpreting them in its own fashion. The order of the day was: the status quo in the west, dynamism in the east. But it was only necessary to have read *Mein Kampf* to realize how uncertain was this status quo which was being proposed to the western powers. Hitler wished to cover his flank on one side, while seeking on the other the key to world empire. Behind the theories of partition stood the will to universal hegemony.

Henceforth it might well seem vain to defend the precise text of the new treaties. As if it were a question of texts! Hitler's will was law; it was the sole "right" which counted inside the German Empire. Whoever wished to treat with this empire came up against this new German "right" and had to compound with it.

Worst of all was the fact that, in order to reach this point, the western powers had been obliged to sacrifice everything that still retained a semblance of the organization of a collective peace. After Munich the League of Nations lost its last vestige of authority. Russia took advantage of its isolation to abandon its policy of assistance. All the regional groupings were menaced. The Little Entente was dead. Only a false promise remained: an agreement determined by the interest of a "chosen" people and the changing will of a dictator. The ground was being cut from under the feet of the western states; no engagement in which they could place their trust remained. Europe, divided according to Nazi wishes, presented zones of influence but not a zone of rights.

It was natural that armaments should immediately be spoken of again. Chamberlain proclaimed England's will to be strong. By this, Hitler felt himself frustrated. He confided his chagrin to M. François-Poncet when the latter visited him in his eyrie at Berchtesgaden. England was causing him pain—it did not wish to understand. Why on earth should it resound with a call to arms when the specter of war had been dispelled forever?

These calls were to become increasingly insistent; here was the ransom from the policy of partition. In a world where right no longer governed relations between states, and where third parties seemed to be abandoned to the will of the strongest, a great power could not remain what it was save by the constant maintenance of its strength.

Hitler had a final means of preventing a return of the "specter of war." He could calm the apprehensions of England and France by giving the promised guarantee to Czechoslovakia. Had he kept his word just once, Europe would have been reassured. But he did not dream of doing so. Either Czechoslovakia became a docile instrument in his hands, or he would break it. In order to avoid the promised guarantee, he saw to it that the problem of the Polish and Hungarian minorities (upon whose solution he had made the execution of his promise depend) remained unsettled. His agents fostered the animosity of neighboring peoples of Czechoslovakia, so that he might have a pretext for solving the "problem" as and when he judged best.

In fact, as a result of pretended agitations by Slovak and Hungarian minorities, he was to decide to intervene once more in the affairs of Bohemia. The way he went to work showed his character. Since his refusal to guarantee the Czech frontiers perpetuated a vexatious argument and revealed his bad faith, Hitler laid the blame on the cause of the "misunderstanding"—and suppressed Czechoslovakia.

This crime was perpetrated on March 15, 1939.

The cunning with which it was prepared, the cynicism with which it was carried out, the violence which was applied during a whole night against the unfortunate Hacha to compel him to ask for the wiping out of his own country, all these events mark one of the darkest pages of contemporary history. The Führer surpassed himself when he attempted to justify his action in the eyes of the world. His whole argument meant that the Reich was free to re-establish order on its frontiers as it saw fit; but Hitler invoked the Munich Agreement by which the western powers had supposedly recognized his right to act as he pleased in Central Europe, which amounted to saying that the Munich Agreement, concerned with Czech affairs, had given Hitler in advance the liberty—and the right—to violate the engagements contained in this very agreement. Hitler's will settled the matter; after first having interpreted the treaties, it removed them and later stood in their stead. It determined the relations among the powers.

A violent controversy arose immediately. On March 14

(the eve of the day the crime was perpetrated) the French Government had recalled that the Munich Agreement, "regarded in Germany itself as a fundamental factor in the peace of Central Europe and as a decisive stage in the relations of mutual confidence among the principal European powers, had created *an indisputable solidarity of intentions,* particularly in the matter of Czechoslovakia."

The very next day Hitler replied by confronting the western powers with a *fait accompli.* Then he cited the "accord" between the Reich and President Hacha. Had not Czechoslovakia the *right* to disappear if that was its wish? When the French Government definitely refused to recognize the legality of this shameful agreement it was told that it had been well understood that Czechoslovakia would no longer "be the subject of an exchange of views." [1] In vain M. Bonnet (citing the numerous steps he had taken to prove the continuing interest which France had in the affairs of central and eastern Europe) pointed out that such an allegation was manifestly false; Hitler would not budge. Once and for all, he had made up his mind that he had the right to govern his vital living space alone; [2] he would allow no one to challenge the justice of a policy which he had the force to impose.

M. Coulondre, the new French Ambassador in Berlin, drew the only logical conclusion. "Obviously it is vain to hope that any argument other than force can successfully be brought to bear on the Führer. The Third Reich has the same contempt for treaties and engagements as had the empire of William II. Germany is still the country of scraps of paper." The unfortunate thing was that the most recent of

1. Conversation, Weizsäcker-Coulondre, March 18, 1939.
2. "The German conception of the Munich Agreement, completed by the German-British declaration and the Franco-German declarations, was that it gave the Reich the right to organize central and southeastern Europe as it saw fit with the tacit support of the great western powers or at least their toleration. For months this conception had been given daily publicity in the leading German newspapers which served as mouthpieces for official circles. The French Embassy correspondence repeatedly revealed this fact." Report of M. Coulondre, March 19, 1945.

these scraps of paper—the Munich Agreement—had replaced all the earlier engagements between nations. When
it was torn up, there no longer remained anything on which
to found a "legal" resistance. Hitler had succeeded in unset-
tling the whole fabric of international law. Juridically,
Europe found itself more disarmed in March, 1939, than it
had been in September, 1938; for in September the prospect
of a German occupation of Czechoslovakia had almost provoked war and only the hurried conclusion of the agreement
of the 29th had prevented hostilities; while, six months later,
the saving agreement having been violated and Czechoslovakia ocupied, Europe did not stir. Nothing more clearly sums
up the triumph of the policy of partition over the established
order of European rights than this comparison. The Old
World had never been so lacking in direction as during this
crisis, a crisis both moral and political.

However, the act of March 15 did contain the possibility
of redressing the situation. It put an end to the policy of
Munich. "The Munich Agreements no longer exist," reported M. Coulondre to his government; "the psychological
foundations on which the potentialities of the declarations
of September 30 and December 6 might have developed
have been destroyed. . . . We are in the presence of an entirely new situation."

This "new situation" was characterized by the fact that
Hitlerian Germany had thrown off the mask and was giving
free rein to its imperialism in seizing foreign countries. If
this danger which menaced the world was to be combated,
if violence was to be resisted, it was no longer possible to
associate with the Third Reich; it was necessary to reorganize a new system of rights and security outside, and against,
Germany.

A final period of political and diplomatic efforts began.

In the troubled months between the Munich Agreement
and the occupation of Prague, the eastern European coun-

tries realized that their existence was at stake. If the policy of partition succeeded, if European unity was shattered, it would be the end of their liberties and of their independence.

Rumania's first reaction was to protest against the decisions which struck at the integrity of Czechoslovakia. The Rumanian Government refused to participate in the partition of Subcarpathian Ruthenia—in which Colonel Beck urged it to share.

Its second reaction was to demonstrate its solidarity with the established European order of things, as maintained up to then under the aegis of the western powers. A month after Munich King Carol paid an official visit to the Court of St. James's. The King and his suite received a most cordial reception in London and later in Paris. But the problems of armament and economic collaboration which he raised did not sufficiently impress his hosts. The illusions created by the recent Four-Power Pact were not yet entirely dissipated. The pacification so dearly bought was still too fresh for people to wish to contemplate the cost of a new war. Since Europe seemed wedded to the policy of collaboration among the great powers, the King on his return stopped at Berchtesgaden. Hitler spoke to him with complacency of his peaceful intentions toward the Danubian countries, and Göring fulminated against the "Bolsheviks." During this time the Iron Guard, a Rumanian political formation which the Nazis considered as their spearhead in the east, indulged in "revolutionary" exercises in several Transylvanian towns. Determined to replace the traditional policy of the country by a movement in line with the Axis, the Iron Guard believed that its day was at hand. The King made up his mind to oppose the movement. On his return to Bucharest a violent campaign of repression ensued, which claimed many victims. The leader of the "Legionaries," Corneliu Codreanu, fell, together with his principal lieutenants.

Hitler regarded this repression, so closely following the King's visit to Berchtesgaden, as a challenge to his person and to National Socialism. Trembling with rage, he threatened Rumania with the worst. The Reich prepared a "punitive expedition" toward the lower Danube. The western powers warned the Rumanian Government of the danger; but neither France nor England was disposed to contemplate the possibility of war three months after Munich. It was in such circumstances that I was appointed Rumanian Minister of Foreign Affairs on December 23, 1938.

My task was urgent: to appease the fury raging in Berlin, which, at a time when European solidarity no longer existed, might be fatal to my country; and then to consolidate the ties binding my country to its friends in western Europe and the Balkans. The Rumanian Government negotiated an economic agreement with Germany. This was the only way to avoid certain contingencies which would have weighed heavily on Rumania's policy and friendships.

The negotiations had begun, when the German armies invaded Bohemia. Then our friends feared for the fate of Rumania. We received alarming messages from Paris, Belgrade, and Warsaw. "It is possible that tomorrow the Reich will follow the same course against Rumania and Poland which served it so well against Austria and Czechoslovakia," reported the French Ambassador to his government on March 19, 1939.[1]

These anxieties were not without foundation: later on, proclamations drawn up in the Rumanian language were to be found in the luggage of the German occupation troops in

1. In the same report of March 19 M. Coulondre wrote: "One fact would seem to indicate that, at the moment when the Hitlerian leaders were contemplating operations against Bohemia and Moravia, they also envisaged penetrating further toward the east sooner or later. According to present information, it seems that the German Army actually tried to occupy the whole of Slovakia and even Subcarpathian Russia. . . . Now the complete occupation of these regions, which would have led the German Army to the Rumanian frontier, only made sense politically or militarily, if other operations were in mind against either Rumania or Poland. At the present moment, it is in this direction that the best-informed circles in Berlin incline to believe the immediate menace lies."

Bohemia. It seems as if it really had been foreseen that the German "expedition" might penetrate further to the east.

The Rumano-German economic agreement thwarted these plans. This was signed at Bucharest on March 23. Although favorable to the Reich, it was not disadvantageous to Rumanian economy and it did not embarrass Rumania's economic relations with other countries in any way. Its principal merit was to save Rumania from invasion and allow it to gain a period of time which might have been precious. For the west was taking action at last. Five days after the occupation of Prague—March 20, 1939—the British Government addressed an appeal to France, the U.S.S.R., and Poland, inviting the governments of these three countries to join it in common consultations. On March 31 England gave a guarantee to Poland. On April 13 England and France jointly guaranteed Rumania and Greece. The ties between the east and west were thus drawn closer. "Europe" seemed to be reawakening and affirming its unity and its solidarity afresh in face of danger.

At this point, the German Government invited me to pay an official visit to Berlin. It desired to mark the *détente* which had come about in the relations between the Reich and Rumania as the result of the conclusion of the economic agreement. I accepted, and at the same time I announced my intention of paying visits to the governments of the western countries.

This journey in search of Europe, made a few months before the war, I have endeavored to retrace in the following pages.

CHAPTER I

TRAIN JOURNEY WITH COLONEL BECK

Recapitulation of German-Polish relations. Pact of Nonaggression of January 27, 1934. Colonel Beck's "principles." Hitler's assurances. The crisis (January 21, 1939). The Polish leaders' great illusion. Beck's message to Hitler.

I LEFT Bucharest at noon on April 16, 1939. The Berlin train ran through Moldavia until nightfall, crossed into Polish territory, and passed through Lemberg, Cracow, and Katowice during the night, reaching the Silesian frontier the next morning.

Shortly after midnight, the special coach of the Polish Foreign Minister was attached to our train. I had been warned that Colonel Beck was anxious to see me before my visit to Berlin. I joined him in his carriage, and we continued our journey together until dawn. So there and then I was in the thick of the European drama.

The man who had come to meet me, to unburden his anxieties, and to entrust me with certain messages, was no longer he whose imperturbable smile and haughty self-composure had long been familiar to me. I had always been intrigued by this audacious minister, none of whose ideas I shared, but whose bold evolutions amid the pitfalls of politics I watched with interest—and no little apprehension. He had covered himself with glory in the first World War while serving in the Polish Legion. Afterward he had devoted himself to diplomacy, to which he brought an astute mind and nonchalant, feline graces. This supple cavalier considered himself a clever calculator: he explained events in a fashion all his own, distrusting the "chattering" of the foreign offices and believing in his ability to grasp "the reality of things." Having come to power while still very young, under the protective wing of Marshal Pilsudski, and having maintained himself for more than seven years in the Polish Ministry of Foreign Affairs—he was the doyen of the European foreign ministers—he considered that he had followed certain political developments sufficiently long to know all their ramifications. His personal ambition had grown in proportion to his national ambitions; and thus he was inclined to overestimate the possibilities of his policy and the forces on which he relied for support.

I had never seen him in doubt of the success of his undertakings. For the first time that night, in the train, I discovered signs of anxiety in him. His furtive glance, in which there shone a glint of fever, the nervous gestures of his long hands, the unusual pallor of his face, everything about him betrayed an emotion which his voice, calm as usual, did not succeed in dissimulating.

The blow which everyone had expected, whose imminence he alone had obstinately denied, had fallen on him. Hitler had broken his word. After occupying Prague and Memel, he had put his cards on the table concerning Poland: he wanted Danzig.

"Oh, well, he won't get it," Beck said decisively. "If he counts on me to give it to him, he is making a mistake! I am the last person who could abandon Danzig. After five years of perfect entente, during which I have in no wise failed in my engagements, he has sought to strike me a mortal blow. I have already parried the blow, as was required. The English are my friends; Danzig is in safe keeping, and I am still on my feet. But I do not want war. I remained in office so that I could work for peace. I want them to realize this in Berlin; and I want them to know also that I have not changed my policy, and have abandoned none of my principles. It was to save peace that I avoided taking any irretrievable step."

This attitude, at once combative and conciliatory, was in keeping with the fighting spirit of Colonel Beck. By reason of its chances and the risks, it conformed even more to his needs as a gambler. He had just begun the highest game of all, on the outcome of which the integrity of his country, his honor as a minister, and the peace of the world depended.

So that he could use every chance, Beck was ready to talk with Berlin after having bound himself up with London. But it was necessary for Berlin to lend an ear to his explanations. Hitler, however, furious at England's intervention in Polish affairs, had recalled his Ambassador from Warsaw. As for M. Lipski, the Polish Ambassador in Berlin, he tried in vain to reach the German Chancellor or the latter's Minister of Foreign Affairs during the critical days. Beck, wishing to strike where it was necessary, was prepared to use any means.

I realized that I was the means my Polish colleague required. I listened to his account of his contentions with the Third Reich more attentively because my own apprehensions on this subject had anticipated his. From the Baltic to the Black Sea, were we not all exposed to the consequences of Hitler's rages; and did we not all share the same terrible anxiety, as we asked ourselves which of us would be attacked first? Rumania had vainly sought to reconcile the opposite tendencies of Poland and Czechoslovakia, the two states to which it was bound by ties of alliance and sincere friendship. It had witnessed the collapse of the policy of security in which it had placed its trust. Czechoslovakia had fallen; Poland seemed to be threatened. When would it be Rumania's turn? At this critical hour, the policy of the Warsaw government (which aroused active suspicion in Poland itself, where public opinion was demanding with increasing insistence a return to the old friendships and a reinforcement of the old alliances) was being followed with agonized curiosity by the foreign offices of friendly states. I was happy to be able to learn from Colonel Beck himself what thoughts had guided him and what hopes he still entertained.

Here is the account that Colonel Beck gave me during the night of April 16–17, 1939. It is taken from my notes, and is completed by extracts from official documents.

The Minister began by recapitulating the events that had preceded the crisis.

Relations between Hitler's Germany and Pilsudski's Poland had been perfect up to the beginning of the winter of 1938. These relations had been developing in conformity with the spirit and the letter of the pact of nonaggression, concluded on January 26, 1934. The terms of this pact were identical with those of the nonaggression pact signed by Poland with the Soviet Union two years previously. Beck liked to emphasize symmetry, which determined his policy. "I received instructions from the Marshal," he used to say, "which I have always scrupulously followed. Thanks to my policy, Poland has been able to ensure its security to the east as well as to the west without impeding its liberty of action. So as not to arouse suspicions of any sort, either east or west, I have signed nonaggression pacts with our great immediate neighbors; but I have always avoided treaties of mutual assistance. Thus I have pursued an *independent* and strictly logical policy."

In reality, the perfect balance which Beck desired to maintain did incline toward the west—which fact the Minister did not deny. Not that his patriotism was tainted by any love for Germany, as has wrongly been suggested. A faithful disciple of Marshal Pilsudski, the founder of this policy of equilibrium, Colonel Beck denied that he had ever admitted that any foreign influence could alter his national sentiment, which was as ardent, as proud, and as uncompromising as that of any of his compatriots. But he recognized that between him and the leaders of Germany there were certain affinities of thought which must lend a particular significance to the pact of 1934. Like many Poles, Beck had little faith in the ideology of Geneva, denouncing its chimerical char-

acter and mercilessly criticizing the schemes of collective
security which, according to him, tended to create a dangerous and illusory situation. In this respect, his judgment was
influenced by the old resentments which had been provoked
in Poland by the Locarno Pact and the policy of rapprochement among the western powers. At Locarno, Poland did
not get the guarantees which it felt were its right. Aspiring
to the role of a great power, it felt itself belittled. Its resentment was quickened when, the Locarno policy having had
its day, the western powers busied themselves at Geneva with
the extension of their system of security to the east, and as
the eastern pillar of this policy chose not the Poland of M.
Beck but the Soviet Union of M. Litvinov. In spite of the
good intentions which it paraded in the League of Nations,
the Soviet Union did not inspire its Polish neighbor with
complete confidence. An engagement for mutual assistance
which gave the right of entry into the territory of a menaced neighbor appeared to them to be a two-edged sword.
Warsaw felt that it was a ticklish matter to accept such an
engagement from a power lying so near to Polish territories
where there were strong ethnical minorities.

M. Beck believed he was faithfully interpreting his countrymen's wishes when he sought to disengage himself from
multilateral and collective pacts (i.e., from a system which
sometimes stopped at the Rhine, and at others sought a
point d'appui in Moscow). The Minister clearly showed his
preference for what he considered simpler and more direct
methods, which would permit Poland fully to enjoy its prerogatives as a great power by taking its security into its own
hands. To do so, Poland must come to an understanding
either directly with its neighbors by exchanging pledges of
nonaggression with each, or else by contracting precise,
bilateral alliances with more distant friendly states. So a
special system of security would come into being, founded,
not on humanitarian considerations or on the precepts of an
international law still in the process of formation, but on a

realistic appreciation of common interests which needed to be united and opposed interests which needed to be reconciled. M. Beck believed that he had succeeded in organizing such a system, by his pacts with the U.S.S.R. and the Reich, and his alliances with France and Rumania.

"By the accomplishment of such a work," said the Minister to me, "I have given proof not only of my patriotism but also of absolute impartiality. It is quite as unfair to accuse me of Russophobia as to call me a Germanophile. I have never followed a policy hostile to the Soviet Union; but I know Russia; and I have never allowed myself to be guided in this respect by the illusions of a westerner. The western powers understand nothing whatever about Soviet Russia, just as they understood nothing about tsarist Russia. They go from one extreme to the other, pursuing different and contradictory policies in turn. The French and the English have jumped from the policy of the *cordon sanitaire* to that of pacts of mutual assistance. The Germans have done just the opposite. At Rapallo they established extremely intimate relations of a political and economic order with Russia; while today they erect an Anti-Comintern Pact against the Soviet Union. As for me, I have never fallen into these excesses. We are too near to the Russians not to know them. We shall therefore never take a wavering course. No Anti-Comintern Pact for us! It is not my duty to advertise the Third International or to combat it officially. I recognize only the Soviet state. When I was at Moscow, I did not visit M. Stalin. This all-powerful man held no official position; he was only the Party Secretary. Pacts of mutual assistance, like Anti-Comintern pacts, have the same defect: they draw Russia into Europe and bring it into continental affairs. On the other hand, nonaggression pacts stop it at its frontiers. This is how I understand security. After the crisis of last September (the Munich crisis), our relations with Russia were strained. I took care to re-establish the former position—namely, the status quo in our relations. The closer relations

I effected then did not indicate the adoption of a new attitude toward Germany but only the re-establishment of that equilibrium which is indispensable to our independence. With this precise aim in view, I have striven to improve our economic relations with Russia. The result of these efforts—which, by the way, interest me only from a political point of view—has been most satisfactory.

"My policy with respect to Germany has been based on the same principles. I have avoided all sentimentality, and have taken account only of the realities of the situation. If sometimes I may have felt particularly satisfied with the pacific work that I have accomplished with Germany, it is because I believed that the German leaders were as realistic as I was, and as desirous of escaping from the complications of the Geneva procedure. Of that, moveover, they have always assured me."

It may not be entirely without interest to insert here the assurances and encouragements which Hitler and his colleagues had lavished on the Polish Minister of Foreign Affairs in order to stimulate his statesmanlike "realism."

"*I regard Poland as a reality which nothing can change or cause to disappear.*" This is what Hitler had stated in 1933, when he was preparing his pact with Poland. He was to use similar phrases, for years to come, on every possible occasion. As late as September 12, 1938, he declared at Nuremberg: "Since a great patriot and statesman in Poland, Marshal Pilsudski, was ready to sign a pact with Germany, we immediately agreed; and we have begun an arrangement which is of more importance to European peace than the sum of all the babblings uttered in the temple of the League of Nations at Geneva."

The reality and eternal duration of Poland on the one hand, and the inanity of the babblings of Geneva on the other: there, not unintentionally, Hitler expressed the main point of the political thought of Marshal Pilsudski and his disciples. To emphasize this community of thought, it was only necessary to stress the magnitude of the great common interests of the two countries, and to give solemn assurances that the Reich would never resolve the few difficulties that might remain between Berlin and Warsaw in other than a friendly spirit.

This Hitler did not fail to do.

"War of any sort could only bring Communism to Europe—that Communism which is a terrible danger. . . . Poland is a bastion (*ein Vorposten*) on the Asiatic front. The destruction of Poland would be a disaster for the states which would thus become neighbors of Asia. The other states ought to comprehend this role of bastion which Poland is fulfilling." Here again the Führer expressed an idea well fixed in the best Polish minds. On such data as this, which the Polish leaders accepted from the start, it remained only to develop the idea of the twin destinies of the National Socialist Reich and "realistic" Poland in face of the menace of Asia. To the Polish Ambassador to Berlin (January 26, 1934) Hitler confided his uneasiness with regard to Soviet machinations:

"The moment might well come when our two states may have to defend themselves against an invasion from the east. The policy pursued by former German governments, and particularly by the Reichswehr. which consisted in a collusion with Russia directed against Poland, was the greatest political absurdity. On one occasion Hitler himself had had a violent controversy with General von Schleicher, who sought a rapprochement with Russia, to the detriment of Poland. Such a policy would end by increasing the greatest danger which menaced Germany—namely, the Soviet danger. . . ."

Here Hitler touched a point on which the Poles were particularly sensitive: of all the things which menaced Poland, a collusion between the Reich and the U.S.S.R. was the worst conceivable. If Warsaw could be convinced that

National Socialism would remove this danger forever, then in Poland Hitler would find precious auxiliaries for his foreign policy. It was necessary to stress the point. On January 31, 1935, at a shooting party, Marshal Göring in turn made an important confidential statement to Count Szembeck, Polish Undersecretary of State for Foreign Affairs:

"In theory, one might imagine how a new partition of Poland might be effected by means of German-Russian collaboration. In practice, however, it would be impossible to carry out, because the partition of Poland would compel the Reich to have a common frontier with the U.S.S.R., a thing which would be extremely dangerous for Germany. For this reason, Germany needs a strong Poland, so as to form with it a barrier against Russia. Only Chancellor Hitler has so apprehended the problem of Polish-German relations. Before his advent, after Stresemann and even before, the Reich had other aims. At the beginning of 1933, when General Schleicher handed over to Hitler, the General explained to the Führer what Germany's policy toward Poland should be. General Schleicher's idea was to promote an entente between Germany, France, and Russia. The suppression of Poland was to be undertaken subsequently by means of an entente with Russia. During the whole time that General Schleicher was giving these explanations Hitler said nothing. It was only when he parted from the Chancellor, who was about to retire, that he said to Herr Göring: 'As for me, I shall do the contrary.' "

It should be noted that this recital does not entirely correspond with Hitler's own version of his conversation with von Schleicher. The Chancellor mentioned a "violent controversy"; Göring only recalled the Führer's disapproving silence. But the purpose of these revelations was the same: Warsaw must be convinced that Hitler sincerely believed on thing: that the Reich and Poland had common interests regarding the U.S.S.R. It was equally necessary to prove that the Third Reich, having cut itself off from Moscow by its doctrine and action (contrary to German political tradition), would prudently and naturally seek the best and most sincere relations with Poland.

This thesis was to be defended and reinforced by innumerable declarations and assurances.

"As for Russia," said von Ribbentrop to Count Szembeck on August 14, 1936, "Chancellor Hitler cannot countenance any compromise. The slightest deviation from his policy as regards the Soviet would inevitably open the door to Bolshevism. Poland is quite as menaced as Germany; therefore the two counties must collaborate."

As for Göring, he repeated (February 16, 1937) in the presence of Marshal Smigly-Rydz the words he had spoken to Szembeck:

"The Chancellor has overturned the situation by adopting the thesis once and for all that all contact with Communism is excluded."

On this occasion Göring elaborated his ideas on the necessity of German-Polish collaboration.

"As it is well understood in Germany, Poland is in a position to pursue a truly independent policy of considerable scope, on the condition that it has a Reich to deal with which is benevolently disposed toward it. . . . The Polish-French alliance offers no threat to the Reich, since the Reich is well aware that this alliance is of a strictly defensive character."

Implicitly, Göring let it be understood that a Polish-Soviet agreement would not be interpreted in Berlin as being "strictly defensive." He did this to prevent Poland's adhesion to the more extensive system of security that was being discussed at this period. But he was preaching to the converted. Beck was quite as suspicious of collective security as were the German leaders. The Polish Minister was far from dissatisfied to hear the principles repeated which Hitler had definitely stated in 1935, when he informed the Polish Ambassador that "he was resolutely opposed to any western cooperation with Russia, since European solidarity, of which he was a supporter, ought to stop at the Polish-Soviet frontier."

Similar assurances followed throughout 1937 and 1938, expressing in precisely formulated terms the same essential "truths," which the Reich liked to pronounce because it thought them useful, and Poland liked to hear because it believed in them. On January 5, 1939, at the beginning of the terrible year destined to reveal the depths of Hitlerian thinking, the Chancellor again proclaimed:

"As regards Russia, the community of interests between Germany and Poland is complete. In the eyes of Germany, Russia, whether tsarist or Bolshevik, is equally dangerous. . . . For this reason, a strong Poland is purely and simply a necessity for Germany."

This constant repetition of the principles of German policy in the east would not have been sufficient to calm all Poland's apprehensions had the Berlin government not found the necessary words to define its attitude toward the international rule of the Free City of Danzig. Here, indeed, was to be found the touchstone of German-Polish relations. Would the Reich also give the necessary assurances on this point? Hitler did so without hesitation.

"The Polish state," he stated in his speech of February 20, 1938, "respects the national situation in the State of Danzig; and this city, as well as Germany, respects Polish rights. So, despite all the disturbers of the peace, the way has been successfully smoothed to an entente which, beginning with Danzig, has today finally taken the poison out of German-Polish relations and transformed them into a sincere and friendly collaboration."

In the same spirit, but still more precisely, the Chancellor had declared to M. Lipski four months previously, on November 5, 1937, that "nothing would be modified in the juridical and political situation of Danzig" ("*An der rechtspolitischen Lage Danzigs wird nichts geändert werden*").

That same day the two governments had proceeded to a solemn exchange of declarations "on the subject of the reciprocal treatment of minorities." And from then on the official spokesmen of the Reich had not failed to take their cue from the Führer and to exalt the virtues of an entente which brought to nought the intrigues of the "disturbers of the peace," braved the worst trials, and was indispensable to European harmony.

In his reference to the procedure of the German Government at Warsaw, Beck indicated how closely these assurances and encouragements corresponded to his own *principles*. And, indeed, how could he have failed to appreciate their correctness and strength? In comparison with the "babblings of Geneva," which left the security of states dependent on the untried force of some articles of the Covenant, the promise of a manly and farseeing people seemed to him a guarantee of quite another sort. Moreover, he was a soldier, not a jurist—a soldier who had managed to keep his position as head of a Ministry of Foreign Affairs longer than had any diplomat. The possibility of pursuing "a far-reaching independent policy" seemed to him not only more desirable but in fact less risky than to rely on an indeterminate system of security. Nor was he insensible of the tremendous resurgence of vitality which shook the neighboring German people in 1938. Why should he hamper the action of people whose language he so well understood? Munich did not find him alongside his former allies. He remained "independent" while claiming his part of the spoils of Czechoslovakia. He got Teschen, and knew the joy of the conqueror when he stood on his balcony to be cheered by an enthusiastic crowd.

The memory of this joy had not faded before an untoward piece of news reached Warsaw. On October 25, 1938, a few days after Munich, Herr von Ribbentrop suggested to M. Lipski a general solution—*eine Gesamtlösung*—of all "mat-

ters in suspense." The City of Danzig should be reunited
with the Reich, and "extraterritorial means of communication" should connect the Reich with East Prussia.

Beck was surprised. "Never had such claims been put to
me," he said. "I had every right to be furious, but I did not
lose my temper, and I sent Lipski precise instructions. I recalled the Führer's latest pronouncements, which had been
reassuring and less ambiguous than ever. I extolled the virtues
of the 1934 agreement, which had shown its full force at the
time of the greatest perturbation Europe had known since
the end of the World War; and, while accepting the idea
of a Gesamtlösung, I categorically refused the incorporation
of Danzig into Germany."

The Germans did not then push the conversations to the
limit. They had first to liquidate Czechoslovakia and seize
Memel. Beck still had time to outline a scheme of higher policy. To his Hungarian and Rumanian neighbors he proposed
a tripartite partition of Subcarpathian Russia. Although
warned by the Rumanian Ambassador that this plan was
bound to fail, he nevertheless went to Galatz to put the suggestion to King Carol. The King and his ministers categorically refused profit at the cost of an allied and friendly
country. Discontented and disappointed, Beck returned to
Warsaw, where he was repeatedly to hear more and more
about Danzig.

The words Hitler spoke to him at Berchtesgaden on
January 5, 1939, were still cordial. Danzig was only mentioned casually. All the same, these words perturbed the
Polish Minister, and next day he asked Herr von Ribbentrop
to inform the Chancellor "that he had always been optimistic after his interviews and contacts with the German statesmen; but that this time pessimism had taken hold of him,
and that, especially concerning the question of Danzig as
put by the Chancellor, he saw no way of reaching an understanding."

The Government of the Reich did not intend to frighten

the Poles. It still wore the velvet glove. On January 25 Ribbentrop, paying an official visit to Warsaw, was fulsomely amiable and did not press the Danzig question. Between friends, such affairs could be arranged quietly and amicably. Ribbentrop proposed a "gentleman's agreement." Beck gladly agreed. The word pleased him. Here was evidence of reliable relations such as could only be established between strong peoples. To tell the truth, those "gentlemen" with whom he was dealing had treated Austria and Czechoslovakia most unceremoniously. Not that that unduly disturbed Colonel Beck. Were not those two small states destined to disappear sooner or later? Poland was in no danger. It could trust the Reich because, if need be, it could stand up to it. And in any event, the agreement seemed harmless. It stated that:

"In case the League of Nations should withdraw from Danzig, this withdrawal would immediately be followed by a Polish-German declaration that the status quo in Danzig would be maintained until Poland and Germany reached an understanding."

So parity was maintained between the two great powers which were prepared to substitute the prestige of their joint action for the weakening authority of the League of Nations. Beck's "realism" permitted him to think little of Poland's withdrawal from the League of Nations, whose guarantee seemed to him to be of less value than the word of a "gentleman." (This was also the opinion of his partner, Herr von Ribbentrop.)

In the midst of all this, Hitler made a new speech. On January 30, 1939, he said:

"Five years ago we made a nonaggression pact with Poland. It would be hard at this moment to find any difference of opinion among the true friends of peace on the value of this agreement. It is enough simply to ask what would have happened to Europe had this liberating entente not been concluded five years ago. . . ."

Nevertheless the eddies of Hitler's policy in Europe had spread to Poland. Public opinion was stirred; opposition had found its voice, and the students were indulging in noisy street demonstrations. At this juncture Beck received two new official visits, those of Count Ciano and myself. I had reached Warsaw on March 2, 1939, and spent three days there as the guest of the Polish Government. Beck had shown no uneasiness then, when spring was in the air. He reminded me of this six weeks later when we met in the train.

"You remember how undisturbed I was in March?" he asked. I remembered. I had found the situation somewhat strained in Warsaw. Political circles were reproaching the Minister of Foreign Affairs for having allowed himself to be fooled by a dishonest partner. Beck alone was impassive. He affected an absolute calm. What had he to suspect? He claimed that he maintained full confidence in the word of the German Chancellor. "My confidence," he had said to me at the time, "is based on profound experience. Ever since 1935 all the explanations which Hitler has been kind enough to give me have proved exact and right. They have never been belied by the facts. *I have spoken to him as man to man, as soldier to soldier.* He has always kept all his engagements. Up to date he has never deceived me." When I reminded him that Beneš also had received more than one assurance before being struck down, Beck had replied with some warmth: "That is not the same thing. Czechoslovakia has always seemed to me to be a caricature of Hapsburg Austria. Everything about it was wrong and temporary. Ever since January,1938, I knew that Germany, after occupying Austria, was going to annex the Sudeten. The German plan might have extended to the Baltic States had I not hastened to occupy Vilna and tighten the bonds between Poland and Lithuania. As for the western powers, they had not made up their minds to oppose Germany. They might go to the brink of the precipice (up to Munich), but they were not ready to take the decisive step. That is why Poland faced up to the international situation as it judged best. Only one problem remained to be solved: that of Czechoslovakia. It was solved."

To this the Minister added: "Regarding Czechoslovakia, I think that the crisis has not ended. I do not know Germany's actual intentions toward that country, but one must keep one's eyes open, and we may expect new surprises very shortly."

The Minister did not realize how right he was; but, going beyond the collapse of Czechoslovakia, the surprise in store was to open up a new problem in Europe, one which would concern him much more closely. At first he did not perceive the danger, being absorbed by the changes taking place in neighboring states, in which he still believed that he could actively participate. So he did not seem to take too much to heart my reproach that he had contributed to the weakening of a country friendly to mine, and whose existence was an essential factor of the security of Poland as well as of Rumania. He still believed that he was perfectly secure. The Danzig affair did not worry him. "It is true," he told me, "that Danzig is more National Socialist than Germany itself. But my last agreement with Ribbentrop, and Hitler's recent declarations, cover me against any surprise." When I asked him if the calm he affected did not come from the fact that he attached very little importance to the matter of Danzig, he replied with animation: "Certainly not! We must have Danzig. We shall never allow it to be reincorporated in the Reich. Situated as it is at the mouth of the Vistula, this port handles seven million tons of our exports, while ten millions go through Gdynia. *If they touch Danzig, it means war.* But why should they touch it, since the fate of this city can always be settled amicably between Germany and ourselves?"

I had asked myself at that time whether Beck was sincere when he set such confidence in himself and his policy, against the great uneasiness that was troubling Europe. He could not have been unaware of the seriousness of certain changes which had taken place, and his long experience of affairs must surely have warned him of still other changes which were about to occur. However, he gave no sign of this; and, when I left Warsaw, my host's optimism had seemed to be impossible of change.

Beck went on with his story. He now came to the most critical period of German-Polish relations. Ten days after Beck had assured me in Warsaw of his absolute faith in Hitler's word, Germany invaded Bohemia; Prague was occupied; and Czechoslovakia fell. A few days later the Reich assumed "the protection of the political independence of Slovakia" and claimed for itself the right "to proceed to effect military installations and maintain garrisons along the eastern and western frontiers of Slovakia." So it threw its arms around the Polish Republic. Then, on March 22, a new forward push occurred. The German armies occupied Memel. The Reich's embrace tightened. The day before, March 21, 1939, Herr von Ribbentrop had summoned M. Lipski to the Wilhelmstrasse to discuss Polish-German relations in their entirety. The German Minister had changed his tone. He was surprised that Warsaw had not yet given a definite reply to the German suggestions. This delay estranged the Chancellor. The Führer "was still ready to maintain good relations with Poland"; but it was necessary that the "incomprehension of the true intentions of the Reich should cease." Herr von Ribbentrop was urgent. He suggested a meeting with Beck at once, and demanded an immediate reply to this proposal—so that the Chancellor "might not come to the conclusion that Poland rejected all his proposals."

M. Lipski understood. He telegraphed to his chief:

". . . The suggestion of a fresh meeting, the date of which Herr Ribbentrop wishes to hasten, is proof that the Germans have decided to carry out their program to the east without loss of time."

It should be noted that during this conversation the German Minister did not breathe a word about Memel.

"It was as though he wanted to neutralize us just when the Memel business was to be settled," observed M. Lipski. He did not dream that this "business" was to be settled at dawn next day.

Beck perceived the danger but did not yet realize the catastrophe. He decided not to accept the suggestion of a direct discussion with Ribbentrop, and confined himself to giving precise instructions to his Ambassador in Berlin (March 27), emphasizing his desire to maintain the best possible relations with the Reich, "as in the past" and "into the most distant future." He again restated the position Poland meant to hold regarding Danzig:

1. The Polish Government was ready to study with the German Government the question of a new simplification of the railway and motor transit traffic between the Reich and East Prussia and also new facilities; but it intended to grant these facilities "within the framework of Polish sovereignty."

2. Regarding the Free City of Danzig, the Polish Government considered that "a solution might be found, based on a joint Polish-German guarantee, which would take account of the national aspirations of the population as well as of Polish interests."

By this firm but polite refusal to entertain the German claims, Beck hoped to steer the conversations along the path of a friendly understanding in conformity with the spirit and the letter of the agreement of 1934. Was he not indeed maintaining the principles which had so happily governed German-Polish relations during the last few years? And was he not agreeing to take the thorny problem of Danzig from the jurisdiction of the League of Nations (an organization for which Warsaw, like Berlin, saw no future), to leave it to the care of a Polish-German collaboration destined to draw still tighter the bonds between the two states?

Herr von Ribbentrop refused to be convinced. He gave M. Lipski a cold welcome (March 26) and expressed his dissatisfaction with M. Beck's reply. The Ambassador noticed "his marked coldness" and "his nervousness." Ribbentrop observed that "his offer of a broad understanding had not been taken into consideration"; with insistence, he again put forward all his claims. The two representatives parted without having been able to reconcile their respective points of view. On this occasion it was plainly evident that Germany was getting ready to carry out its full program. After Prague, Bratislava, and Memel, it wanted Danzig. And it meant to move quickly; the wind was fair and success was smiling on it. Why wait for fresh international complications? England was beginning to react. Churchill was taking an increasingly bolder stand in the House of Commons; the London press was storming; Chamberlain himself, infuriated by the seizure of Prague and feeling personally affronted, seemed ready for anything. He had just (March 20) proposed to France, the Soviet Union, and Poland that they should take security measures in common. The Reich had no time to lose if it wished to settle by itself, in a tête-à-tête with the Warsaw government, the problems it had raised with Poland.

During these historic days Colonel Beck felt the ground tremble under his feet. The crisis which his people had feared, but in which he himself had not been willing to believe, had been reached. He realized its extreme gravity. He was not duped by the fact that the difference between the two theses was small in appearance. At first sight, the difficulties did not seem insurmountable. What did Germany want? To reincorporate Danzig in the Reich while permitting it to remain in the Polish economic sphere. What did Poland want? To allow liberal self-administration to the German population but still to retain Polish-German control. How could such a difference of opinion, arising between two peoples who for years had proved their desire for collaboration, lead to war? "In reality, it is only an affair of nuances," declared M. Franassovici, the Rumanian Ambassador, to his German colleague, seeking to discover his intentions. "You are mistaken," replied Count von Moltke, abandoning for once his habitual reserve. "It is not a question of nuances but one of colors. You see this map of Europe? On it Germany is marked in yellow and the Free State of Danzig in blue. Well, the little blue spot must disappear. There must be yellow here. It is absolutely essential. It is a question of the Führer's prestige. Things are very serious."

Count von Moltke had no malicious reference to his master's former taste for painting in mind. He referred to political prestige, that imponderable element which, as soon as it enters into a problem, however seemingly insignificant, immediately makes its issue a matter of triumph or collapse. The Führer had set himself a program to realize, a great mission to fulfill. He was in mid career, and could not stop.

But Poland, too, had a charge to keep. It could not bend to the unreasonable demands of a policy in perpetual movement, which, having substituted bilateral engagements for the principle of a general order of things, now sought to replace collaboration by arbitrary decisions at the will of a single individual. These decisions endangered not only the precious territory connecting Poland with the sea but its entire situation and that national independence which it cherished like a sacred flame. The tragic example of Czechoslovakia, acute at that very moment, showed what fate was in store for a country obliged to yield, if only on a single point, to the demands of the Third Reich. M. Lipski had realized that clearly. In his last interview with Herr von Ribbentrop, when the Minister asked him on what grounds Poland was so suspicious of Germany, the Polish Ambassador had replied that "recent events had occurred so swiftly, and had changed so many agreements and ententes that it was not surprising if public opinion was aroused."

Beck himself had ultimately seen what was at stake. He

understood it the better because the problem of Danzig for him also was linked with a question of personal prestige. More than for any other Pole, it was impossible for him to cede Danzig to Hitler. It was a "man to man" affair between him and the German Chancellor. For Beck had given his country a solemn pledge to act in such a manner that his policy would avoid all complications on the subject of Danzig. If he was to face the anger already mounting against him in Poland, he had to defend Danzig at all costs.

When he reached this point in his exposition, the Minister repeated what he had said to me in Warsaw: "*If they touch Danzig, it means war.*" And he added: "If I have remained in office during these tragic hours it has been to *incarnate* that immovable decision. We shall not let Danzig go. During the crisis, people have asked why I did not resign. More than once I thought of doing so. I could concentrate on the treatment of an ailment that I have neglected too long, and take that care which the doctors are urging on me. I could disappear and abandon my place to a successor on whom no responsibility would rest as regards the agreement of 1934. But you know me. I am not the man to bow to the storm. Weakened in health, sorely beset by events, attacked in the press, and spat upon in the street, I still mean to stick to my post, for I am convinced that my going would aggravate the situation still further. The present crisis will lead inevitably to war, if no one dares to stand up to it. Believe me, I am the only man who can still avoid the worst. I assure you, no one knows Germany and the Germans better than I do."

That showed how his mind had worked during the long years of conversations with Berlin, as well as the hold which the ideas of subtle propaganda had obtained over him. Certainly he was compelled to recognize that Hitler had tricked him, and that the Chancellor's friendship had only been a ruse by which the better to get Poland at his mercy. He recognized equally that any fresh concession might be fatal to Poland, for Hitler was not the man to be content with an initial success, but would work out "his program" to the bitter end. But Beck could not, and would not, believe that Hitler's Germany, after having "finally" broken with the Soviet Union, could afford the risks of a war with Poland. "I confess," he declared to me, "that I have wrongly estimated the importance of the Polish factor in Hitler's foreign policy; but I do not think I am wrong in my estimation of the Soviet factor. Unlike all his predecessors, Hitler knows the *reality* of the Bolshevik danger. He has always fought it. Because of his doctrine, his past, and his national and political reason for existence, he cannot come to terms with it! *I know* that therein lies the central, the primary, the decisive problem for Hitler's Germany—to which all other problems are secondary. Therefore, what can Germany's interest be in making war on Poland? To weaken Poland would be to play Russia's game. If the Polish 'bastion' were to fall, the gates of Europe would open to the Soviet's forward drive. Do you believe that Hitler wants that? *I know* that he does not! Certainly he wants Danzig; but he will never consent to pay such a price for the Free City."

Beck was thus convinced that resistance ought to be offered in the matter of Danzig, and that this could be done without irremediably provoking war. But resistance should be put up without anger while carefully calculating the steps to be taken, and restraining ill will. Above all, the door must be left open to Germany and no steps be taken toward Russia, so as not to compromise Poland's chances. Any such move toward Russia might be fatal. Were Poland to approach the Soviet Union, the Reich would no longer have any reason to spare it. For the presence of Poland on Russia's side would increase the very danger to fight which Hitler regarded as his mission. To change the position which Poland occupied in the political system of the Third Reich would be to make the fatal gesture which would automatically bring about war.

Such was the reasoning which certain strongly held ideas inspired in Beck, and which he ascribed to his "realistic" judgment and his knowledge of men. And such were the data on which he believed that he could establish his plan of action.

He would continue to stand up to Hitler, in his own way, by strengthening Poland's international position and by showing himself more uncompromising in the Danzig affair than any other Pole. But he would know how to escape the worst—war. He would not disturb what he regarded as the deep and unalterable reason of the German-Polish peace: the common attitude of the two countries toward Russia.

Hitler had broken his word to him, but he, Beck, knew how to defend himself. Great Britain was holding out a helping hand to him. Pocketing many grievances, it was interesting itself in the security of Poland. Beck had decided that he would profit by the occasion and grasp England's hand. But he intended to remain "whole." He would not compromise on his "principles"; he would not identify himself with the political system proposed by Chamberlain—that westerner who understood nothing about Russia; and he would oblige Great Britain to adjust its policy to his, adapt itself to Poland's system of security, and choose Poland as the principal pillar, the independent pillar, of security in the east.

His reply to the British note of March 20, 1939 (in which London proposed a "consultation" . between the French, Polish, Soviet, and British Governments), was, in its way, a masterpiece of diplomacy. "Will you ask Lord Halifax [he ordered Count Raczynski, the Polish Ambassador in London] whether, given the existing difficulties, the inevitable complications, and the loss of time involved in a multilateral negotiation, and given also the rapid course of events . . . the British Government might not envisage the possibility (without prejudice to the later outcome of a general negotiation) of concluding a bilateral pact with us without delay."

There was Beck's entire foreign policy. He desired an entente "without delay," for he was pressed for time and he wished as quickly as possible to stay the diplomatic offensive of the Reich as well as the agitation of Polish public opinion. But he refused to let himself be caught in the jaws of the vice of any system of general security. Against the Reich he would put the British alliance, without provoking Hitler by a Russian alliance. He would be at once resistant and supple; and while linking himself up with England he would not abandon the hope of some day effecting a reconciliation with Germany.

He therefore proposed to the British Government a bilateral pact; and he stuck to his formula, even though for the sake of the cause he had to accept the unilateral declaration in favor of Poland which Chamberlain made in the House of Commons on March 31.

Between March 21, when Ribbentrop opened diplomatic hostilities, and March 31, the day of the British guarantee, only ten days had elapsed. Beck was proud of having redressed the situation so quickly and decisively. "As you see, I have not lost any time. It did not take me more than ten days to land on my feet again. The Prague business is not going to be repeated. Hitler has found someone to talk to."

But it was important that Hitler should want to talk. The Chancellor, however, had broken off conversations in Warsaw as well as in Berlin. Furious at Beck's maneuver, which had tripped him with the British guarantee, Hitler had recalled his Ambassador and was undoubtedly preparing some new blow.

In the meantime, Beck had decided to enter into explanations just as he had decided to resist. He believed that he

could save the peace, just as he had saved Danzig. He was
sure he possessed decisive arguments, which he must use at
all costs. Such were his reasons for coming to meet me.

I had followed with keen interest Beck's recital of these
events so heavy with the threat of danger. It was the tale of
a profound misunderstanding, which held, alas! all the elements necessary for a great historical drama.

As I listened while Beck expounded the subtle arguments
with which he hoped to convince and appease Hitler, I did
not get the impression that this misunderstanding could be
dissipated.

"By the agreement I have just signed with Great Britain,
I have completed our system of security without changing
its direction. After all, the alliance with Great Britain is
simply a natural and logical complement to our alliance with
France. Hitler has always known of the alliance with France,
and the Chancellor took no offense at it when he concluded
his *friendly pact of nonaggression* with us in 1934. He expressly recognized its strictly defensive character. How can
the British alliance be more embarrassing to the Reich than
the French alliance? If ever France, by reason of its commitments, had to go to the aid of Poland, is it not certain (given
the close ties binding London to Paris) that Great Britain
also would be drawn in, pact or no pact? By accepting the
British offer of a pact of mutual assistance, I have simply
consented to give juridical expression to a system of security
which already existed in fact. This agreement has in no way
modified Poland's attitude toward Germany. It has not
changed the position that Poland upholds in the matter of
Danzig. As formerly, the Polish Government intends to recognize the right of the German population of Danzig to
liberal self-administration. As hitherto also, it refuses to renounce Poland's essential rights. Between our attitude and
the German claims there is a certain 'margin' which allows
of new negotiations. It is certainly not the agreement we

have signed with Great Britain that will prevent our solving in friendly fashion the differences separating Germany from Poland. Neither the British alliance nor the French alliance is the determining factor in Polish security.

"These two alliances are only part of our system of reinsurance. They will only come into play if the direct engagements contracted by Poland with its immediate neighbors fail. I want to stress this argument, because it seems conclusive to me. Poland is reinsuring itself in London, as it did in Paris, against the risks inherent in the instability of European affairs. But it is on the direct pacts of nonaggression—and primarily on the pact of 1934 with the Reich—that our security really rests.

"That is what I should like Berlin to know. I do not feel that I have in any way failed to live up to the engagements I have undertaken toward the Reich. It would have been quite different had I accepted the pact of mutual assistance literally, as it was put forward by Great Britain. This pact was, indeed, so conceived as to bind Poland not only with the western countries but also with Soviet Russia. Poland, however, wanted none of this multilateral pact, desired by England; for it would have obliged Poland to abandon its principles and change its position. A pact of mutual assistance with Moscow could not fail to alter the profound, eminently European sense of the German-Polish Agreement of 1934. Polish foreign policy would appear to have taken a new direction which might raise just alarms in Berlin. That is why we rejected the British offer. I am ready to give a formal assurance that Poland will never engage itself in such a path. It will resolutely defend its interests but it will not change the basic lines of its foreign policy. I reaffirm my conviction that, as long as the essential bases of the European order remain unaltered, there will always be some way for neighbors to reach an understanding."

Such were the explanations which Beck believed he ought to furnish to Hitler. By the solemn assurance never to change the "direction" of his policy, he believed that he was striking the most sensitive chord in Hitlerian ideology. He was so sincere in his attitude, and so certain that by it he could ultimately banish the threatening specter of war, that he fought fiercely to the end, to the last day of the tragic month of August, 1939, to reject all offers and injunctions by his allies, and any participation whatsoever in a system of general security. He was convinced that in this way he kept a hold on peace.

In reality, he delivered himself to Hitler, bound hand and foot. Rigid in intransigence and isolation, he offered himself to the tender mercies of an implacable adversary. Hitler could ask nothing better than to know that Beck remained faithful to his "principles." This obstinacy was—as Hitler knew—such as to compromise not only the relations between Poland and Russia but even more the whole Allied policy of security. On the eve of going into action, the German Chancellor wanted elbowroom more than anything. Chamberlain's policy of "encirclement" worried him. If England succeeded in bringing into a single security system the pact it had just concluded with Poland and that which it was preparing to negotiate with the U.S.S.R., the Reich's freedom of movement would suffer. By showing his hand, Beck allowed Hitler to make his arrangements in time. From then on Hitler was free to counter the efforts of the Allies to bring Russia into their schemes; he could paralyze the west, and have Poland at his mercy. He was not a man to let such opportunities slip.

Hitler's idea of "the great European interests"—which he had often discussed with the Polish Minister—would certainly not check his advance. The German Chancellor was not bound by the conceptions or arguments of which he made use. His mind was free, and his words had wings. The systems and doctrines he advanced were to serve his aims, not to hamper his movement. When he gave assurances, they bound the assured, not himself.

An affair such as Danzig might have had a thousand successive meanings to him, and he might have given a thousand different explanations of it. But the day he decided to proceed to action, one thing only counted for him—the success of his enterprise. As Count von Moltke had said, the little blue spot of Danzig must disappear from the map. This spot must be of the same color as Germany. This was absolutely essential even though the map of Europe were covered in blood.

Not having grasped this truth, the Polish Foreign Minister pursued a new chimera. He did it resolutely and courageously, for he was a brave and intrepid man. In taking leave of him, I bore away the disturbing image of a human being obstinately struggling against destiny. Turbulent when things were quiet, smooth and calm during a storm, Beck had the proud and violent spirit of an old soldier. His patriotism was ardent but touchy, and he accepted the word of an adversary more readily than the assurances of a friend. So while he was dangerous to others (for he had no "prejudices" as to third-party rights), he was more dangerous to himself. He believed that he had shown himself supremely adroit in disentangling his country from the toils of the Geneva policy, so that he might entrust its safety to the explosive passions of the greatest destroyer in modern history. His romantic transports, which he mistook for realism, were not without grandeur. He had the rare radiance of the elect who seem ordained to determine events but who are, in reality, the instruments of destiny.

CHAPTER II

HITLER PREPARES

Berlin on the eve of Hitler's anniversary. A "look round" with von Ribbentrop. Talk with Göring. Audience at the Imperial Chancellery. The Führer expounds his policy. The military review of April 20, 1939.

M Y first day in Germany was destined to be spent in Breslau. My hosts had arranged this so that I might arrive in Berlin before noon on the next day as the schedule demanded. This was done so that on the threshold of the Third Reich certain legitimate apprehensions might be allayed. Before I was face to face with the men and the institutions of the regime, I was free to consider the past. The city of Breslau, whose most amiable Lord Mayor did me the honors, still had the air of an earlier age in the shadow of its old churches. Despite the tremendous development of its industrial suburbs, there prevailed in it the peaceful atmosphere of a provincial city, full of memories and haunted by dreams. Conscientiously I made the tour of the historical monuments; and that evening, utterly worn out, I slept deliciously in the principal box of the Stadttheater to the familiar and cheering strains of a Viennese operetta.

By morning the scene had changed. Herr von Ribbentrop, in uniform and surrounded by his leading associates, awaited me at the Friedrichstrasse Railway Station in Berlin. A military fanfare sounded; and then, to the strains of a military march, I reviewed the magnificent guard of honor which, with colors flying, received me as I stepped from the train. In those feverish days, when a "still greater Germany" was being planned, Berlin liked to receive its foreign guests in such a manner, and from the moment of their arrival to put on a show of force calculated to seduce, convince, and intimidate them. Nothing less could prepare these foreigners for the agitation awaiting them in the German capital. Berlin, which at this moment was being decorated to make a glorious celebration of the Führer's fiftieth birthday, was continually shaken by acute spasms of enthusiasm and fever. Rejoicing to have burst the limits imposed upon it at Versailles (not so much because these limits were unjust as because they were *limits*), the Reich was tipsy with success and hope. Eloquent public speakers roused the imagination of the crowds; all kinds of theorists—publicists, historians, geopoliticians—added their voices to those of the party leaders in the justification of and demand for new enterprises. Legendary heroes, vigorously brought forward again by the apostles of Pan-Germanism, played their part in the debates: Siegfried the dragon killer and the Hohenstaufen emperors, ancient masters of Europe, showed Hitler the way and urged him to go forward—to complete his program, reach Germany's natural frontiers, and fulfill the imperial destinies of the German people. Infinite gratitude and unbounded confidence rose toward Hitler, supreme incarnation of every German desire. The anonymous crowd, convinced and conquered, and obedient to the orders of the special police, suffered itself to be assembled by the hundreds of thousands, sometimes in interminable processions, sometimes in motionless and trembling masses before the dictator's tribune.

At first sight, none of these popular manifestations indicated xenophobia. Germany's aspirations were immense but vague, and paradoxical as it might seem, did not appear to be directed against foreign nations. It seemed as if Germany wanted the whole world to take part in the good fortune of its rebirth—by sharing power with certain great powers and carrying all the small ones along with it. Formulas of good will to foreign states, sometimes addressed to France, sometimes to the British Empire, and often directed also to the states of southeastern Europe, were devised by the leaders and circulated among the crowds. It was only when the possessive sympathy of the Germans came up against the uneasy reserve or resolute resistance of neighboring peoples that it changed into a sense of insult and into anger. Then the German claims took a definite shape and, instead of being vague, acquired a terrible precision. In the rousing of the German people, cleverly organized by its masters, there was something infinitely farther-reaching than schemes of conquest in the direction of Danzig and the territories of the east. The Reich felt the call to remake the world. The success of the National Socialist party inside the country was a stimulant, an example of what Germany might, and ought to, accomplish abroad. As a shrewd observer of the German phenomenon has written,[1] "The Reich assessed its mission in Europe to be the equal to that of the National Socialist party in Germany. Europe was called upon to direct the world; but to do that Europe itself needed to be directed. Germany had only been rescued from the disorder and anarchy into which democracy had plunged her by the triumph of the authoritarian principle. The same would be true for Europe. . . ."

This claim to direct a world established on new bases was to be exposed in detail in a work which during the war became the breviary of German political thought.[2] "Thanks to its superior political capability, the German kernel, as a determining center, is organizing around itself, into a political community, a group of territories peopled by those of other races, which ethnically may be completely autonomous. In this community, German direction and the autonomy of the foreign peoples will combine in an organic hierarchy."

This plan referred less to western Europe, which the Reich regarded as "a zone lying outside its sphere of active intervention," than to the countries of eastern Europe,

1. Claude Moret, *L'Allemagne et la réorganisation de l'Europe.*
2. Karl Richard Ganzer, *Das Reich als europäische Ordnungsmacht.*

where Germany intended to act as it would. But it still affected the entire political order of the Continent, for it struck at the ideas of law, morals, and politics upon which Christian and European civilization had been built.

These ideas, however, were more firmly established in the consciousness of the European nations than democracy in Germany. The old Europe was built to resist attack; and Hitler could neither force it by the violence of his speech nor lay hold of it by any kind of *Putsch*.

This old Europe, however, had no desire to fight. It sought to avoid fuss, and at times consented to submit to the Führer's caprices. But immediately it reasserted itself. Great or small, the states could renounce neither the prerogatives of their power nor the virtues of their liberty. They all refused to accept a retrogression which would have driven them to seek the security of an authoritarian regime in the heart of a medieval empire (such as that toward which the admirers of the Hohenstaufens wished to lead them).

The discrepancy between the level on which the great majority of nations lived and that on which the Hitlerian tyranny moved contained potentially all the elements of catastrophe. The Third Reich, collecting enormous forces for the impossible adventure, was well aware of the indefinable resistance on all sides. Hence its sharp fits of ill-humor and its great bursts of anger whenever "the German people" discovered that the world had no wish to think as it did.

The diplomats of the medium and small countries who passed through Berlin during this time of disturbance found their receptions change without warning from hot to cold, from the most flattering of welcomes to the most distrustful of attitudes, from a show of sympathy to alarming warnings, from the most amiable speeches (appeals, assurances, and encouragements) to words full of threats. However clear their consciences might be, however slight their possibility of action, they had continually to plead not guilty (according to a usage which has become general and tends to settle relations between great and small powers in the manner of the wolf and the lamb). They had to prove that their country did not intend to employ its feeble forces to attack its big neighbor; that it had no desire to "encircle" anyone; and that it would take good care not to trouble the current whose violent waters had their source in some powerful empire.

In contrast, the pacific pronouncements made to these diplomats had a somewhat strange echo in martial Berlin, with flags and banners waving, and resounding with processions.

The immense welcoming city gave to its foreign visitors an impression of uncertainty and unease. I was the more aware of this because the memory of a certain event still left a shadow. Was it not at the very railway station where I had just received a warm welcome that a month earlier a similar flourish of trumpets had greeted M. Hacha? Received with all the honors still due him, the improvised President of unhappy Czechoslovakia had been escorted with full ceremony to the Wilhelmstrasse, there to undergo proceedings that were continued until very late at night, unltimately to be brought to the point where he himself asked for the suppression of his own country.

To that same place I was escorted by the Chief of Protocol two hours after my arrival. Gravely polite, Herr von Ribbentrop welcomed me in his office. Standing below Lenbach's famous portrait of Bismarck, the Minister invited me to make with him the usual survey of the situation. He spoke easily, sometimes volubly, freely making use of well-worn phrases the better to express his thoughts and to prevent any digression. In the manner usual at that time, when the Nazi leaders sought to make events subject to their ideas, his exposition soon became special pleading: His mission was to repair the wrongs done to the Reich at Versailles: that was his entire policy. With head thrown back, lips drawn, blue

IN RIBBENTROP'S OFFICE

"Standing below Lenbach's famous portrait of Bismarck, the Minister invited me to make with him the usual survey of the situation."

(See page 58.)

IN THE FÜHRER'S APARTMENT

"Sunk deep in the corner of his chair, as if he wanted to take up the least possible space, he prepared to defend the essential qualities of his policy . . . which were, according to him, moderation and modesty."

eyes steely with resentment, he was pleased to enumerate the grievances on which the Reich based its action against the world. He recalled the policy of reparations and of disarmament, the "rape" of the colonies, the isolation of Austria, the creation of Czechoslovakia—that enemy state in the heart of the German community— the "absurd" Polish Corridor, and the "impossible" situation of Danzig. It was necessary to be careful: the sense of injustice was a lever capable of provoking the world to revolt and turning it upside down. By redressing the wrongs committed against his country one by one, and without bloodshed, the Führer had respected international law. But his forces were growing stronger, and it certainly was unwise to set an obstinately hostile lack of understanding against his will to create a better order. The Führer wanted peace, only peace. The Reich had reached its natural frontiers; it had filled its vital living space; and had no other desire than to consolidate its positions and develop its empire in peace. . . .

In giving these final assurances, which were in violent contrast with the state of mind prevailing in Berlin, Herr von Ribbentrop became again the Minister of Foreign Affairs. Was not his role to play down German national claims the better to assure their total realization by successive stages? To reassure Europe, it was necessary to interpose the soothing assurances of a wise diplomacy between the increasingly lively apprehensions of neighboring peoples and the vehemence of German desires. Herr von Ribbentrop lent himself to this with little enthusiasm or conviction. He was in no humor to please, even by false pretenses, and even while seeking to reassure his hearers—in well-rehearsed language—he clearly indicated that should anyone try to check the Reich on its course, it would certainly not be he.

Yet Germany had never needed to reassure the world more than in the spring of 1939. Its last success had alarmed its friends as well as its enemies. Everybody saw the Reich in a new light; the cloak had fallen from the excuses it had offered to disguise its intentions and serve its purpose. By the occupation of Bohemia (March 15) the Reich had passed from the policy of national expansion to that of aggression: claims founded on racial community had given way to military imperialism. Instantly the Reich was seen to be dangerous to all its neighbors who had tried hard to believe that Hitler would restrict his claim to German territories.

The structure built at Munich tumbled like a house of cards. The signatories of the short-lived compromise, western powers as well as Germany, had been forced to acknowledge the miserable failure of their attempts at conciliation. The French Government had hastened to inform Berlin (March 17) that it regarded the action taken against Czechoslovakia "as a flagrant violation of the letter and the spirit of the agreements signed at Munich," and that it could not recognize the legitimacy of the new situation. Britain had taken a similar stand. It had refused to recognize the conquest and was prepared to show an even more violent reaction to any new incursions on the part of the Reich. On March 20 Mr. Chamberlain proposed to the governments at Paris, Moscow, and Warsaw that they should "join with His Majesty's Government in immediate consultations with a view to offering common resistance to any new German challenge." The first effect of this proposition was the conclusion of the Anglo-Polish Agreement. It also initiated negotiations between London, Paris, and Moscow. The threat Hitler's policy offered to the general peace was made clear. All eyes, even those which had so long been wilfully blind, were finally opened. Europe seemed to be searching for some means of uniting against a common danger.

This violent reaction had thrown certain German calculations into confusion. The Munich Agreement and its corollaries (the Anglo-German Pact of September 30, 1938, and the Franco-German Pact of December 6, 1938) were now only scraps of paper. The security of the west could no longer be balanced against the freedom of action which the Reich claimed as its own in the east. Besides, this precious freedom of action was everywhere being shattered: England and France were strengthening their ties with Poland, negotiating with Moscow and guaranteeing Rumania and Greece. The eastern "space" was again being invaded by the diplomacy of these "foreigners from the west."

It only needed the intervention of another continent to show Hitler the vanity of an effort which sought to subject part of Europe to his law. This intervention came on April 14, 1939. In a message addressed to the German Chancellor and to Mussolini, President Roosevelt stated that "hundreds of millions of human beings are living today in constant fear of a new war or even a series of wars. . . ." The President indicated the causes of this profound uneasiness:

"Three nations in Europe and one in Africa have seen their independent existence terminated. . . . Reports, which we trust are not true, insist that further acts of aggression are contemplated against still other independent nations. Plainly the world is moving toward the moment when this situation must end in catastrophe unless a more rational way of guiding events is found. . . . I am convinced that the cause of world peace would be greatly advanced if the nations of the world were to obtain a frank statement relating to the present and future policy of governments."

It is scarcely likely that Hitler, on receiving this message, was able to read in it the signs of destiny. Nor, underlying those words so seldom used in diplomatic conversations, did he perceive the force which was to contribute powerfully to put an end to his unlawful ambitions. Perhaps he smiled, like Herr von Ribbentrop when he was speaking to me of the President's strange message:

"Mr. Roosevelt would like to be assured that we shall never attack or occupy countries such as Norway, Denmark, Holland, Belgium, France, Poland, Greece, and Russia. . . . But I ask you: which of these countries really feels itself in danger? If any one of them desires a declaration from us, we are ready to give it directly—but not through the medium of an American president!"

The smiles of the German leaders could not hide their annoyance. The world had awakened a little too soon—for the Führer's program had not yet been entirely carried out. The efforts which still remained to be made (which nobody, though faced with the gravest threats, dreamed of renouncing) were henceforth to encounter a fierce resistance. The German leaders were not, be it said, inclined to overestimate the strength of this resistance; they knew the gaps in the military preparations of France and the absolute lack of preparation of the British; they did not fear the west. The confusion caused by the Munich Agreement in the countries of eastern Europe would be favorable to the Reich; Geneva's prestige was diminished; and it was difficult to organize a new system of collective security in time. So far as the Americans and the Russians were concerned, the former were far distant, the latter uncertain, and the European allies could not be sure of their collaboration. The military force at the disposal of the Reich gave it a definite advantage over all neighboring states, and this advantage could not be neutralized if the Reich acted in time. Consequently, the diplomacy of the Reich pursued a double aim; on the one hand, it needed at all costs to prevent the collusion of the great empires which could establish several fronts; on the other hand, it needed to prepare a definite program which could swiftly be put into operation while Germany still could count on superior strength.

Herr von Ribbentrop, in his analysis of the situation, gave me no indication of his future intentions. It was for another, much greater than he, to carry me further into the political thought that was directing the German Reich.

Meanwhile, I carried on with my program. It included a visit to the Air Ministry, where Marshal Göring awaited me. The Marshal had just returned by air, after spending a few

days in Tripolitania as the guest of his colleague, Balbo. The
work that the Italians were doing in their African colonies
had deeply impressed him, and the first words he addressed
to me were a vehement protest against the "madmen" who
had deprived a great power like Germany of all colonial
outlet. "But we shall recover our colonies, I promise you!"
And as this last word recalled to him other grievances that
concerned me more directly, he spoke to me with some
asperity of the guarantees which Rumania had just accepted
from France and England. Less correct in his expressions
than Herr von Ribbentrop and with a less studious courtesy,
Marshal Göring, despite his gross bulk, reminiscent of a Roman emperor during the Decline, had a certain communica-
tive frankness which encouraged conversation. Since he had
intervened at the moment of the German-Rumanian tension
to appease the Führer's anger and suggest a means of conciliation, he believed that he had a right to speak more freely
to me than his colleagues on the Anglo-French guarantees.
But it did not annoy him to be contradicted, and the rather
lively dialogue that ensued occasioned him no ill feeling.

"You have called the English and the French to your aid.
You want them to fight for you?"

"We are determined to fight for our independence and
our frontiers ourselves, Herr Marshal."

"How long have you been a diplomat, Monsieur le Ministre?"

"Only for a few months. But I have been a soldier for
twenty-five years."

This reference to my service in the Flying Corps caused
the Marshal to unbend. He continued in a more affable tone:

"Still, you ought to realize that this guarantee is useless.
When Germany promises its military aid it gives it, because
it is able to. Listen to this: if the Bolsheviks ever attacked
your frontiers, my aircraft would be there in a few hours
to protect you. But England cannot aid you. For selfish
motives, it is trying to draw countries to its side in which

it has no concern. Then, when danger threatens, it drops them. The help promised by England is absolutely inoperative. Have you asked yourself, Monsieur le Ministre, by what channel British assistance could reach you in case of war?"

"I have never given it a thought, Herr Marshal."

As Göring seemed amazed by such a reply, I explained:

"Why should I worry about it? If the Russians attack us, I know that you are ready to defend us—as you have just assured me. If the Hungarians march against us, our own forces will be quite sufficient. Who, then, would you have attack us?"

With a smile the Marshal declared: "Perhaps you are right."

Thereupon he changed his tone and spoke to me gravely of the policy of encirclement.

"This policy directed by London is dangerous. Above all it is dangerous for you. The Reich remembers 1914; it will never allow itself to be encircled; never again does it want to fight the whole world. It will therefore defend itself fiercely and will attack the enemy front at its most vulnerable and weakest points. If Rumania is our friend, we want to see it great and strong. If it takes part in the policy of encirclement, we shall abandon it to the designs of its Hungarian and Bulgarian neighbors."

I replied without hesitation: "There is no policy of encirclement. There is no country, great or small, which dreams of attacking Germany. Any aggressive political or military encirclement of the Reich is absolutely out of the question. I should not say the same of a certain psychological encirclement which seems to be taking shape. But that does not arise from a policy directed by the governments. It arises from a feeling of fear and insecurity which tends to unite all the peoples of Europe regardless of frontiers. I leave it to your judgment to decide what policy has aroused such a sentiment. I shall confine myself to recalling to you the

regrettable impression that the occupation of Czechoslovakia made throughout the world. And may I recall to you
certain expressions, such as 'vital living space' and 'sphere
of influence,' which foster a profound and general sense
of uneasiness in the world. This uneasiness exists in my country. It exists also in Yugoslavia, Poland, and Turkey, as I
have seen for myself. . . . It exists everywhere; it has gone
the rounds of Europe; and this may well be the encirclement
of which you complain. But it is for you to put an end to this
uneasiness. You can do so by making an effort to give definition and precise limits to the principles that govern your
policy. You ought to do this, for everyone today knows
your strength; and strength, like honor, has its obligations."

I had no illusion that I had convinced the Marshal. I was
grateful to him for letting me speak without interruption.

The next day, April 19, I was received by Herr Hitler
at the Imperial Chancellery.

After having crossed the court of honor, not without
emotion, and ascended the monumental staircase, in company with Herr von Ribbentrop and M. Radou Croutzesco,
Rumanian Minister in Berlin, I entered the immense gallery
leading to the private apartments of the Führer. At the head
of our procession marched a red-haired giant, Freiherr Dörn-
berg, the introducer of ambassadors. I had known him in
Bucharest, where as a young diplomat he had served as an
attaché at the German Legation. I remembered some society
theatricals in which he had acted in a fairy tale of Perrault's,
together with the six little girls of my friend, Jean de Haute-
cloque. He had played the part of the ogre—with such talent
that little Hop o' My Thumb had never dared to remove his
seven-league boots. This incident of the boots came back
to mind as I followed the ogre who, with huge strides, led
us to the threshold of the well-padded door, behind which
was the master of Germany.

When the door was opened and we stepped into the pres-

ence of the Führer I had to make a serious effort to get rid of
the false pictures which filled my mind. I looked in vain for
any evidence of that mysterious attraction with which he
had been clothed in the imagination of the crowds. The
man looked just like the many photographs which we saw
day by day. He was smaller and more paltry than I had
thought—at first sight he seemed astonishingly negative.
I had been told often enough of his piercing eyes, the irresistible charm of his voice. I felt nothing of the sort. There
was nothing out of the ordinary about him. The color of
his eyes and the timbre of his voice were equally dull and
caused neither discomfort nor confusion. Dullness was also
the prevailing note of his uniform (maroon and black). His
manners, on the other hand, were of an agreeable simplicity;
there was no bombast about him, and he could be extremely
polite. His man-to-man attitude was direct and natural and
inspired that peculiar feeling of confidence of which more
than one political leader was to be the victim.

During the course of the conversation, which quickly
became a long, passionate monologue, I thought that I
grasped the secret of his uncanny power over the masses.
When, pursuing a formula or an idea, he warmed up enough
to show something of himself, the sound of his voice, and
still more the significance of his words, his choice of arguments and the succession of his thoughts, seemed in strange
harmony with an invisible force that surrounded him. Then
he became a demagogue in the ancient sense of the word:
the man who lends his voice to the crowd and through
whom the crowd speaks. His personality took on a mysterious amplitude. He spoke to the accompaniment of a cease-
less thunder, and the illusion was complete. One felt that
his double stood behind him—a collective double, the
"mass," the countless crowd, the people—and his discourse
gave the impression of a great army on the march. Sheer
weight, rather than quality, gave importance to his ideas.
Had the masses possessed a single voice to express themselves,

they would have chosen his arguments, used his phrases, and spoken as he did. He was the crowd-man, destined to unite a thousand sources of mediocre and often vulgar ideas into an irresistible torrent.

Even the most reserved of those who spoke with him could not escape the grip of his power. He had the gift of instilling a sense of isolation into those who resisted him. Met by the tide of his vehement speech, which seemed to beset and encircle the mind, one never felt oneself small—but one did feel alone. It was not with a man that one spoke but with a million men.

Hitler asked me to be seated on the couch, while he sat facing me in an armchair. He was disposed to listen. I knew that such an opportunity must be used as quickly as possible. Once the Führer began to speak, it would be impossible to interrupt him.

Profiting by the courteous reception he had accorded me, I spoke frankly to him. I expressed the hope that the new economic agreement between the Reich and Rumania would, as its preamble stated, help to "consolidate the peace" between the two countries. In signing this accord Rumania had had in view not only its own interests but also the entire European situation. It had considered that a wise regulation of interchange between Central Europe and the countries of the southeast, in a spirit of continental collaboration, was necessary the better to insure the general peace. In the same spirit Rumania had accepted the unilateral guarantee given by France and Great Britain. This guarantee covered its independence and territorial integrity; it was not directed against anyone; and by reinforcing the security of a country which held a key situation on the Danube, it served the general interest of peace. Rumania hoped that the system of guarantees, as well as the method of economic collaboration, might become general so as to unite all the European countries in the service of peace.

I then reviewed the relations existing between my country

and the neighboring states; and (recalling my conversation in the train with Colonel Beck) I expressed with some strength my conviction that Poland was sincerely animated by the most pacific intentions toward the Reich.

Hitler had let me speak without interruption so that when he spoke in turn, he might remain master of the conversation. He did not like dialogues; when once he began to speak, he had ears only for his own inspiration.

He began by speaking to me of my country, and he did so with kindly feeling:

"Our economic agreement is good, because it is based on natural interests. It is durable. They say that we forced it on you. That is absurd. The exchanges established by this agreement strengthen your position. You give us food, we give you machines. Your position is better than ours. You can live without our machines, while we cannot live without food-stuffs. But do not let us speak of superiority or inferiority. We wish to develop the best relations with you on a basis of perfect equality. It is in our interest that you should produce as much as possible. It is in your interest to receive our machines, because they are excellent and will constantly improve. We have the firm intention of making the best machines in the world."

Carried away by his burst of good will, he went so far in his amiability as to speak ill of the Hungarians.

"They say that I want to restore the grandeur of Hungary. Why should I be so ill advised? A greater Hungary might be embarrassing for the Reich. Besides, the Hungarians have always shown us utter ingratitude. They have no regard or sympathy for the German minorities. As for me, I am only interested in my Germans. I said so frankly to Count Csaky, who sat just where you are now. And I have said so without equivocation to the Regent Horthy and to Imredy: the German minorities in Rumania and Yougoslavia do not want to return to Hungary; they are better treated in their new fatherland. And what the German minorities do not want, the Reich does not want either.

"Of course, there would obviously be a reason why we should protect the Hungarians. They were on our side during the Great War. But that is not entirely correct. It was we who were on their side, to help them in the war which Austria-Hungary had so unwisely started. If I had been in power in 1914, I should not so simply have submitted to the consequences of the ultimatum of Berchtold, Tisza, and company. I should have intervened in the negotiations between Austria-Hungary and Serbia. It was absurd to go to war in order to save the prestige of Austria-Hungary. The old Hapsburg Empire was an anachronism—a state impossible to defend because of its injustice toward the nationalities composing it. It stirred up hatred, used the Magyars against the Rumanians, the Czechs against the Germans, the Slovaks against the Hungarians, and so on. That is why, in spite of my Austrian origin, I did not fight for Austria-Hungary. I insisted as a German on enlisting in the German Army. If I had been at the head of Germany when the last war broke out, I should have put forward the division of Austria-Hungary on ethnological lines; the Germans to Germany, the Poles to Poland, the Serbs to Serbia, the Rumanians to Rumania. The principle of nationality, you see, ought to be the basis of every durable order. That is why I shall not touch Rumania. I shall not encourage any claims directed against it—as long, of course, as I may count on its friendship."

This last reservation gave the Führer's assurances a contingent value. However, it was true that Hitler seemed no longer to cherish any hostile intentions toward us or to be preparing any imminent move against us. The economic agreement had succeeded in quieting Germany. I could not ask for more. Scarcely a month had elapsed since the man I was speaking to, this ardent champion of the principle of nationality, had seized Czechoslovakia. At that moment, Rumania's position had caused its friends the most acute uneasiness. In his report of March 19 (communicated to me by the French Government) Ambassador Coulondre had expressed the fear that Hitler, when occupying Bohemia, had had it in mind to "penetrate further east." It seemed to me, after listening to Hitler, that an immediate threat was no longer to be contemplated as regards Rumania. This was all that could be hoped for in those times of provisional security when, for a country on which the Reich cast covetous eyes, every day gained might enable the peace-loving powers to recover, regain contact, and attempt joint measures of preservation.

The condition upon which Hitler would grant us his confidence was evidently not of a nature to favor our participation in a move toward a general agreement of assistance.

"The Anglo-French guarantees," declared the Chancellor, "will be of no use to you. But I shall not take exception to them. I know your weakness for France. My attitude would be quite different were you to take part, alongside the Soviet, in this vast plan of encirclement which the government in London is preparing. Such a plan endangers the existence of the Reich, and we are determined to defend ourselves by every means."

This warning (so similar to those which Hitler did not cease to give Beck) was obviously important. The Nazi leaders, the Chancellor as well as Göring, seemed disposed to regard any agreement with the Soviet Union as a provocation to Germany. But, to be certain of the favor of the Reich, it was not enough simply to take heed of this warning. The words which Hitler was to address to me on the question of Poland were to show how little hold Beck's "principle" (of keeping Russia outside his political combinations) had gained on the Führer.

"The fault of M. Beck," Hitler told me, "is that he has turned to London. I shall never understand the change that has come over Poland's attitude. It is a change which may prove fatal to it. Beck's arguments are of no value. His story about reassurance does not hold water. The Anglo-Polish engagement is in flagrant contradiction of the agreement which I concluded earlier with Marshal Pilsudski. In case of a conflict between the Reich and any other power, a conflict in which England would be led to participate, Poland is pledged to take up a position against Germany. I am told in reply that I approved the existence of the Franco-Polish Agreement. That has nothing to do with the case. In 1934 I took note of the Polish engagements then existing, but I do not accept a subsequent enlargement of these engagements. In the conditions created by these new engagements, I should never have signed my agreement with Poland! There you have the reason why I no longer attach any importance to it.

"Nevertheless, I had the best of intentions toward Pilsudski's Poland. I respected its frontiers and all the absurd provisions of Versailles. I prevented the German press from protesting against the scandalous way in which the German minorities were treated. I paid no attention to infamous attacks such as these. . . ." Here Hitler brandished in front of me a packet of Polish newspapers which, it appeared, violently attacked Germany and its leaders.[1]

"In all circumstances, I have shown the Polish people my understanding and friendship. Only recently, I made Poland an offer that will abide in the annals of history as an act of incredible generosity. If Poland had understood it, it might have helped us to resolve all matters outstanding between us—and which in any event cannot remain as they are. I offered Poland an understanding regarding the German City of Danzig. This city, in conformity with its express will, must be reunited with the Reich. Nothing, absolutely

---

1. I hastened to note the titles of the Polish newspapers cited by Hitler, so as to speak about them to the Polish Ambassador. M. Lipski told me that they were "rags" published in Danzig (not Poland), which the German propaganda services continually put before the Führer.

nothing, can stop that. In exchange, I proposed that Danzig should remain economically bound to Poland. I have always recognized that this city was the prolongation of Poland's economic territory. I also asked for an extraterritorial right of passage to Danzig and East Prussia. In addition, I was ready to recognize formally all Poland's frontiers; and I was prepared to promise not to raise any political or territorial claims against Poland for twenty-five years. Still further, I was disposed to place the new Slovakian state under the protection of a tripartite regime—German-Magyar-Polish. Such a collaboration could assure peace in Central Europe for years to come. That is the extraordinary offer which Poland refused. I assure you that Poland certainly will not soon see another. M. Beck has joined up with the western powers. He has settled his own fate. I do not know what will follow, but one thing is certain: the solution that will be reached will no longer consider Poland's interests in the same way. As for the Danzig affair, it must be settled with the utmost dispatch—and it will be, whatever political schemes M. Beck may have!"

The Chancellor had finished that part of his monologue which was addressed to the Rumanian Foreign Minister. Thereafter he spoke to the traveler who on the morrow was to continue his journey to London and Paris. I felt that I was becoming a more important auditor. Through my humble self, the Führer was talking to the western chancelleries. His voice became graver and more contemplative. Sunk deep in the corner of his chair, as if he wanted to take up the least possible space, he prepared to defend the essential qualities of his policy against the accusations of bad faith which had been leveled against them. According to him, these qualities were moderation and modesty.

"I am accused of being unlimited in my desires. What injustice! I have always been careful to set precise limits to my claims and my enthusiasm. For nothing is more precise than the ends I strive for. I am fighting against the Treaty of Versailles: that is the fight of my life. So far, I have always been the victor. I have still a few battles to wage. I shall win them. I am not fighting against the interests of any other people. I fight for Germany's just cause. That is why I know how to set limits on myself. I limited myself with respect to England, with whom I have signed a naval agreement. I limited myself with respect to France by renouncing Alsace-Lorraine once and for all. That was a painful gesture, which I alone had the power to make. I made it without qualification or mental reservation. With me, the whole German people, the youth, the army, and the press, have loyally and forever renounced those provinces for whose possession France and Germany have so long fought. I have limited my intentions with regard to Italy by giving up the numerous Germans of the Tyrol which Italy annexed in 1918. I knew that, if I had to fight on behalf of all the Germans scattered about the world—Italy, Yugoslavia, Rumania, and Russia—I should have to wage war all my life. But, for my part, I want peace. In the struggles I have undertaken and won, not a drop of blood has been shed. I have limited my claims regarding Yugoslavia, with which I am happy to maintain the best relations. I have the same wise and moderate attitude toward Hungary. I had limited myself as regards Poland, and it is not my fault if M. Beck has not seen fit to allow his country to profit by the advantages gained for it by Marshal Pilsudski. I intend to respect the frontiers of Holland, Belgium, and Switzerland. I shall never attack these countries. People attribute to me the preposterous idea of wanting to enlarge the battle front at their expense in case of war. I am accused of laying claim to the Belgian and Dutch colonies. Nothing of the sort. We do not want other people's colonies. We refuse them even when they are offered us (for there are well-intentioned people—obviously neither Belgians nor Dutch—to offer them to us).We want our own colonies, and we shall end by getting them. As to the battle front, why should we begin again the same mistakes we made in 1914?

We have no interest in enlarging this front; quite the contrary. We shall concentrate all our forces at the point where we must go through; and there are no fortifications which could hold out against the technical means at our disposal. The Maginot Line will not change the way of the war.

"I intend to extend the German Reich to its natural limits, and no more. If I have occupied Bohemia, it is not for the pleasure of making conquests but to prevent the continuance, within the German living space, of an alien, hostile wedge driven into the body of the Reich."

Here the Führer understood that he needed to be more explicit. The affair of Czechoslovakia decidedly had a bad press; and the theory of "limits" would hardly suffice to calm opinion. The good intentions had been so contradicted by facts that a further argument was necessary to maintain the "right" on Hitler's side. He set about defending the right of the strongest with the quibbles of a crooked lawyer. I was astonished at his ferocity. Doubtless he had recently discovered that the improbable stereotyped reply his ambassadors had been ordered to make to the complaints of the foreign chancelleries—that Bohemia itself asked, through its president, to be incorporated into the Reich—was such as to aggravate still further the uneasiness caused in Europe by the occupation of Prague. At all costs it was essential to repel the offensive conducted by the foreign newspapers, news agencies, and radio stations, if only that German propaganda might retain its initiative, its freedom of action, and the unhampered use of the excellent "ethnical" argument which it intended to turn to account in the Danzig affair. The troublesome reaction of European public opinion must not be allowed to check the realization of a program which was far from being completed. If Hitler consented to defend himself and to that devoted his whole zeal, it was the better to be able to attack.

"I never wanted to annex the Czechs, I assure you. My sole thought was to liberate the four million Germans who found themselves in an intolerable situation in Bohemia. But this problem immediately raised the question of the other nationalities. The Hungarians, Poles, and Slovaks all demanded their rights. So I was obliged to re-examine in its entirety a question which had only been partially settled at Munich.

"You will recall that Hungary and Czechoslovakia appealed to us to fix their new frontiers by arbitration. The western countries were not consulted, for they had no concern in that region where the role of maintaining peace is exclusively ours. The Reich and Italy issued the Vienna Award; neither France nor England protested against this action, which nevertheless departed formally from the Munich arrangements. How could they have protested? Germany and Italy were approached by the interested countries themselves, which intended to address themselves to them and to them alone.

"But the Vienna Award did not put an end to the claims of the neighboring states. You Rumanians know better than anyone else the stubbornness with which the Hungarians and Poles sought to divide Subcarpathian Ukraine between them so as to have a common frontier. You were opposed to the idea; so were we. But I did not wish to play a thankless role, and I ended by yielding to the insistent demands of the Hungarians. . . . Since, at that moment, Slovakia manifested its desire to gain its independence, I realized that there could no longer be any question of maintaining a state that was breaking up itself." [1]

Without taking into account the bewilderment caused by such explanations, Hitler pretended that in his good faith he had been surprised by his adversaries' lack of understanding.

1. This version of events, which attributed the initiative in the dismemberment of Czechoslovakia to the neighboring countries, and notably to Hungary, was put forward by Hitler again in his speech of April 28, 1939.

"Why should this solution be in opposition to the Munich Agreements? What could these agreements accomplish against a decay which was in the nature of things? And by what right did England claim to intervene in order to prevent the normal, natural evolution of the situation in Central Europe?"

The Führer's voice suddenly became sharper, his utterance more nervous and abrupt. He left his chair and spoke standing, pacing up and down the room. The monologue developed into an oration. Hitler had embarked on the subject which obsessed him: England's resistance.

"The English are determined not to understand. Instead of coming to an agreement with us, as I have so often proposed to them, they insist on blocking our path and seeking a quarrel with us. They do not admit our political power. They stand in the way of our economic development. They seek allies against us everywhere. They undermine our influence and raise illusory barriers against us; they maintain a campaign of hatred and prepare a general war, the responsibility for which they already seek to put on us. With what do they reproach us? We only want what is our due. We want our colonies, which we need; they are essential to our economic life, to our sense of strength and honor. We wish England, whose empire we respect, to respect in turn our own sphere of interest, and the space without which we cannot live."

Here the orator, carried away by his eloquence, showed the core of his thoughts. Germany, coming too late in the partitioning of the world and having no intention of accepting the lot God sets apart for the poet, dreamed of a new distribution of the good things of the world. This conception, which incorporated his most cherished ambitions as well as his thirst for power, had been put to the British by Hitler when he asked the same question that the Emperor William put to Joseph Chamberlain and King Edward:

"Will you share the world with us?" And again the British had replied: "No."

This determined and implacable "No," which Hitler thought he heard whenever he called up the image of "perfidious Albion," filled him with a rage that was "heroic and sacred." His manner and countenance were changed, his voice became loud and threatening, while a strange light shone in his eyes. Rage unleashed his soul, which threw off the constraint of *limits* it had provisionally imposed on itself and showed itself for what it really was, violent and ungovernable. Was it not nursing the boldest schemes, which might, as political combinations offered, open up the exotic region of the former colonies, or the east as far as the Kuban and the Caucasus, or the most fertile African territories? It seemed as though the Führer had only established those famous limits of which his moderation boasted so that he might the better rely on them when he concentrated his forces to strike at one particular point. He had limited himself regarding Austria when his armies were penetrating into the Rhineland; he had given assurances to Prague when he annexed Austria; he had agreed to guarantee Bohemia when he took the Sudeten from it. And, after occupying Czechoslovakia, he left the remnants of that country to its neighbors, well knowing that soon it would be the turn of Poland and Hungary. But it was toward England that his policy, masked though it was by unending equivocations, had to make its greatest effort, in order to penetrate to the coveted world outside. His mind was given entirely to this, the culminating point of his successes. His gains in Germany and Central Europe would be of no value, and he could not give a world significance to the imperial destinies of the German people, unless he succeeded in the final showdown with Britain either by gaining its collusion or by destroying its resistance.

Therefore the mere suggestion of a quarrel with Britain enraged him; the statesman became the partisan, and his frustrated imagination became frenzied. It threw off all limitations of frontier, expanded into limitless zones of influence, occupied Lebensraum and was lost in the infinite. . . .

"Oh, well, if England wants war, it will have it. It won't be so easy a war as it thinks, nor one on the old pattern. England will no longer have the whole world at its side. At least half the world is with us. And it will be a war of destruction beyond belief. Besides, how can England think of a modern war when she cannot mount two divisions on any front?

"As for us, our misfortunes have been of use. We shall fight with other arms than those of 1914. We shall fight ruthlessly, to the end, with no consideration. We have never been as strong as we are now. To the invincibility of our armies must be added the genius of our technicians, engineers, and chemists. We shall astound the world with our methods and inventions. So on what do they rely to hold us in check? Their air force? They may perhaps succeed in bombarding a few towns, but how can they measure up to us? Our air force leads the world, and no enemy town will be left standing!"

Here Hitler suddenly broke off his terrifying prophecies to ask in a calmer and graver voice:

"But, after all, why this unimaginable massacre? In the end victor or vanquished, we shall all be buried in the same ruins; and the only one who will profit is that man in Moscow." (*"Am Ende werden wir alle, Sieger und Besiegte, unter den gleichen Trümmern liegen, und nur einem wird es nützen, dem da von Moskau."*)

As though seeking in advance to rid himself of such a responsibility, the Führer added sorrowfully:

"And to think that it is I—I who am accused in Germany of being an impenitent admirer of the British Empire, I who have so often tried to establish a lasting understanding between the Reich and England (an understanding which today I still consider necessary to the defense of European civilization)—to think that it is I who must envisage such a conflict! And this entirely on account of the incomprehension and blind obduracy of the leaders of Great Britain!"

With these words of disillusion (which still held something like a gleam of hope), the Chancellor closed the very long audience he had given me.

As I left the Imperial Chancellery, I thought over what I had heard. I tried to separate what should be forgotten (tempting as it might be taken at its face value) from what should be retained. When Hitler asserted that he would never attack Belgium or Holland, when he solemnly avowed that he would in nowise support the Magyar claims against Rumania, when finally he made it clear that any agreement with Moscow meant an attack on Europe, his duplicity was not in doubt. His threats to Poland seemed to me to carry more truth. Hitler had fully decided that he would not revive the "generous" offer he had recently made to Beck. Danzig he must have, and perhaps much more. He was not interested in the Polish Foreign Minister's explanations. Beck had told me that if the Reich touched Danzig it was war. After hearing both parties I thought I was right in believing that Polish affairs were in a very bad way. The war for Danzig was bound to come sometime. Was a respite possible? I had the feeling that Hitler had not fixed the precise date of intervention. He was wondering how he could isolate Poland. He wanted to avoid a general war. Not that he would recoil from it if he thought it inevitable. He knew that he was better prepared, militarily, than his adversaries. The picture he had painted of a future war was not a deterrent. It was his warning to the "others"; because history would hold them responsible: he only recognized the responsibility he had assumed to his own people, whose high destinies he had pledged himself to realize. Such a mission raised him above all judgments and risks.

However, the wish to do something different from his predecessors obsessed him. He did not want to have the whole world against him. He must have at least half the world on his side. And he seemed to have retained a faint hope (before looking, moreover!) of finding this requisite half in the one nation toward which his so-called sympathies had always driven him: in England. Perhaps it might still be possible to arouse a spirit of "understanding" in London, which would make a comprehensive settlement (whether in connection with Danzig or anything else) possible. By that means, on a world basis, things could be tried that had misfired on the restricted basis of Munich—the allocation of spheres of influence. The words Hitler had spoken to me regarding England, sometimes threatening, sometimes insidious, seemed to convey such an idea. What was clear was that the country toward which this disingenuous argument was directed, the country which Hitler needed to divide the world with him in equal portions, had no substance: it existed only in the Führer's imagination. England, such as it really was, in no way justified any such illusions. Having founded its policy on an order governed by equilibrium and on a commonwealth held together by mutual consent, how could England countenance anything that would upset international order and national rights by force, and shake the very foundations of the civilization, grandeur, and existence of the English people? This "dream" of Hitler's must inevitably drive him along the road to catastrophe.

However, it is not entirely without interest to remark that, when everything seemed fated, since Beck was determined to defend Danzig and Hitler was determined to take it, the Polish Minister of Foreign Affairs turned toward Germany, while the German Chancellor looked toward England: both with the same hope of receiving some saving indication of understanding.

Each seemed to rely on someone else's good will in order to ward off misfortune. But Hitler's Germany on principle could not renounce a single point of its program. It had begun a movement which no one could stop; the world must yield. The vain hope that the British would give way in their idea of liberty was, in any case, only the inevitable conclusion of a long train of fallacious reasoning. Hitler used a specious dialectic to deceive others—and doubtless himself. His words, deliberately measured, sounded like the steady ticking of the clockwork of an infernal machine.

He had ascribed to himself the role of reformer. He wanted to create a New Order in which the old values would be bereft of their substance: Europe of its historical significance; the world of its equilibrium; law of its concept of equity; morality of any sense of charity; and religion of the presence of God. He believed that he could achieve all this if he proceeded "modestly"—that is, by degrees. The supermen could then colonize the heavens and the earth with German men and gods.

Of all this, the evident end was disaster. An impossible, iniquitous will possessed Hitler's mind and doomed him to catastrophe; and this catastrophe threatened to be the more extensive and general because the forces capable of opposing the evil in the German people were still scattered and unready.

This was certainly the chief impression I got from my visit to the Reichskanzlei. It was only too much to be feared that the vibrant and tense individual in whom every man with common sense recognized the vanquished of the future would first win a series of awful victories against a negligent world taken unawares.

My official visit finished the evening of April 19. There had been not the slightest incident, for which I was profoundly thankful.

But there was still one trial in store.

I had fixed my departure for the next day, but this was April 20, Hitler's birthday. All Germany was celebrating the Führer's fiftieth anniversary with fervid enthusiasm. A gigantic military parade had been arranged in Berlin.

Herr von Ribbentrop wished me to be his official guest on this occasion. So the invitation had been phrased when it was sent to me at Bucharest. I had not accepted this part of the invitation, since I wished my visit to be strictly diplomatic. Only the German people in the year 1939 had cause to fête Herr Hitler. The German Foreign Office had not insisted, and the program arranged had been in accordance with my desires.

Once in the capital of the Reich, however, I was subject to more pressure. First Herr von Ribbentrop, and then Marshal Göring, strongly urged me to attend the military review. I replied that I could do so as a private individual, my mission having ended the evening of April 19. It was agreed that I should go to the diplomatic stand accompanied only by the Rumanian Minister in Berlin. But the officials kept a last-minute surprise for me.

On the morning of April 20, as I was preparing to go to the Rumanian Legation, I heard voices raised in an adjoining room. It was the Rumanian chief of protocol, my friend Georges Croutzesco, arguing with Herr Fabricius, the German Minister to Rumania, and a representative from the Wilhelmstrasse. The two Germans seemed to be putting forward an argument that Georges Croutzesco strongly objected to. I learned that two open cars were waiting at the door of the hotel: I must hurry, so that I might appear with two other guests of honor in the procession that was making its way to the Führer's special stand. I also made my protest, citing the previous understanding. Neither of my visitors would give way; they had received a formal order to fetch me so that I might take part in the ceremonies among the "guests of honor." I asked who were these guests with whom I was to share the honor of being received in the Chancellor's box. The reluctant reply was given that they were M. Hacha (the "President" of what remained of Czechoslovakia) and

Monseigneur Tiso (chief of the "independent" republic of Slovakia). I saw red and said that I set no store whatever on being paid so extravagant an honor. It was of no avail. The courteous but implacable pressure tightened around me; time was getting short and it was necessary to go. A happy inspiration saved me. I was suffering at the time from the aftereffects of a liver complaint, which compelled me to adhere to a strict diet, about which all my hosts knew. The only way I could avoid a scandal was to simulate an attack of "liver." I played it up with appropriate moans; then, before the staring eyes of the two German diplomats, I flung off morning coat, collar, shoes, and the rest, and in an instant I was in bed, carefully tended by my secretaries, who had instantly grasped the significance of the "crisis."

Protocol had lost the game. It was not severe with me. After a series of telephone calls, Herr Fabricius came to tell me with a smile "that, should the crisis pass, I could watch the parade as I wished." I got dressed again at once and went along with Georges and Radou Croutzesco to the diplomatic box.

From that point I saw the celebrated march past which was intended to demonstrate to the world the surpassing power of the mighty German war machine. For all of six hours the motorized troops of the Reich moved in a steady procession of tanks, mortars, howitzers, and big guns—a grandiose display which began gaily with a joyful fanfare of trumpets under the cloudless spring sky, dragged on for hours with a besetting clangor of metal, finally to seem like the unending vision of Hell or a ghastly nightmare to the nerve-shattered spectators.

A six-hour nightmare, an agonizing prelude to the six-year tragedy to come.

Hitler, erect and motionless, never took his eyes from the immense army on the march. It was as though he was letting the army speak—supreme and irrefutable argument—so that by it he might win the full comprehension of the world.

Easily to be seen, at the foot of the presidential tribune, in a special little box like a gilded cage, one saw MM. Hacha and Tiso, who had resigned themselves to participation in the Führer's triumph. Not without some disquiet, I saw the stall originally intended for me at their side—still vacant.

CHAPTER III

THE FEARS OF LEOPOLD III

The small countries after the Munich Agreement. Audience with
the King of the Belgians. Monarchs and the problem of security.

IN the train that carried me to Brussels I made a mental
résumé of the impressions I had gathered at Berlin. I also
drew up a brief telegraphic report for the Rumanian Government:

"From my conversations with Hitler, Göring, and von
Ribbentrop, I believe the following conclusions may be
drawn:

"1. The so-called policy of 'encirclement' annoys and
disturbs the German leaders. Their dissatisfaction is really
due to the action taken by the western powers to assert
themselves again in eastern Europe, in which region, following the Munich Agreement, the Reich intends to stand alone.

"2. This annoyance is chiefly directed against England.
The interventions of the United States (which they denounce as 'incitements to war'), as well as President Roosevelt's last message, are laid at the door of British diplomacy.
France is treated more gently; they consider that it has acted
more circumspectly.

"3. The anger with England may bring the question of
the colonies onto the agenda. The German leaders seem convinced that in the end the former German colonies will be
restored to the Reich 'peacefully.'

"4. The tension between Berlin and London may lead to
conflict. However, Herr Hitler made no secret of his hope
that a peaceful understanding with England might still be
reached. For this 'England would have to understand'—that
is to say, recognize the predominant position of the Reich
on the Continent and agree to the division of the world into
zones of influence.

"5. The German leaders are aware of our point of view regarding the Anglo-French guarantees. 'I rely on your explanations,' Hitler said to me in these words, 'that these guarantees are pacific and unilateral.' But the attitude of the Reich might change toward us and consequently its support of Hungary might be increased, were we to try to change these guarantees into bilateral pacts or to seek Russian assistance.

"6. So long as we hold our present position, we shall still be able to obtain munitions and arms from the Bohemian factories that are now in German territory.[1]

"7. These facts will enable me, in the course of my visits to London and Paris, to explain to our western friends the obstacles which face our policy of security. I shall insist on the fact that we consider that it is absolutely necessary for Great Britain and France to be represented in eastern Europe, since it would be a dangerous mistake to leave in this part of Europe one sole arbiter who would inevitably become master. I shall also show that it would be unwise to make us party to any new commitments, for that would lay us open to instant and direct danger and risk compromising peace instead of consolidating it."

I reproduce the terms of this report, certainly not to appear to be justified by events but rather to recall as exactly as possible the difficulties of the little countries facing the imminent general conflagration. Certain western European statesmen had regarded the Munich Agreement as a compromise made to gain time. In their opinion, it should have allowed England and France to offset the lead that the Reich had gained in armaments. This reasoning could be defended from a military point of view. But, in the realm of politics

1. Czechoslovakia had been the principal purveyor of armaments to the southeastern countries. When the German armies occupied Bohemia, the deliveries in course of execution were stopped. It was impossible to carry out the Rumanian armament program without the consent of the Reich.

it was Hitler whom Munich allowed to gain time, since the system of security which united the great and small European states in one community—imperfect, certainly, but capable of perfection—had been completely demolished by it. The ties between the western powers and the Danubian and Balkan States had weakened; certain regional groupings had disappeared; confidence diminished; the Soviet Union, offended and distrustful, withdrew its powerful support from the policy of mutual assistance. The Reich profited by the general disorder to consolidate its positions. For months it had been at work without meeting any resistance, arbitrating between some countries, threatening others, stirring up grudges and suppressing opposition. Western Europe made no move. When Mr. Chamberlain, on March 20, 1939—five days after the occupation of Prague—revived the idea of a new organization of security, Germany was so far ahead of events that the situation was completely changed. It was no longer Hitler who took an aggressive stand against the peace of Europe, but the general security which sought to reorganize itself against Hitler. On the ruins of the ideology of Geneva and the labors of the League of Nations, the Third Reich had taken its defensive positions. It regarded every move toward continental solidarity in which it did not share as aggressive, an attempt at "encirclement," an "incitement to war," an intolerable provocation. The weight of German strength endowed these absurd epithets with a strange consistency. They expressed one of those political "truths" which might be a heavy burden on the world for several years to come. And already they were exercising a strong influence on neighboring peoples, who no longer dared to look to their security save with an uneasy conscience. To wish for peace in those times meant risking offending the German Chancellor. Therefore, when President Roosevelt emphasized the great uneasiness that pervaded the world and Hitler in a shocked and threatening

manner asked which of the small countries considered itself
threatened by him, there was a profound silence from one
end of Europe to the other.

There was nothing heroic about this prudence; it was
determined by events. It was impossible for the small states
to participate openly in the "peace offensive" until a precise
agreement had been reached among the great powers. The
German rejoinder would have been immediately directed
against the weakest points. The example of Czechoslovakia
showed how dangerous it was for a small country without
effective support to lay itself open to the anger of the Reich.

Munich had had still other consequences. The small countries were forced to approach Germany directly to obtain
from it certain guarantees which the international system
could no longer provide. The Reich was ready to consider
these matters, but only gave the desired guarantees in exchange for new engagements. It demanded that the countries
having recourse to it should renounce any policy of "encirclement," as well as any idea of rapprochement with Russia.

For the countries which had been obliged to seek such
guarantees, often with the approbation of the western
powers, the return to the system of collective assistance was
full of snares. It was equivalent to the violation of engagements entered into with the Reich, and might automatically
incur sanctions on the part of the German Government.

The truth is that, after Munich, the *sense of lawfulness*
attached to the policy of collective security had disappeared.
German "dynamism" had become a factor in the order of
things; it had won the right to take its part in Europe; and
the New Order no longer justified caring in the least for
the security of others. If anyone wanted to recreate a system
of general security, a new lawfulness had to be established.
But the Germans, by virtue of the positions they had taken,
fought any idea of "change." To accomplish a broader organization it was therefore necessary to advance over open
ground under enemy fire. That was a risk which the weakest

countries could hardly take. They were all, therefore, caught up in a tragic dilemma: should they invite Germany's wrath by identifying themselves with the efforts of the great powers in recreating a broader scheme of pacts of assistance, or should they try to find security in isolation and stand alone in face of Hitler's Reich?

At Brussels, I was to find anxieties which were also those of my own country. No one was more acutely sensible of them than King Leopold. His political insight gave him a clarity of vision that was almost painful, which at times numbed his will, showing him the risks which the small nations were running, and revealing beforehand the uncertainty of the policy of the western powers and the dangerous reactions of the totalitarian states.

The King received me early in the morning—an hour after my arrival in Brussels. He was sitting at his desk, which was laden with newspapers and files. The sight was familiar to me; in Bucharest I had left a sovereign just as assiduous, who received his ministers in the early hours of the day. I could not help remarking on this in presenting King Carol's compliments to King Leopold. The sovereign smiled and asked what were my impressions of Berlin. His gaze was clear, his manner serious and somewhat shy, extremely pleasant; he looked like a young blond archangel yoked by fate to the labor of government. Yet, notwithstanding certain hesitations as he spoke, he had formed his own personal judgment and had fixed ideas. Well in advance of others, he had perceived the first rumblings of the thunder which foretold the storm; and, like a good shepherd, his only thought was to find shelter for his flock. It was evident, alas! that he labored under an illusion in believing that by his own efforts he could avoid the cataclysm which threatened the world. I was unhappy to have to strengthen this illusion still more, but I was bound to acquaint him with what Hitler had said to me concerning his country: "I shall never attack

Belgium or Holland. . . . I intend to respect the frontiers of these countries. . . . People credit me with the preposterous idea of wanting to enlarge the battle front at their expense. Why should we begin again the same mistakes we made in 1914?" King Leopold listened to me with interest. A gleam of hope enlivened his uneasy countenance. He made me repeat several times the reassuring words of the German Chancellor. All he wanted was to be able to believe them. Hitler's reassurances corresponded in essence to certain trends that showed in the King's policy. Leopold III was inclined to believe that, if he followed a "wise" and "independent" policy, he could avoid the worst. The worst was swift invasion and lengthy occupation, a repetition of the somber tragedy in which Belgium had nearly foundered a quarter of a century earlier. The King was haunted by memories of the last war. The joys of victory had not erased from his memory the sight of his fatherland trampled under foot by armies marching toward the west. *At any cost* the repetition of such a calamity must be avoided. To have every chance on his side, the King thought himself able to correct the serious defects of Belgium's geographical situation by following a farsighted policy. Belgian territory must cease to be regarded by its neighbors as a corridor. Therefore care must be taken not to tie Belgium politically with the threatened territories of its western neighbors, either by way of coalition or alliance. The idea that a coalition, even though it might bring victory in the long run, could not in any event bring effective aid to Belgium in time became an obsession. With anguish he spoke to me of Britain's lack of military preparation, and he did not hide his fear that, with things as they were, the aid promised to a small country by Britain might compromise it rather than protect it.

On this matter, the King asked me what Rumania expected from the Anglo-French guarantees. I gave him the fullest possible explanations. I spoke to him of our fear of having to face the Reich alone, of our desire to see the western powers again assert their position in eastern Europe; and of our firm hope, in view of the gravity of the international crisis, of seeing Great Britain making an effort to recover lost time. I told King Leopold that we understood his point of view as to the necessity of our following a reserved and prudent policy; and that, like him, we were determined to provoke no one by spectacular alliances. But this was a question of method, not of principle. Europe could not be saved by progressively retreating before a power which had no consideration for anyone. The salvation of the small as well as of the great countries depended on the possibility of holding the invading forces of the Third Reich in check. So long as it was impossible to restore equilibrium (a period particularly propitious to crises capable of leading to war), a small country certainly should not lay itself open uselessly; but, as soon as a coalition of countries inspired with good will could be realized, no state wishing to safeguard its independence should withhold its support.

The King agreed. His sympathies were with the western powers. But he blamed them for having lost so much time that their recovery might coincide with the crushing of the small countries. Either from "method" or from "principle," he thought, above all it was necessary to be prudent.

Such prudence was not a hindrance to action. There were other means than premature association with the idea of collective security by which the threatened danger might be averted. Why should not the small countries come to an understanding among themselves to establish by common accord certain principles which would interest everybody in the maintenance of peace? The King dreamed of devising a plan of continental economic collaboration. He hoped to be able to convene an international conference—"if there was still time"—to which the Scandinavian, Baltic, Balkan, and Belgian-Dutch groups would send representatives. It was for those countries not divided by violent competition or ideological passions to make an appeal to the sentiment of European solidarity by grouping and adjusting among themselves their economic interests. Peace was still possible—at least the King hoped that it was—if it were possible to set "a disinterested effort and the unanimous protest of those peoples who hate war" against the ambitions which were stirring up trouble.

As I listened to the projects of the King of the Belgians, I thought of Herr von Ribbentrop's harsh expression and pinched lips; again I saw Hitler pacing up and down and gesticulating like a madman; I heard the distant metallic clatter of the interminable military review in Berlin. . . . And I thought that, with or without prudence, Leopold III would find it very hard to shelter his flock.

The case of King Leopold was not unique in Europe. There were three other sovereigns who, faced with similar difficulties, reacted in the same manner. When the historian, making a close study of the constituent elements of the great European crisis of 1939, pauses to consider the particular dramas of the middle-sized and the small countries, he will link four names in his judgment: Leopold of Belgium; Carol of Rumania; Boris of Bulgaria; and Paul, Regent of Yugoslavia.

These four princes, who were quite dissimilar in nature, had the same idea of their mission as head of state. Caught by fate in their youth, they faced up to danger in the same way, met it with the same personal inclinations, including a marked liking for "independence," some authoritarian fancies of self-confidence, fed by the desire to do the right thing, and an immense, youthful ardor.

King Boris (whom I did not know personally) was considered the most calculating of the four. He was clever, and he knew how to bend men and institutions to his will. He alone among the other sovereigns linked his fate to that of Hitler.

Kingship was not Prince Paul's real vocation: he preferred

art to politics. Nostalgia for the happy times spent in England stayed with him in the care-laden atmosphere peculiar to a Balkan government. His regency was charged with the heaviest burdens; at home, enemy brothers to be reconciled; abroad, a policy of appeasement to be pursued in face of implacable neighbors. It was necessary for him to develop the qualities of a clever tactician.

King Carol, too, had an aptitude for tactics. He feared multilateral engagements which embarrassed his liberty of action without giving him security. He preferred not to have danger hidden from him by misleading formulae, so that he might use his own means of avoiding it. He did not shun risk, but he relied on no one in facing destiny. He wished to run the state as he ran his motor cars, with himself at the wheel. Politics were a passion with him, down to their smallest details. He loved power, action, and intrigue. Brilliant in everything except the role of constitutional monarch, he failed to reign because he wanted to rule. Conflict was attractive to him, and his dream would have been to have had to fight each time for the power in his dispensation. So he ended by regarding himself as the rival and adversary of all the party leaders, and would have liked to battle with them for favors in the people's suffrage. Some totalitarian theories suited him, in so far as they made the head of the state the effective possessor of all the powers of government. But King Carol, despite his weakness for authoritarian formulae, only inclined toward the Axis powers when he judged the cause of the Allies irremediably compromised.

The King of the Belgians was certainly quite different from his Balkan "cousins." He had neither King Carol's authoritarian impulses, nor the great flexibility of Prince Paul, nor King Boris' desire to serve the Axis and make it serve him. Besides, he reigned in a country where constitutional rule was deeply ingrained, and where the methods of the Axis had not succeeded in weakening any essential position. Nevertheless, certain of his words seemed very familiar to me; I had heard them more than once at the Courts of Bucharest and Belgrade. After Munich, the King of the Belgians became suspicious of international engagements of collective security. In Belgrade, in Bucharest, and, of course, in Sofia, the kings and princes became equally suspicious of them. King Leopold thought that each country should try to serve the cause of general peace in its own way, but that its first task was to save its own particular peace. The other sovereigns thought the same thing. The King had placed his whole reliance on a policy of "independence," sheltered from the violent passions that were rending the world. His cousins, too, talked a great deal about independence. Finally, the King thought that in those difficult times the duty of a sovereign was to sacrifice his own person and to put his ideas resolutely at the service of his country. The others thought likewise, and did not hesitate, each according to his character, to assume major responsibilities. Here doubtless was discernible the influence of certain Nazi and fascist theories, which undermined confidence in the efficacy of democratic methods (in the national sphere as well as in the larger sphere of international collaboration), and which led the heads of state toward authoritarianism.

But there was something more serious than this. The great ship of general security, which for several years had been making water fast, had finally gone on the rocks at Munich. In the space of a few days it had foundered. Lifeboats hastily launched were trying to pick up survivors. It was in an atmosphere of "every man for himself" that certain heads of state took the helm and tried to save their own by whatever means offered.

However, the catastrophe drew nearer. It was to put an end to illusions as well as to the last-hour maneuvers; and was to engulf—singly or together—all those in Europe who still clung desperately to peace at any price.

CHAPTER IV

THE STRENGTH OF ENGLAND

Channel crossing. London: the Court, the government, public
opinion. Mr. Winston Churchill over coffee and cigars. His moral
and political opposition to National Socialism. His plans for a
"Great Coalition" (speeches of May 9, 1938, October 5, 1938, and
April 13, 1939).

TO reach England in bad weather, a price must be paid;
and there is no diplomatic immunity. I crossed the
Channel lying flat on my back with my eyes closed, trying to
forget the relentless discomfort of the rough sea by visual-
izing all that Europe owed to the narrow, wind-swept straits,
dominated by the British Fleet, and where seasickness raged.
Was it not behind this bulwark that the fundamental values
of European civilization had sheltered in times of great crisis?
Hitler's envious speeches regarding the inaccessible maritime
empire echoed in my ears and mingled in a confused murmur
with the rhythm of verses which another German, Friedrich
Schiller, had dedicated to the grandeur of England. God,
looking with terror on the immense fleet which Philip II of
Spain was sending against the British Isles, says: "Must my
Albion be lost? Must it disappear, this race of heroes, this
last bulwark against oppression, this supreme defense against
tyrants? No!" He cried. The Almighty breathed, and the
Armada was scattered by the winds.

Our winds were more merciful. They blew us toward
Dover, where a most comforting welcome awaited us. At
Victoria, a gentleman in mufti with all the attributes of a
civilian and a gentleman greeted me with a warm smile. I
had been beset by uniforms on the Continent, which clothed
both military and nonmilitary figures—soldiers, diplomats,
or functionaries. I was grateful to Lord Halifax for his well-
ironed top hat, the impeccable cut of his overcoat, and the

magnificent umbrella hooked casually on his left arm. I was specially thankful for the benevolent concern for me, and the friendly and distinguished ease by which he established the note of absolute confidence in our relations from the outset.

The atmosphere of comfort and civility which surrounded one in England seemed to defy the political and moral crisis raging everywhere else at the beginning of 1939. One enjoyed its benefits, but not without asking oneself, with some anguish: Did Great Britain understand? Had it grasped the full magnitude of the storm gathering over Europe? Did it know that, when the tempest broke, although it might be the last to be attacked, it, of all the world powers, would be the principal objective?

In England it is not good form to betray one's apprehensions or to make much of one's troubles. It might have been only a seeming composure, in keeping with the traditions of English education and behavior. But one might also ask whether a country so well brought up would be able to defend itself against the immense tide of churlishness that was rising on the Continent.

I asked myself this question whenever, following the program arranged for me, some corner of old England roused my emotion. I put it to myself, above all, when at Buckingham Palace, so remote from the Reichskanzlei, where I had the honor of being received by the youthful sovereigns of the British Empire.

I was the traveler who had just seen Hitler. Naturally it was on him that the conversation turned. "What is he like?" the Queen asked me. "Did there seem to be any suggestion of exaggeration when he received you?" I replied that he could be very simple in manner if he wished, but that that made him all the more to be feared. The Queen observed very sensibly: "If he is simple, it might be that he is really great, unless it should be greatness of another sort. . . ."

It was certainly something "great": the greatest cataclysm

that had ever threatened the empire whose noble and tranquil majesty was symbolized by the two gracious human beings before whom I stood.

Nevertheless, Britain had been warned. Attention had been called to the danger by one whose incomparably clear vision was unequaled in Europe. Britain, it could be supposed, understood the nature of the evil, its extent, and its power. I had the privilege in London of meeting Mr. Winston Churchill in the course of a dinner given by our Legation. At that time he held no public office. His political role, great as it really was, appeared to be of secondary importance; he led neither the Government nor the Opposition; and his words as well as his thoughts committed no one but himself. But Hitler, who closely followed his actions, had recognized him to be his chief opponent. Churchill had realized what was afoot.

After dinner I sat by Mr. Churchill over a cigar, and heard him expound some of his ideas, of which I was partly aware from his recent speeches. No one could speak better than he the ancient European language of diplomacy (with a marked English accent, as was fitting), which aroused in everybody who was still loyal to a common civilization, independent of race and nationality, the same uneasiness and the same resurgence of pride.

Contrary to so many sociologists and geopoliticians, who tried to give scientific explanations of the profound upheaval which events in Germany proclaimed, this man of venerable culture and generous disposition had realized that Nazism, leaping "out upon us from the Dark Ages," intended to win its first battle—the decisive battle—in the realm of man's thought and conscience. And it was precisely there that the fiercest opposition should be made.

"People say," Mr. Churchill had stated in an address to the American public,[1] "we ought not to allow ourselves to

1. An Address to the People of the United States of America, October 16, 1938.

be drawn into a theoretical antagonism between Nazidom and democracy; but the antagonism is here now. It is this very conflict of spiritual and moral ideas which gives the free countries a great part of their strength. . . . Cannons, aeroplanes, they can manufacture in large quantities; but how are they to quell the natural promptings of human nature, which after all these centuries of trial and progress has inherited a whole armoury of potent and indestructible knowledge?"

Mr. Churchill was right. Even more than the vast natural resources of the future United Nations, the natural promptings of human nature were to decide the battle already foretold in the spring of 1939. One of the greatest of the many contributions of this British statesman was the moral support that he provided, which was to bring victory to the cause his country ultimately espoused with all its might.

The high, disinterested ideal which Mr. Churchill set against the Nazi ideology was of a peculiarly British character. It was embodied in "a liberal constitution, in democratic and Parliamentary government, in Magna Carta and the Petition of Right." [1] The civilization which Mr. Churchill defended was a regime where parliaments make the laws and independent courts of justice maintain them; where the ruling authority is subordinate "to the settled customs of the people and to their will as expressed through the Constitution"; and where the people have a "respect for law and sense of continuity." [2] But, while exalting the political ideal of his own country, Mr. Churchill could find words of more universal application, which stirred men's hearts wherever the love of liberty rose against the threatening danger of foreign tyranny. Is not civilization really the definite expression which men gave to their ideal of liberty at certain epochs? It includes not only political and juridical achievements but those verities by which the individual is

1. Speech at the Free Trade Hall, Manchester, May 9, 1938.
2. An Address as Chancellor to the University of Bristol, July 2, 1938.

able to free himself from the fetters which bound him in the realms of thought and belief. It was to defend these menaced verities that Churchill flung his fearless appeals far beyond the frontiers of the British Empire. He knew that "the cause of freedom has in it a recuperative power and virtue which can draw from misfortune new hope and new strength." [1] Mr. Churchill also foresaw that the principles which had moulded Britain's free and tolerant civilization would extend far beyond the confines of that fortunate isle, ultimately to reign throughout "the turbulent, formidable world outside our shores." [2] This hope which he had communicated to his country, and which Britain was to communicate to the world, shone in advance on war and on victory. Mr. Churchill's words pledged the future. Today, a problem of liberty and civilization—of a common civilization and liberty for all—arises at the end of the hostilities, as it arose at the beginning. We cannot now forget the principles and acts which determined the political and moral direction of the cause for which this gigantic war was fought.[3]

Mr. Churchill's conceptions had still another effect. On the national basis, they made impossible Hitler's dream of partitioning the world.

I reported to the British statesman the secret hopes of an understanding which Hitler had outlined in my presence. Churchill was fully aware of this Nazi project. "I know that they are ready to come to an understanding with us! But at what a price? And against whom? Every time Hitler wants to make peace in one direction, it is so that he can the better make war in another! . . ." And Churchill reminded me of a speech he had made a year earlier, on May 9, 1938, at the time of Hitler's visit to Rome, in which he had spoken of the possibility Britain had of making a direct agreement with the Reich.

1. Address, October 16.
2. Address, July 2.
3. Cf. Appendix IV, p. 234.

"There is another foreign policy which you are urged to pursue. It is not to worry about all these countries of Central Europe, not to trouble yourself with preserving the Covenant of the League, to recognize that all that is foolish and vain and can never be restored, and to make a special pact of friendship with Nazi Germany. . . . But when we are told we must make a special pact with Nazi Germany, I want to know what that pact is going to be, and at whose expense it is to be made. Undoubtedly our Government could make an agreement with Germany. All they have to do is to give her back her former colonies, and such others as she may desire; to muzzle the British press and platform by a law of censorship; and to give Herr Hitler a free hand to spread the Nazi system and dominance far and wide through Central Europe. That is the alternative foreign policy. It is one which, in my view, would be disgraceful and disastrous. In the first place it leads us straight to war. The Nazi regime, elated by this triumph, with every restraint removed, would proceed unchecked upon its path of ambition and aggression. We should be the helpless, silent, gagged, apparently consenting, spectators of the horrors which would spread through Central Europe. . . ." [1]

This categorical reply, contrary to the ideas of all those who had spoken and were still to speak of a direct entente between Britain and Hitler's Reich, contained all the arguments which a character at once as human and as British as Mr. Churchill's could consider. It was difficult for an Englishman to cede colonies and to allow a great country as restless as Germany to return to the high seas. It was even more difficult for an Englishman to link himself up with a regime which waged open warfare against all the guarantees which Britain regarded as being essential to the security of individuals and nations. But what seemed utterly impossible was to give a European power a free hand to expand at will by the violation of other countries. This meant transgressing

1. Manchester speech, May 9.

not only all the laws of morality but also those of the established policy—the policy of the balance of power—which had for long assured the peace of Europe and Britain's constant greatness. Compromise of any sort was bound to be unstable; the Nazi Reich would proceed by successive stages, it would begin by demanding "its rights" and end by asserting its strength. It wanted to be a friend so that it might become master, and regarded equality as only a passing phase, leading necessarily to hegemony.

Mr. Churchill took up this line of argument with me:

"What can we divide with them? The world? But the world is not ours. And if, in a moment of aberration, we should cede to Hitler what does not belong to us, on the morrow we should not be able to keep what does belong to us. Herr Hitler reproaches us for believing what he himself wrote in his book. How can we not take him at his word, when the security and the very existence of our empire are in question?"

It was evident that no compromise was possible. *Mein Kampf* made clear the meaning of a partition into zones of influence. No longer could there be agreement between the Reich and England, once Hitler had written his book and Churchill had read it.

The plans Winston Churchill drew for European policy foresaw the means of defending peace by common resistance against pressure from Germany. In the same speech in which he had rejected the idea of a special agreement with Germany (May 9, 1938), he proposed a complete system of alliances designed to prevent "another terrible war."

"I should like," he said, "to see [Great Britain and France] go to all the smaller states that are menaced, who are going to be devoured one by one by the Nazi tyranny, and say to them bluntly, We are not going to help you if you are not going to help yourselves. What are you going to do about it? What are you going to contribute? Are you prepared to take special service in defense of the Covenant? If you are willing to do so, and to prove it by actions, then we will join together with you, if there are enough of you, in active military association under the authority of the League in order to protect each other and the world from another act of aggression."

This proposal was not limited to a principle of collective security; it was a practical suggestion (which Churchill was careful to bring out). It proposed to institute an active military association. In this it departed from the methods of the League of Nations and linked up with the old British idea of the "great military coalition," to oppose a continental power which tended to upset the balance of power. Faithful to the British tradition, Mr. Churchill carefully chose the counterweights he needed. "To be precise," he said, "some of the countries which should be asked whether they will join Great Britain and France in this special duty to the League are Yugoslavia, Rumania, Hungary and Czechoslovakia."

If such a question had been put to these countries in 1938, at least three of them would have replied: Yes!

"In the next place," added Mr. Churchill, "there are Bulgaria, Greece and Turkey, all states who wish to preserve their individuality and national independence, . . . If this powerful group of Danubian and Balkan states were firmly united with the two great Western democracies, an immense, probably a decisive, step towards stability would be achieved."

It is an interesting fact that the first group of countries which Mr. Churchill had in mind for the defense of equilibrium and continental peace comprised the Danubian and Balkan States. This idea was to persist in the minds of the British political leaders. In their opinion, the Danubian and Balkan peoples formed the most evident and certain grouping to counterbalance German power. But Churchill's thinking went further. Despite his mistrust of the system of government of "the enormous power of Russia," he believed that it was necessary to appeal to the Soviet Union, "a country whose interests are peace, a country profoundly menaced by Nazi hostility . . ."

Then would come the rest of Europe: Poland, the countries of the north, the Baltic States, the Scandinavian powers. "If we had once gathered together the forces I have mentioned, we should then be in a position to offer these countries a very great measure of armed security for peace . . . they might easily be induced to throw in their lot with us and 'make assurance doubly sure.' "

Mr. Churchill's project was the logical reply to the "program" expounded by Hitler in *Mein Kampf*. No government, of course, accepted it. Hitler did not let this go unnoticed. It might be said that, when he went into action, he carefully destroyed one after another, in the very order indicated by Churchill, the different points on which the latter hoped to build his system of security. At Munich, Hitler began by shattering the political order prevailing in the Danubian basin; Czechoslovakia was knocked out and the Little Entente split up. He then turned his attention to the Balkans, paralyzing Yugoslavia's political will and winning Bulgaria to his cause. He was to continue with the Soviet Union, with the intention of withdrawing this immense power from the side of the western powers. With the ground so made ready he was to strike a mortal blow against Poland. War was to come along the very road which Mr. Churchill had wished to close.

At the time of my visit to London, only the Czech bastion had fallen. Mr. Churchill immediately realized the disastrous significance of the Munich Agreement. The speech he made on October 5, 1938, will remain one of the finest examples of parliamentary eloquence and perspicacity.

"All is over," he exclaimed. He was thinking not only of Czechoslovakia—"silent, mournful, abandoned, broken, Czechoslovakia recedes into the darkness"—but of Europe, which at one blow had lost some important defensive positions. For him, it was European peace as he conceived it that had been destroyed at Munich. His anguish found expression in memorable phrases: "We are in the presence of a disaster of the first magnitude which has befallen Great Britain and France. Do not let us blind ourselves to that. It must now be accepted that all the countries of Central and Eastern Europe will make the best terms they can with the triumphant Nazi power. The system of alliances in Central Europe upon which France has relied for her safety has been swept away, and I can see no means by which it can be reconstituted. The road down the Danube Valley to the Black Sea, the road which leads as far as Turkey, has been opened. In fact, if not in form, it seems to me that all those countries of Middle Europe, all those Danubian countries, will, one after another be drawn into this vast system of power politics—not only power military politics but power economic politics—radiating from Berlin, and I believe this can be achieved quite smoothly and swiftly and will not necessarily entail the firing of a single shot. . . . You will see, day after day, week after week, entire alienation of those regions. Many of those countries, in fear of the rise of the Nazi power, have already got politicians, Ministers, Governments, who were pro-German, but there was always an enormous popular movement in Poland, Rumania, Bulgaria and Yugoslavia which looked to the Western democracies and loathed the idea of having this arbitrary rule of the totalitarian system thrust upon them, and hoped that a stand would be made. All that has gone by the board."

Mr. Churchill had looked deeply into the possibilities opened up by Munich. He knew which direction the German thrust would take. The countries in the middle of Europe would be led (some by self-interest, others by necessity and in spite of themselves) to make terms with the Third Reich. Germany had set itself up as the champion of revisionism, and had at once won over Hungary and Bulgaria. It had successfully dismembered friendly Czechoslovakia.

The other friendly states, Rumania, Yugoslavia, and Greece, felt themselves bereft of protection. Hard facts forced these states, until then faithfully attached to the League of Nations, to modify their policy. It was no longer sufficient for them to be present at Geneva; from now on, they had to address themselves to Berlin, in order to obtain assurances and guarantees. And Berlin was in a position to impose conditions. Every promise was to be paid for by an undertaking. Henceforth Hitler had the means of progressively dismantling all the work of the treaties.

Hitler's seizure of Danubian Europe was not to be so easy as Mr. Churchill imagined. In analyzing what would happen, the British statesman vindicated in advance the conduct of these states condemned to fall into the "vast system of power politics radiating from Berlin." In fact Greece, thanks to its courage, and helped by its remote situation, succeeded in never having to align itself with the policy of the Axis. After the waverings and compromises of its government, Yugoslavia was to regain its liberty at the cost of the greatest sacrifices. As for Rumania, the first country to be exposed to the German schemes, it was to maintain loyalty to its western friendships until the collapse of the Anglo-French front in Flanders.

The progressive upheaval predicted by Mr. Churchill, which was destined to bring the course of the valley of the Danube all the way to the Black Sea into the orbit of power politics, still lacked a further upheaval, the culminating effect of the policy of Munich—that of the Moscow Agreement. Not only the little countries were to detach themselves from the western democracies. The Soviet Union, whose importance Churchill correctly estimated, was to renounce a system of security which no longer inspired it with confidence. The possible collusion between the Reich and the U.S.S.R., so disturbing to world opinion, would rob the intermediary regions of all autonomy; and these countries, whose independence was so necessary to equilibrium that Churchill saw in their downfall "a disaster of the first magnitude," were to drift helplessly between two powerful forces.

In the spring of 1939 Mr. Churchill did not go so far as this in his forebodings; but even so, they were remarkably exact. There was a direct relation between the safety of the western powers and the position of the countries of central and eastern Europe. The cry of alarm which he had uttered expressed a justified national anguish. But the British statesman did not allow himself to be discouraged by his own forebodings. Immediately he felt in England, and in Europe, a clearer understanding of events and a will to face them, with extraordinary tenacity he returned to his former proposal of a great alliance.

On March 15, 1939, the Germans seized Prague. On April 7 Italy invaded Albania. Mr. Chamberlain's government, profoundly shaken by these events, inaugurated a policy of resistance. On April 13 Mr. Churchill announced in the House of Commons that "this is no time for half measures," and put his ideas forward with vigor. "If peace is to be preserved there seem to be two main steps which I trust are already being taken or will be taken with more decision immediately. The first, of course, is the full inclusion of Soviet Russia in our defensive peace bloc." Mr. Churchill did not think that this would be easy. Russia already seemed "uncertain," and "I do not at all think that we should be well advised to ask favors from anyone." But use should be made of "the deep interest that Russia had against the further eastward extension of the Nazi power." Despite his reservations, Mr. Churchill seemed more anxious than he was in 1938 to see Russia enlisted on the side of Britain.

He was equally anxious to renew relations with the southeastern states. After the disappearance of Czechoslovakia, and with close collaboration between the Reich and Hungary, it was no longer possible to speak of "Danubian organization." Stress must be put on the Balkans. "The second main step which, it seems to me, we should take, and which I cannot but feel that the Government are taking, is the promotion of unity in the Balkans. The four Balkan States and Turkey are an immense combination. If they stand together, they are safe. They have only to stand together to be safe. They will save their populations from the horrors of another war and, by their massive stabilizing force, they may well play a decisive part in averting a general catastrophe. If they allow themselves to be divided, if they depart at all from the simple principle of 'the Balkans for the Balkan peoples,' they will renew the horrible experiences which tore and devastated every single one of them in the Great War, and the Balkan Wars which preceded the Great War."

Mr. Churchill's plan had acquired greater urgency. No longer was it a question of inducing each of the southeastern states individually to take part in a general military alliance; it was necessary to bring about a closely cemented regional organization, able to play "a decisive part" in preventing the outbreak of war.

This idea was fully justified by the way events were moving. The four Balkan States—Rumania, Yugoslavia, Greece, and Turkey—had closed their ranks and consolidated their entente. The leaders of this entente kept close contact with one another, hoping to give to their community of aims and interests the character of a political and military organization.

Mr. Churchill realized better than anyone how immediately useful such an organization was. The British statesman expressed himself as follows: "Here let me say, with regard to the action of our country over the centuries, that in all the great struggles in which we have been engaged we have survived and emerged victorious not only because of the prowess of great commanders or because of famous battles gained by land and sea, but also because the true interests of Britain have coincided with those of so many other States and nations, and that we have been able to march in a great company along the high road of progress and freedom for all. This is certainly a condition which is extablished in the policy that we are now pursuing in the Balkan Peninsula."

Mr. Churchill had so spoken hardly ten days before I had the privilege of meeting him. I profited by the interview to assure him, as Temporary President of the Balkan Entente, that my colleagues and I firmly hoped that we could bring about the union he recommended. Straightway he spoke of Bulgaria. He believed that Bulgaria could be won over to the cause of the entente by the cession of the Southern Dobruja. I was not quite so sure. I feared that the Axis might already have succeeded at Sofia, through the same maneuvers which had insured its complete success at Budapest. If that were so, any cession of territory would be not only useless but dangerous, for it would needlessly weaken the strength of our entente. Mr. Churchill refused to be convinced; he believed that the Balkan Union was indispensable to the Balkans and to Europe, and that everything must be staked on its achievement. Later on, his insistence was to influence the attitude of the entente toward Bulgaria in some cases; but it seemed fairly certain that the Axis had got ahead of us in the Bulgarian capital; and the proposals which we could make lacked the breadth of the German and Italian promises.

The ardor with which Mr. Churchill attempted to bring the greatest number of countries into his system of alliances impressed me profoundly. "I know," he told me, "that I am accused in Berlin of pursuing a policy of encirclement. But there is nothing wrong in encircling an aggressor. We do not want to combine to make war; we wish to combine to defend ourselves. Our association must only be directed against an eventual aggressor: that is not a crime; it is a duty, an act of wisdom. If Germany does not want to make war, if it does not want to impose its decisions and its will on anyone by force, it has only to join our union; we ask nothing better than to give it all proper assurances to calm its apprehensions."

DINNER AT THE RUMANIAN LEGATION, LONDON
Lord Halifax and Grigore Gafencu.
(See page 97.)

THE AUTHOR WITH MR. CHURCHILL, LORD VANSITTART, AND MR. ATTLEE

Mr. Churchill "spoke of war and peace quietly, while smoking his cigar and taking his coffee."

(See page 109.)

I thereupon repeated the explanations which I had given Marshal Göring concerning our participation in the supposed campaign of encirclement—namely, that there was no concerted political encirclement, that no one thought of attacking Germany, but that a psychological encirclement was taking shape, a feeling of fear and insecurity which tended to unite all the European peoples. . . . "It is just that!" exclaimed Mr. Churchill; "a psychological encirclement." (He was to develop this idea, a few days later, in a broadcast to the American people.) [1]

I can still hear the conviction with which Mr. Churchill uttered these words. There was nothing martial in his manner. He spoke of war and peace quietly, while smoking his cigar and taking his coffee. His energy was pre-eminently humane and pacific; but it was no less endowed with a fervor that could move mountains. What struck me most about him was that his natural eloquence seemed to be contemplative; before convincing others, he sought the arguments best adapted to the strengthening of his own personal conviction. His phrases, ruled by artistic appreciation, were always perfect in form; but he was not satisfied with words, and he did not seek to move other people, or himself, by easy means. He roused enthusiasm by an appeal to reason.

1. "If there be encirclement of Germany, it is not military or economic encirclement. It is a psychological encirclement. The masses of the peoples in all the countries around Germany are forcing their governments to be on their guard against tyranny and invasion, and to join for that purpose with the other like-minded States. Nothing can now stop this process except a change of heart in the German leaders, or a change of those leaders. . . ." (An address Broadcast to the People of the United States of America, April 28, 1939.)

CHAPTER V

THE POLICY OF THE FOREIGN OFFICE

The conversion of Mr. Neville Chamberlain. Exchange of views with Lord Halifax. England resists Hitler and assumes its responsibilities on the Continent. It gives "guarantees," treats with Turkey, and begins negotiations with the U.S.S.R. General compulsory military service.

WHEN Mr. Churchill spoke to me, his ideas had already taken on a semi-official character, because the British Government had adopted them and was striving to put them into effect. It had appealed to the governments in Paris, Moscow, and Warsaw (March 20, 1939). It had given guarantees to Poland (March 31), and to Greece and Rumania (April 13). It was negotiating with Turkey and the U.S.S.R. In short, the Churchill program was being followed—though not without regrettable delay.

Mr. Churchill had not been hard on the government for this delay. Some time previously he had roundly denounced the errors of the British political leaders: "So far as this country is concerned, the responsibility must rest with those who have had the undisputed control of our political affairs. They neither prevented Germany from rearming, nor did they rearm ourselves in time. They quarreled with Italy without saving Ethiopia. They exploited and discredited the vast institution of the League of Nations and they neglected to make alliances and combinations which might have repaired previous errors, and thus they left us in the hour of trial without adequate national defense or effective international security." [1]

Mr. Churchill was too steeped in British parliamentary traditions not to leave the judgment of the responsible lead-

1. Speech to the House of Commons on the Munich Agreement, October 5, 1938.

ers of the British Empire to history. Moreover, he was convinced that the motives of the leaders in power had always been "perfectly honourable and sincere." Thus he was the first to support Mr. Neville Chamberlain's new policy. On April 13, 1939, the Prime Minister rose gravely from his seat to announce to the House of Commons that Great Britain intended to give guarantees to Greece and Rumania, to avoid the "disturbance by force or threats of force of the *status quo* in the Mediterranean and the Balkan Peninsula." Mr. Churchill had immediately lent his support: "The great majority of the House, I believe, supports the Government in the policy which they are now adopting in building up a strong alliance of nations to resist further aggression. . . . [The Prime Minister] has an absolute right to the aid of all in the country in carrying out that course." This categorical approbation was preceded by a few remarks in which there was only the merest hint of accusation: "We can readily imagine that it must have been a great disappointment and surprise to the Prime Minister to be treated in this way by a dictator in whom he placed particular trust, and in whom he advised us to place particular trust. Everyone knows that his motives have been absolutely straightforward and sincere. We all sympathize with him, and we all sympathize with ourselves, too." So it was that the grave problem of responsibilities was settled in Britain.

Mr. Chamberlain came to an attitude almost identical with that of Mr. Churchill. But while the latter had formed his judgment by political reflection, Mr. Chamberlain was reaching the same conclusions because of his defeats. In the case of the Prime Minister, the reaction was neither so logical nor so long standing as Mr. Churchill's, but it was accompanied by more bitterness and irritation. Mr. Chamberlain had wanted to trust Hitler. He had refused to reject offhand the honeyed words with which Hitler had pictured to Britain the possibility of a complete understanding with the Third Reich. Should not everything be tried so that catastrophe might be avoided? To be truthful, Mr. Chamberlain's ideas concerning Europe had never differed very greatly from those of Mr. Churchill. The Prime Minister was too British himself not to have constantly sought to maintain a state of equilibrium on the Continent. But he had hoped to be able to enlist Hitler in the defense of this order. In short, the British Prime Minister, like Herr Hitler, had cherished a chimera: the Reich, as Chamberlain imagined it, had no more reality than the Britain Hitler wanted.

Mr. Chamberlain had certainly always acted in good faith. His good faith took him to Munich. He went there after he had twice experienced Hitler's ill-humor. Never had a British Prime Minister, to satisfy his conscience, consented to make such heavy and costly sacrifices. Deplorable as it was, in view of the consequences, the action which led up to Munich (itself only the result of a long series of collective errors which favored the development of a state of political and military insecurity) had at least had an undeniable moral quality. Thanks to Mr. Chamberlain's attitude and to the personal steps he took, it showed a most praiseworthy effort to appease bellicose intentions. As a pretext, Hitler had raised the Sudeten question. Accepting this pretext as the real cause of the European crisis, Mr. Chamberlain was preparing the future; that error was redeemed by his good faith, for when, five months later, Hitler violated the Munich engagements, Mr. Chamberlain's indignation found an echo in the whole of the British Empire. From that moment the empire, despite its lack of military preparation, was morally ready to fight.

I found this firm, unshakable resolution in all the ministers of the government, and all Members of Parliament and all the journalists whom I met. With an impressive unanimity, the same conclusions were drawn from the fact that Hitler had broken his word: that an entente with the Reich was impossible. Peace was no longer a matter of confidence but of force. The world must be united against the common danger.

This general opinion was given to me by Mr. Chamberlain himself most directly. Lord Halifax had taken me to the Prime Minister, so that I might tell him what Hitler had said to me about Britain. I was received at the House of Commons in the room reserved for the Prime Minister. My account, which was as precise as I could make it, did nothing to brighten Mr. Chamberlain's expression. After listening to me in silence, he said with a frown: "He is a liar."

There was nothing more to be said to that: the phrase was to decide British policy.

Lord Halifax received me at the Foreign Office, where a number of high officials of his ministry were present. I was accompanied by V. V. Tilea, our Minister in London. Very kindly and frankly my host told me of the steps that England was taking to establish as extensive a system of security as possible. I endeavored to show him as plainly what a country in Rumania's position could do in the cause of peace.

After Prague had been occupied, Britain had followed delaying tactics, to prevent another surprise such as that which had presented the western powers with a fait accompli. On March 20 Lord Halifax had informed the House of Lords of the new direction of British policy. He said, in effect, that, at a time when the various states can see no sure guarantee against successive attacks directed in turn on all those who block the way of ambitious schemes of domination, "then at once the scale tips the other way and . . . there is . . . very much greater readiness to consider whether the acceptance of wider mutual obligations in the cause of mutual support is not dictated . . . His Majesty's Government have not failed to draw the moral from these events and have lost no time in placing themselves in close and direct consultation . . . with other Governments concerned . . ."

That same day the British Government had addressed a note to the governments in Paris, Moscow, and Warsaw, urging joint consultation immediately any fresh action was taken against the political independence of a European state. Mr. Chamberlain thought that such an engagement ought to be the first step toward the organization of a system of mutual assistance against violations of international law. Since negotiations with a view to accomplish such a great undertaking might take time, and in view of the gravity of the international situation, the British Government, against its normal practice and traditions, had given guarantees to three states which seemed particularly menaced: Poland, Rumania, and Greece.

The British leaders did not regard these as final measures. Mr. Chamberlain had termed the guarantee given to Poland a covering note, preceding the actual insurance policy. While realizing that this procedure meant a break with tradition on the matter, so great that it would need a special chapter in history for its explanation, the Prime Minister tried to show that it was still in keeping with tradition, since it did not assume indeterminate and limitless obligations which might have to be carried out in unforeseen circumstances.

Mr. Chamberlain, who accepted bold innovations only under the force of circumstances, hoped that he had not broken with tradition: "What we are doing now is to undertake a specific engagement directed to a certain eventuality —namely, if such an attempt should be made to dominate the world by force." Against an abstract principle of collective security he set a more practical and concrete conception. To go from a covering note to a final insurance policy, he had to give a broader and more general character to his foreign policy. His moves must lead to the constitution of a *system* of security. This system arose in crisis—the European crisis—and not out of the calm deliberations of the League of Nations. It took on the quality of an alliance—that great alliance in the interests of peace, which Mr. Churchill, who had no fear of writing new pages in history, had advocated for more than a year. Everything the government did conformed to Mr. Churchill's project. By reinforcing the points most immediately threatened—Poland, Rumania, and the Balkans—Mr. Chamberlain hoped to ward off the threat of war. Thereafter appropriate formulas would have to be found to induce the Soviet Union to back the guarantees given to the eastern countries. So Europe could be brought within the framework of a great organization for security.

Lord Halifax invited me to consider with him what chances there were of creating this new policy (so far as it concerned the eastern countries). The head of the British Foreign Office spoke in the first place of the guarantee given to Poland. Mr. Chamberlain had plainly stated in the Commons, on March 31, that "in the event of any action which clearly threatened Polish independence and which the Polish Government accordingly considered it vital to resist with their national forces, his Majesty's Government would feel themselves bound at once to lend the Polish Government all support in their power."

The British Government was aware of Poland's wish not to be party to the negotiations started with the U.S.S.R., following the events of March 20. It had considered the necessity of an immediate move in favor of Poland. But it had not taken Colonel Beck's sensitivities into account. Colonel Beck absolutely refused to admit that a unilateral guarantee might be given to a power such as Poland. That point of view was corrected a few days later, on the occasion of Beck's visit to London (April 6). It was agreed that the two nations should conclude "an agreement of a permanent and reciprocal character to replace the present temporary and unilateral assurance given by His Majesty's Government to the Polish Government." [1]

Meanwhile, Beck (with the purpose of establishing a per-

1. The Anglo-Polish Agreement of Mutual Assistance was concluded on August 6, 1939, three weeks before the outbreak of war.

fect symmetry in Anglo-Polish relations) gave the British Government assurance that Poland considered itself bound to come to England's aid in the same conditions as those specified by the provisional assurance given to Poland by the British Government.

This was agreeable to Britain, since it made possible a more active intervention in Polish affairs, without offending its new partner. Lord Halifax had his own scruples, although they differed from those of Colonel Beck. He did not wish the support given to Poland to be regarded as an encouragement to any warlike attitude. The Minister knew that he could not avoid charges from the Reich on this point. Nazi propaganda seized on everything. Every gesture that might add fuel to the fire would have to be avoided. Lord Halifax took this political duty as a matter of conscience. No minister ever showed a greater sense of responsibility. He had studied the Danzig problem in all its ramifications, and had tried to get an exact statement from Beck as to what conditions Poland would agree to in reaching an understanding with the Reich. His personal inflence had always been on the side of appeasement. In his questions regarding my conversations with Beck, I realized how careful he was being to learn whether the Polish Minister, as he had promised, really meant to make it possible for the German population of Danzig to exercise self-rule within an international framework. I was able to reassure him on this point. Beck's peaceful intentions regarding Germany were above suspicion; and the Polish Government would certainly do all in its power to prevent the crisis. But I made no secret of the fact that the intentions of Berlin, of which I had been advised, were not so reassuring. Citing the German character of Danzig, Hitler seemed determined to incorporate the Free City into Greater Germany. "I am afraid also," said Lord Halifax to me, "that the concessions to which M. Beck might agree will hardly satisfy Herr Hitler."

The ethnical argument favorable to the German thesis

was no more successful in moving the British conscience than it was during the Sudeten crisis. But I still felt that it was embarrassing to them. What could they say to the Germans when they demanded entry into Danzig? I suggested that the reply might be that they should evacuate Prague. If it was decided to resist Hitler, there was the evident danger of fresh arguments, as he chose. He had succeeded against the Czechs by using apparently good arguments in a bad cause. Was he to be allowed to exploit a new Sudeten affair?

I was told that the Germans would not leave Prague even though that was firmly demanded. I replied that this was not the question. The opening of the Polish affair recalled that of Czechoslovakia. Hitler first appropriated the Sudeten; and then, when military resistance had been made impossible, he occupied Bohemia. On ethnical grounds, he had suppressed a state and subjected a foreign people. If he were able to cut Poland off from the sea and to surround Polish territory from Memel to the Carpathian Mountains of Slovakia, it would be the end of Polish independence. Hitler must be told that such an action was impossible *because it was understood what he was up to.* And when, speaking of Danzig, he quoted his *rights*, in order to bring him to a halt he should be reminded of his crime: the occupation of Prague.

This exchange of views was not of much practical value. Still it made it possible for me to see with what meticulous care a man of so great probity as Lord Halifax meant to consider the policy of "encirclement." Quite as convinced as the Prime Minister that it was no longer possible to believe in Hitler's good faith, Lord Halifax tried no less scrupulously to avoid anything that might be interpreted as provocation. Though war might be inevitable, it was still necessary to behave as though it could be avoided. It was in this spirit that he considered Poland. He had not pressed it to come to any understanding with the Soviet Union contrary to its inclination. Beck's arguments on this point had seemed plausible to him. Not to provoke dangerous reactions, he preferred first to feel out Moscow before involving Poland more definitely in the course of general collaboration. This general collaboration in the defense of peace, however, was still the real motive behind the efforts of the British Government. That was the reason for Britain's guarantee to Greece and Rumania.

We came to discuss the Balkans. On April 13 the Prime Minister told the House of Commons that the Government believed it was fulfilling a duty and rendering a service by removing all doubt as to its position. In view of the unrest born of the chain of events that had happened during the last few weeks, His Majesty's Government had come to the conclusion that, "in the event of any action being taken which clearly threatened the independence of Greece or Rumania and which the Greek or Rumanian Government respectively considered it vital to resist with their national forces, his Majesty's Government would feel themselves bound at once to lend the Greek or Rumanian Government, as the case might be, all the support in their power."

In Paris, M. Daladier made a parallel declaration on the same day in the Chambre des Députés. During the conferences which led to this declaration the British Government had shown itself particularly concerned with Greece, while the French Government had pressed for the extension of the guarantee to Rumania.

With affairs as unsettled as they were, such a guarantee cut both ways. It exposed the countries it was intended to cover to the resentment, even to the wrath, of the Third Reich. The day before the declaration Herr von Ribbentrop had made it clear to the countries interested "that he did not think there were still states so disposed as to be deluded by the British." The Reich, said Herr von Ribbentrop, "would regard any participation in the British Government's policy of encirclement as directed against itself, and would draw the necessary conclusions." Ribbentrop recalled the words spoken by Hitler at Wilhelmshaven on April 1: "Whoever is prepared to pull the chestnuts out of the fire for the great powers must expect to get his fingers burned!"

However, the Balkan countries, to whom another threat made no difference, gladly accepted the Anglo-French guarantee. In it they saw the means of closer approach to old allies who not so long ago seemed to want to withdraw from southeastern affairs. The presence of England and France in a region where the Axis claimed exclusive interest seemed to offer, if not certain security, at least a certain amount of freedom. The message of Chamberlain and Daladier linked them again with a Europe dear to them and which they faithfully intended to serve. I was happy to be able to express these ideas personally to Lord Halifax.

I added that the Balkan countries, Rumania above all, hoped that the assistance of the western powers would not be confined to the political sphere, and that England and France would make themselves felt in the same measure on the economic plane. If Germany were to lord it unchallenged over the southeastern markets, it would be hard to stop it wielding the determining influence in the Balkans. The zeal with which the Reich had seized the Danubian and Balkan markets had to be contrasted with the great indifference of the western powers to the economic conditions of these regions. Germany evidently had greater economic interests there than any the western powers could advance. It was neither just nor wise to check the natural play of complementary interests in Europe. But the satisfaction of these complementary interests did not exhaust all the possibilities of the countries of the southeast. There was still a large margin from which England and France could profit; otherwise, the countries in question ran the risk of falling into the closed orbit of German economy. European freedom could not be defended solely by political and military guarantees; efforts should be made so to organize exchange that every country could maintain constant relations with the open market. The

Rumanian Government had concluded an economic agreement of considerable importance with the Reich. It had done
so to end political tension, and to ward off a threat of which
all the friendly powers had warned it. This agreement, concluded as the result of negotiations of whose existence the
British Government was aware,[1] had none of the arbitrary
and improper character attributed to it by some people. It did
not violate Rumania's economic interests and it did not com-
mit Rumanian economy entirely. The Rumanian Government—as its representatives had more than once declared—
wanted to enter into full economic relations with the western
powers. I expressed this desire anew to Lord Halifax while
assuring him that effective economic assistance from England was the more precious to us because it would help us
better to resist Germany's monopolistic tendencies shown in
recent negotiations.

Lord Halifax agreed with my interpretation of the British
guarantee. The British Government had made this most
unusual move to make it perfectly clear that it had no intention of withdrawing its interest in the Balkans. Britain had
never accepted the principle of exclusive zones of influence.
It not only intended to maintain its present relations with the
countries of the southeast, it was also ready to give them aid
in case of danger. The British Government realized that
such a policy demanded a constant effort in the economic
as well as in the political sphere. Sir Frederick Leith-Ross
had just left for Rumania; and the task of this high-ranking
official of the Foreign Office was to strengthen the economic
ties between Britain and Rumania.[2]

1. On March 23, 1939, the day on which the economic agreement with
the Reich was signed, I received the following letter from Sir Reginald
Hoare, British Minister in Bucharest: "My dear Minister,—I hope that
you will not be displeased if I tell you that I am sending the following wire
to London: 'I have maintained the contact with the Rumanian Government since the beginning of the present crisis and I feel justified in record-
ing my opinion that they are handling it with wise circumspection.'"
2. I had met Sir F. Leith-Ross during my visit to Brussels. Sir Frederick
was going to Bucharest "to study the means by which Rumania could be

But the British Government well understood that the guarantees given in the hope of assuring peace in eastern Europe would be insufficient unless they were incorporated in a security system of greater scope. To be complete, this system ought to start in London and Paris and end in Moscow. Warsaw and Ankara were the essential hinges. Therefore, the British leaders, so that they might ultimately reach the Soviet capital—supreme goal of their diplomatic efforts—were taking two separate paths: the southern road, which should bring the western powers closer to Turkey, and through Turkey, to Soviet Russia; and the road of direct negotiations with Moscow, to induce Russia to share in the defense of peace in the east of Europe.

The British Government had made preliminary contact with the Turkish Government. It had indicated to Ankara its desire to see Turkey identify itself with a policy of effective security in the eastern Mediterranean and the Balkans. Lord Halifax was glad to be able to inform me that in principle the reply of the Turkish Government was favorable.

I told Lord Halifax that the Turkish Government had already informed the Rumanian Government of its intention to establish closer relations with the western powers, and that we sincerely hoped the move would be successful. The Rumanian Government realized that the efficacy of the Anglo-French guarantees largely depended on the organization of security in the Balkans. Because of its distance from the Axis, Turkey enjoyed greater freedom of action than its Balkan neighbors. It could openly maintain close relations with the western powers, as well as with the Soviet Union; consequently, it should be an essential pillar of Balkan security.

I was able to prove to Lord Halifax that, prior to the British guarantee, Turkey and Rumania had taken important decisions which had already put them in the camp of the

helped to maintain its position in the world's market, and not disappear into the exclusive economic field of the German Reich."

powers resolved to resist German pressure. I informed the British Foreign Minister of a meeting in Constantinople, on April 8 (the day following the Albanian affair), between M. Sarajoglu, Turkish Minister for Foreign Affairs, and myself. My Turkish colleague, considerably affected by continual aggression against the countries of the southeast, had indicated to me his government's desire to take a determined part in our common resistance. Before entering into precise engagements, Turkey wanted to know just what forces England and France could put behind their policy; but it was determined to make an effective contribution to the strengthening of the Balkan Entente. Certain conclusions followed this meeting. The minutes began as follows:

"The two ministers have reviewed the course of political events since the last Balkan conference. They have observed that the tendency toward hegemony is becoming increasingly evident in Europe, and tends to assert itself in every country, and threatens particularly those of the east and southeast. Moreover it is felt that there is a movement toward an organized effort to show common resistance to this tendency toward hegemony. . . ."

These minutes were completed by certain secret notes, "additional to the conversation," jointly approved by the two parties.

The first rider made clear that: "Turkey and Rumania will make every effort to strengthen the Balkan Entente in all its applications and to increase its potential."

Point 3, which was the most important, was in these terms:

"Should events compel either Rumania or Turkey, or both together, or the entire Balkan Union, to choose and take a definite stand between the two opposing groups, it is fully understood that Rumania and Turkey will join forces—and insist that their allies in the Balkan Entente do likewise—with the group organized and united for the creation of a joint resistance to the tendencies toward hegemony threatening their independence and security."

Later articles outlined the assistance which the two states might mutually offer in case of danger, and Article 6 referred to conversations being pursued by the two states with the western powers:

". . . Rumania and Turkey will strive to obtain all the requisite information with a view to effective military support (troops, material, arms, munitions, navy, and air force), so that their participation in the common resistance may contribute effectively to ultimate success."

These secret notes, whose trend I indicated to Lord Halifax, were evidence of the spirit of the Constantinople conversations. They also show the scrupulous rectitude of the Turkish Government, which, with the full approbation of its Rumanian friends, had just begun negotiations with England.

Turkey, because of its fortunate geographical position, was able to serve the cause of Balkan security, not only by reason of the bonds which it wished to tighten with the western powers, but also because of the close friendly relations it enjoyed with the Soviet Union. I had told M. Sarajoglu when I saw him at Constantinople of the desire of the Rumanian Government to see good relations established between the U.S.S.R. and the Balkan Entente, and I had asked him to let Moscow have an account of our conversations. I was informed later that my Turkish colleague had done this and that the Soviet Government had expressed its thanks. It seemed to me at that time that to ensure the necessary support of the Soviet Union for a broad system of security, it would be better to rely on the offices of the Balkan Entente than on those of the "border states" which separated the Reich from Russia. While Berlin showed increasing and more dangerous irritation over any agreement that might be interpreted as an act of "encirclement," it was difficult to raise objections to the active participation of Russia in the defense of peace in the Balkans. As in other great European crises, the Balkans seemed destined to play a decisive role. If it were possible to set against the intentions of the Reich a united Balkan region whose independence and security were guaranteed by the majority of the great powers, Hitler would not be able to disturb the peace. In face of Axis pressure, Turkey lent itself much better than did Poland as the point where the west and Russia met. And in that spring of 1939 Turkey, supported by its neighbors and friends, had decided to put itself at the service of the cause of resistance.

The idea I expressed coincided with the policy of the British Empire. Lord Halifax did not hide the importance the British Government gave to the full independence of the Balkans and to the strengthening of their unity. He spoke to me in the same terms that Mr. Churchill had used of the necessity of incorporating Bulgaria in the entente. He assured me that the negotiations with Turkey, which were only in their initial stages, would be actively pursued, not only to create new bonds between Britain and that country but also to associate Turkey with the policy of guarantees which Britain had given to Rumania and Greece. Finally, the supreme goal pursued by the British Government was to tie up the intended treaty with Turkey with the agreements consolidating Turco-Soviet friendship. This was one means of reaching Moscow from the south, and of interesting the Soviet Union in the common defense of a region whose security was essential to European equilibrium.

The British Government intended to employ still other means to bring Russia to participate in the defense of continental security. It had decided to reach a direct agreement with Moscow. This, Lord Halifax felt, was the most delicate and difficult problem he still had to solve.

The Government shared neither Mr. Churchill's optimism nor the illusions of the Labor Opposition with regard to the Soviet Union. Russia, it believed, was noticeably reticent, was choosing its own path, and showed no eagerness to accept the proposed formulæ of mutual aid. The British Government was also obliged to take into account the objections raised by Poland, and, to a lesser degree, Rumania. It realized that these two border countries wished to keep clear of a policy which exposed them to a danger that was only too obvious. But it was determined to overcome all difficulties, because Russian support was indispensable in restraining Germany's frenzied ambitions.

The British Government had only a very restricted choice of formulæ whereby to persuade Russia. These formulæ closely considered and politic, had to be framed in such a manner that Russia might be brought in without raising Germany's suspicion. It was necessary, moreover, that the border countries to which the western powers had given guarantees should be included in the new system, always, however, without their being expressly mentioned. Things must be indicated, not said, and the invisible ties properly strengthened.

The British Government had accepted the burden of this thankless task with more firmness than conviction. From the outset it was faced by apparently insurmountable obstacles. I have already mentioned the reply made by the Polish Foreign Minister to the British note of March 20. Beck was agreeable to the exchange of pledges of mutual aid with England but he refused to bind himself to Russia. On his side Count Raczynski, the Polish Ambassador in London, informed the Foreign Office that "Poland found it impossible to sign a political agreement to which Russia was a contracting party." This explicit position led to Moscow's refusal to give favorable consideration to the British note of March 20.

The British Government was obliged to pursue independent negotiations with Warsaw and Moscow. It made new offers to the U.S.S.R. It still hoped that one day it would be possible to unify the efforts which had at first taken such divergent ways. During the month of April there was a steady exchange of telegrams, notes, and *aides-mémoire* between

London, Paris, and Moscow. No proposal won the approval of all three capitals; and it was not even possible to find agreement between London and Paris.

The Soviet Government had entered into the negotiations with some doubt. True, it had not hesitated to accept the idea of a direct agreement among France, the U.S.S.R., and Britain. But the western powers demanded something quite different; they wanted the U.S.S.R. to join in the guarantees they had given to Poland and Rumania. Moscow replied that it was for Poland and Rumania to ask for this or at least to announce their agreement. The British Government, aware of Poland's opposition and of Rumania's reservations (and to a certain extent sharing the apprehension of these countries with regard to Germany, which was ready to take strong measures with any country having a policy of "encirclement"), suggested the use of circumlocution and ambiguity.

"The British Government has noted M. Stalin's recent declaration, by the terms of which the Soviet Union declares itself in favor of giving aid to nations which may be victims of aggression and fight for their independence. It would seem therefore that the Soviet Government would conform entirely to this policy, if on its own initiative, it now made a public declaration, in which, referring to the general declaration mentioned above, and to the declarations recently made by the British and French Governments, it would repeat that, in the event of an act of aggression against a state bordering on the Soviet Union, which the state in question would resist, the aid of the Soviet Government would be given, if the desire for it were expressed, and would be furnished in the most appropriate manner." Lord Halifax's note added: "A positive declaration by the Soviet Government at the present moment would have a quietening effect on the international situation, and would constitute a concrete application of the general Soviet policy as stated above."

The British Government proposed in effect that the Soviet Union should make a declaration of guarantee, as England

and France had done, creating a unilateral engagement. It was only too easy for the Soviet Union to refuse such a proposal, which required the undertaking of important engagements, but in the most uncertain terms.

As for the French Government, though hampered in the same way as the London government, it strove to find more precise formulæ. The Quai d'Orsay drew up the following text on April 14:

"In case France and Great Britain should find themselves in a state of war with Germany, as the outcome of action undertaken by them in giving aid or assistance to Rumania or Poland, victims of unprovoked aggression, the U.S.S.R. would immediately give them aid and assistance. In case the U.S.S.R. should find itself in a state of war with Germany, as the outcome of action undertaken by it to afford aid and assistance to Rumania or Poland, victims of unprovoked aggression, France and Great Britain would immediately give it aid and assistance."

M. Bonnet had found the English proposal too vague. Lord Halifax found the French wording much too clear. The two texts were communicated to Moscow separately. This gave more leeway to the Soviet Government, which informed London and Paris of its response on April 19. During my stay in London the Soviet counterproposal had just arrived and was still being examined. Lord Halifax requested me to ask his French colleague to communicate it to me during my coming visit to Paris. It seemed to me that in these negotiations the British Government was inclined to leave the initiative to the French Government, which showed real ardor and a lively desire to bring them to a head. I promised that I would ask M. Bonnet to inform me as to the latest phases of the negotiations, which were of the utmost interest to me.[1]

I was sorry I could give no effective encouragement to the efforts of Lord Halifax to consolidate the guarantees which Britain had given my country. The cautious policy which

1. Cf. Chap. VI, p. 148.

Rumania was compelled to follow forbade our open participation in an action which the Reich proclaimed as being directed against it. Hitler's threats, which we had just averted by signing the economic agreement, the uncertain attitude which the U.S.S.R. seemed to have taken since Munich, and the speed of Nazi reactions compared to the slowness of Allied conversations all helped to enforce reserve.

I had nothing but approval for the indirect formulæ by which England and France intended to serve security in the east. While realizing how difficult it was so to dispel Russia's reasonable reluctance and to bring the Soviet Union once more to the support of general security, all that I was able to do, to offset the disadvantages of Rumania's attitude of reserve, was to give formal assurance that, in case of war, Rumania would become part of the Anglo-Franco-Russian system of security. With Lord Halifax, just as with the French leaders a few days later, I found appreciation of this position. Negotiations were to continue, without the Rumanian Government being called upon to declare itself openly on a policy to which it was known to have given tacit adhesion.[1]

Unfortunately, there was another point on which Britain's understanding of the needs of a country like Rumania was not to be translated into solid fact. A policy of arresting German expansionism such as the British Government had inaugurated required that all the threatened countries should not only be given certain guarantees but should also be brought to a state of effective defense. The western guarantees were intended to operate only if the guaranteed country resisted aggression "with all its national forces." Now the arming of these national forces demanded an industrial effort which none of the guaranteed countries could make. These countries had not neglected their armies. They had made them into excellent fighting machines, animated by the best spirit and abundantly provided with medium-weight armament. But motorized and heavy armament could only be fur-

1. Cf. Epilogue, pp. 201 ff.

nished in sufficient quantities by the factories of the west.
For years France had armed its eastern friends; but its own
needs, together with a certain delay in manufacture, reduced
its possibilities of export. Rumania turned to the factories of
Czechoslovakia. Very soon the Skoda works were to become
the principal purveyors to the Rumanian Army. When the
Reich occupied Bohemia the Rumanian rearmament program was held up. It was necessary to negotiate in Berlin for
the execution of outstanding contracts. The political significance which might be attached to these negotiations was
evident. The Rumanian Army was becoming tributary to
the Reich. Guaranteed by London and armed by Berlin, Rumania was in a situation in which anything might happen.

King Carol, during his last visit to London (November,
1938), about six weeks after Munich, had drawn the attention of the British Government to the needs of the Rumanian
Army. I returned to the charge, stressing the possible consequences of the seizure of Prague and Pilsen on the military
situation in the east. I had submitted to the competent British
authorities a list of the many orders our Ministry of War
wished to place with Britain. Lord Halifax informed me that
this list would be considered most sympathetically but that,
in view of Britain's own needs and the delay its rearmament
was suffering, it was hardly probable that it could supply Rumania with "anything approaching" the quantities foreseen
by the list.

I could not hide my regret. It was all too evident that, large
states and small, we had not kept pace with events. We were
coming to the hurdle without having really got under way
or having prepared our forces. The policy of resistance
which we wished to set against the policy of violence was
so improvised that it could neither express itself in exact
diplomatic formulæ nor rely on real military power. It was
only too obvious that, given the impossibility the eastern
countries found of obtaining indispensable modern armaments, except from certain factories now controlled by the

Reich, the freedom of action of our countries would steadily diminish.

Yet on this point also Britain, conscious of its past mistakes, was about to take action. It was preparing to back its policy with force. I had the privilege of early information of the great news the British Government had decided to release. During my last visit to the Foreign Office, on April 26, Lord Halifax interrupted our conversation to go to Downing Street, where the Prime Minister was in conference with the Labor leaders. On his return the Minister informed me that Mr. Chamberlain was going to announce to the country the introduction of compulsory military service. "It is a measure," said Lord Halifax to me, "which deviates somewhat from our normal tradition. Therefore, in order to avoid internal difficulties, the Prime Minister wanted first to consult the representatives of the trade unions. General conscription, and eventual mobilization, must be so arranged as not to impede our industrial production at all."

The chief of the Foreign Office had taken his own precautions. Sir Neville Henderson, the British Ambassador in Berlin, had been summoned to London a few days previously, and was on his way back to Berlin with instructions to break the news to Hitler. "We thought," Lord Halifax explained to me, "that it was better for us to tell the Germans ourselves what we intend to do, and why. They must not learn of it through the newspapers." [1]

Lord Halifax's explanation took into account the fact that, two days later, April 28, Hitler was to make an important

1. In fact, on the same day, April 26 (Mr. Chamberlain was to make his declaration during the afternoon in the House of Commons), the British Ambassador handed Baron von Weizsäcker, undersecretary at the Wilhelmstrasse, an aide-mémoire announcing the measures which the British Government intended to take to introduce compulsory military service into the United Kingdom. Sir Neville Henderson was instructed to supplement this communication with a verbal message which began: "Mr. Chamberlain's policy is that of peace. But Mr. Chamberlain believes that the best way of preserving peace is to show in indubitable fashion that England is ready to defend itself, if necessary, against any attack."

DEPARTURE FROM LONDON

"The gentleman who stooped toward me . . . was still impeccably dressed in civil clothes: shining top hat, the perfectly tailored overcoat, the magnificent umbrella."

(See page 131.)

THE ARC DE TRIOMPHE, PARIS

"When 'Last Post' was sounded over the Unknown Soldier . . . I felt how close were the ties which united me . . . like so many other Europeans . . . to the French soldier who lay there."

speech. The Chancellor, whose foreign policy was subject to fits of anger, must not be given any pretext for putting a match to the powder.

Notwithstanding the tactfulness of Sir Neville Henderson's communication to the Wilhelmstrasse, it contained a categorical reply to the words, good and bad, spoken by Hitler regarding Britain. The British Government was not to be moved by either flattery or threats. Against the former it set its political instinct and traditional common sense; against the latter it had decided to bring strength, even though it meant going through with an effort to which it was not accustomed.

I had been witness to the imperious appeal which Hitler had addressed to Britain, and so was better able to appreciate the significance of the reply which was drafted while I was still at the Foreign Office. When Lord Halifax expressed the hope that this move of Britain's would have a salutary effect on Europe, I replied that it was to be hoped that everywhere the importance and gravity would be understood of a decision which ensured a better defense of the cause of law and prevented its further enfeeblement. "In any case," Lord Halifax added with a smile, "the British Government has come to the conclusion that it had to conform to the usages and traditions of the Continent, so as to convince everybody that it is taking things seriously."

The feeling I carried away from England gained in force as the result of this last conversation. The gentleman who stooped toward me as the train pulled out so that he might shake my hand again, was still impeccably dressed in civil clothes: shining top hat, the perfectly tailored overcoat, the magnificent umbrella. But, in spite of himself, his dignified nonchalance seemed to take on a more martial air. He seemed to say with vigorous resignation: "If it must be done, we can do it!" And contrary to all "tradition," this attitude of the diplomat under arms had a very British air about it.

CHAPTER VI

THE TROUBLE IN FRANCE

The internal crisis and its repercussions on foreign policy. The government. M. Daladier, and the peace policy of M. Georges Bonnet. Hitler's speech of April 28, 1939. The Franco-Anglo-Soviet negotiations. France and Italy.

IN no city of the world is the weight of official honors harder to bear than in Paris. To drive in a closed car escorted by two motor cyclists, to be unable to stop as the spirit moves (to admire a view, to go book hunting along the quays, or to stroll along the boulevards), is too heavy a tribute to pay to politics.

The city takes its revenge by showing superb indifference. Just to walk from a hotel upon a red carpet that stretches to the door of a motor car is enough to break that intimate communion established between the traveler and Paris from the moment of his arrival. The only guests whom the capital seems to consider as strangers are its so-called distinguished guests.

The revenge Paris takes can be still more subtle. The city which you cannot approach freely hides the country from you. The whole of the German Reich was in the room where Hitler had received and had spoken to me. It had seemed easy to me to find political England between the Palace of Westminster, Downing Street, and the Foreign Office. In Paris I met brilliant politicians, great journalists, and famous diplomats; but it was hard to find France, hear its voice and know what it was thinking. I attributed this difficulty to the indescribable charm of the lovely capital, which attracted and distracted my attention. There may have been still other reasons. In that spring of 1939 France could hardly find itself.

Germany, one and united under the Führer's orders, was ready for ill deeds. England was again becoming unanimous under the spur of indignation. The seizure of Prague had brushed away all former hesitations; and the whole country, even though it had not been able to reorganize its forces, was ready to resist. But France was still divided. The long and painful European crisis leading up to Munich had shaken its strong moral position. A new sentiment had been revealed to it—that of solitude. The unfair lot that had fallen on its generous people aroused serious dissensions in the French nation. The division was embittered by social crises, and a certain weariness of the regime could be felt.

What, then, was its system of European policy? In 1938, during the Czech affair, the French Government had sounded the intentions of friendly states. None had responded to its appeal without reservations. Yugoslavia was hesitant; the enticing proposals which Berlin and Rome had showered upon it after the death of King Alexander had an increasing influence on its government. Rumania had declared itself ready to help Czechoslovakia—it had persisted in this loyal attitude up to the eve of Munich; but it had not been able to decide in advance to allow Soviet troops to cross its territory. As for Poland, it had resolutely ranged itself among the adversaries of President Beneš and had demanded Teschen. To withstand Hitler, France could count only on Britain's assistance. This assistance was still conditional; for while Britain was ready to support diplomatic resistance, it did not wish to run the risks of war with the few divisions at its disposal.

In these circumstances the French leaders came to the opinion held by almost the whole of Europe: extreme measures must be avoided.

These politicians have been greatly reproached for their faintheartedness, of which Germany knew how to make the most. I have no wish to take part in a debate on the problem of responsibilities. Such problems arise today in every country, and it is not for foreigners, however friendly, to seek to solve them. I shall refrain from judging the French political leaders whom I knew regarding the political necessities, traditions, and even the commands of their fatherland. It is still permissible for me to compare them with the statesmen of other countries whom I had occasion to approach in 1939. Truth obliges me to say that these Frenchmen were no less well informed than, and seemed quite as well intentioned as, the best of their foreign colleagues. Better than anyone they understood the danger which threatened Europe, and they found clear and precise words to define it. Their desire to save the peace was obvious; and they spared no efforts to offset Hitler's policy by as broad and solid a system of alliances and understandings as possible.

If France seemed uncertain and irresolute, if the support always given to the continental order established under its ægis in 1919 was felt to be weakening, the fault was less due to its leaders and institutions than to the sum of conditions determining French public life. At that time deep unrest prevailed in France, which disturbed its material welfare—that amazing fluency of life which all foreigners envied. Had France a foreboding of the maniacal power about to sweep down upon it and deal it the most devastating blows? Was it already conscious of the complete lack of preparation of its closest allies and the insufficiency and obsolescence of its own means? Faced with the numerical superiority of the enemy forces, was it secretly aware that no effort of its own could preserve it any longer from danger, and that its pre-eminence among the nations, its world influence, its very existence were threatened?

The sad unrest of a too clear-sighted people caused a strange phenomenon of dissociation. Innumerable Frenchmen allowed themselves to be drawn into the relentless toils of merciless social and political conflict. These conflicts put everything in question; the strongest interests and the most unreconcilable ideas were commingled; hatred was aroused between parties and classes; and all this internal trouble was hurled into foreign policy, thus giving the people a false impression of the international situation. Foreign propaganda made the most of this prolonged crisis to increase the confusion it had helped to create. In the opinion of many honest citizens, some of whom were thirsty for justice and others trembling for their material possessions, some foreign doctrines, mutually hostile, embodied the theories and regimentation capable of satisfying their own aspirations. Seen through the fog of domestic passions, nations across the border which followed their schemes of power and influence with inflexible severity seemed to be living symbols, to some of the idea of order, to others of the idea of revolution.

It is time to state that this confusion, which was dangerous to the national structure, not only raged in France but reigned more or less over the whole of Europe; and that it was the ace of trumps in Hitler's hand. Throughout the Continent, under the influence of insidious propaganda, internal and international affairs were being confused in a sort of fog. People everywhere followed with "interest" what they believed they saw in the "experiment" of the totalitarian states. They hoped to find there a remedy for their ills. The word "authority" was in vogue; the prestige of democracy was lessened. In Warsaw, Bucharest, Budapest, and throughout the Balkans the new ideas had not only stirred up movements of insurrection but also strongly influenced state policy. Either so that they could strengthen relations with Berlin, or so that they could resist the German policy, governments used the current formulas to increase their own power. As for the masses, whose special virtues totalitarianism recognized, they showed their acceptance of the principle of authority by parading with outstretched arms, wearing green, maroon, or black shirts. The adoption of the outer forms of Nazism was supposed in some cases to guarantee independent nationalism. In point of fact, it consolidated the grip Hitler's national policy had on the neighboring countries.

Above all the French community, always swayed by the principles of liberty, justice, and property, was confronted by a totalitarian system, through which its old enemy of 1918 had brought about a staggering readjustment. In a country of so ancient a civilization as France, this had not led to the formation of armed bands sporting colored shirts. But the ill went further, penetrating the mind where reigned perpetual unrest as to first principles. Were some of these principles to be sacrificed to others, or as in the French Revolution must one "declare war on the king"? Moscow offered one solution; Berlin proclaimed another. The more the French distrusted one another, the more they trusted the ideologies which appeared to be the source of the strength of the nations whose foreign policy was aimed at France. The more they fought among themselves, the more they were led to solve the problems of their consciences, concerning only their own country, with the aid of foreign arguments and the unwitting service of foreign causes. This despite a patriotism probably stronger and more singleminded than any, but one which external influences almost succeeded in paralyzing completely.

In 1939 the split between these antagonistic patriots was not very marked; but it was obviously to be expected. Veterans of the World War were ready to accept defeat in the mistaken and culpable hope of so preventing anarchy and "saving order." On the other hand, some of the people were only to wake up when the German armies invaded Soviet territory. Then, in a profound and complete reaction, partisan passions were to release the sense of national patriotism in the masses, and the recalcitrant to identify themselves with the fatherland in incredible devotion. But in 1939 no one foresaw when and where the redeeming call would be raised to free patriotism from bias and, in the agony of the ordeal, proclaim that France still stood.

This was why the occupation of Prague had not caused the same decisive reaction in France as in Britain. Up to then the French had committed fewer faults in foreign policy than the British. They had tried to maintain the continental order established at Versailles in ways which England had not supported. When they were forced to bow to the demands of the Reich, they were only following the British example. M. Daladier accompanied Mr. Chamberlain to Munich because he was aware of the weakness of the British Army.

Britain redressed its position on March 15, 1939. France's change-over was less complete. The extremist political parties showed no interest in resistance: the extreme left, because Moscow had dropped out of the orbit of collective security; the extreme right, because it saw nothing but good in the authoritarian language of the Axis. France seemed to have lost the significance of Europe. It listened to those who preached resignation and advised it to cultivate its empire as wise Cincinnatus had cultivated his garden—by renouncing the idea of power. While the government, when receiving guests from abroad, still pursued the broad lines of a foreign policy whose foundations were already sadly shaken, France seemed to be absent.

It was still more affecting suddenly to find France at the crossroads of the imperial highways, which meet at the Arc de Triomphe. I had laid wreaths at the foot of various memorials, and I believed that this act of official piety could hardly trouble me further. But, when "Last Post" was sounded over the Unknown Soldier at whose feet I had just spread my country's colors, I felt how close were the ties which united me, like so many of my countrymen, like so many other Europeans, like all the veterans of the last war, to the French soldier who lay there. We owed to him the victory; to him we owed the hope we had put in France and in Europe. "The Last Post" resounded with a strange and disturbing note. It seemed to announce the new danger which threatened the victory. And one felt that France *was there*, laid open to disaster and pledged to sacrifice: the first objective of the threat aimed at the supreme values, it faced destiny with that quiet fervor which, in the minds of all those still faithful to it, linked it to the very conception of eternity.

A feeling of invincible confidence mingled with the anguish that seized my heart.

After this ceremony, I was happy to be able to meet all my French comrades of 1916 at the home of Captain Goulin, leader of Farman Unit No. 5—my old squadron.

The members of the French Government welcomed me with the affectionate cordiality always accorded to the representatives of Rumania. I was all the more moved because I sensed that they carried the same heavy load of bitterness that recent events had laid on my own country. We wore the same mourning—that for Czechoslovakia, our friend, who since the common victory had been the connection and the effective political bond between France and all the countries associated with the French continental system. For France, and for its most faithful friends, the Munich Agreement and the occupation of Prague had had more immediate, more decisive consequences than they had for Britain. While the disturbance of balance in Europe only threatened the British Empire's world situation, it had already upset the continental position of France. We felt, French leaders and representatives of eastern countries, that we clasped hands over the ruins of our common organization of security.

France's solicitude for my country was not diminished in the least because of this bitter experience. M. Edouard Daladier, with dogged energy, had made it his personal concern to see that the Anglo-French guarantee should be accorded to Rumania as well as Greece. I went to the rue St. Dominique to express my country's thanks to the President of the Council. I found there a man whom the occupation of Prague had affected just as it had affected Mr. Chamberlain. It had roused in him the same anger. M. Daladier was at the end of his patience, and he did not hide the fact. His straightforward nature reacted violently against Hitler's gross dishonesty. Like his English colleague, M. Daladier felt that henceforward it was impossible to come to terms with deceit.

M. Georges Bonnet, calmer in adversity because he was deliberate and was disposed to maneuvers, gave me a long interview at the Quai d'Orsay to explain the means by which he still steadfastly hoped to save the peace. He no longer cherished illusions regarding Germany; the Munich policy was finished, completely. Moreover, the Minister had only accepted this policy to gain time and stave off a military catastrophe. Munich had never appeared to him as the beginning of a "new era" but rather as the inevitable result of a constant show of weakness toward Germany, and the equally inevitable consequence of the inadequacy of the system on which European peace was based. In the face of danger, all France's alliances showed themselves to be inoperative. The alliance with Poland had not prevented that country from taking its own course. The Franco-Soviet Pact, lacking practical means of application, was merely platonic. The agreements with countries of the Little Entente were not enough to hold Germany in check. The neighboring countries had refused to facilitate Soviet assistance.

Advantage must be taken of the breathing space, bought so dearly at Munich, to re-establish the organization on more solid foundations. Collective pledges of mutual assistance were no longer sufficient. More precise agreements were necessary, correlated into a complete, general system of security. Britain, first, must accept its responsibilities. That it had decided to do. Next, by mutual agreement, France and Britain ought to guarantee the eastern countries. This they had already done in the case of Poland, Rumania, and Greece. They were on the point of making new ties with Turkey. But this was not all: the most important step still had to be taken. It was essential to bind Russia to the cause of peace. The participation of the Soviet Union was indispensable and would be decisive; the French Government had associated itself with the efforts of the British Government to bring this about. M. Bonnet stressed the great importance he attached to the Soviet contribution. He wanted it at all costs. I was struck by the clearness of his decision.

French policy, as M. Bonnet explained to me, was similar to but not identical with that of the British Government. It had seemed to me that the first thought of the British statesmen was the preservation of the balance of power. They were ready, if necessary, to accept the risk of war, if they could bring the strongest possible coalition to bear against the aggressor. But this coalition must safeguard a balanced order. Certain members of the Conservative Cabinet were prejudiced against Soviet methods and "procedures." They yielded but halfheartedly to the conditions which the Russian negotiators brought forward in increasing numbers. More than one Englishman was tempted to believe that Colonel Beck's thesis (according to which an Anglo-French-Polish alliance was enough to ensure Europe's salvation) was sufficiently advantageous. These reservations, while they did not affect the perfect good faith with which the British Government was trying to reach an understanding with Moscow, were to bring about more than one crisis in the course of the negotiations.

No such preoccupations checked the French Government. It wanted peace. It wanted it for a reason at once very simple and strong: it was afraid that war would be fatal to France. The time gained at Munich had not been used to the full. M. Bonnet knew by heart the precise extent of the armament of France's allies and friends. France still might have to bear alone, or almost alone, the onslaught of the enemy armies. To save France, it was necessary to save the peace. This was no longer possible *with* Germany—as people had believed at the time of Munich—it was now only possible *against* Germany. This could only be realized if the weight of the Soviet masses counterbalanced the German masses. Faced with the threat of war on two fronts, Hitler would

stop. M. Bonnet had less faith in the value of collective engagements than in the effect of a powerful counterpoise to
Hitler that could be brought to bear in good time. Only a
precise agreement with Russia could redress the situation.
Such an agreement was demanded by the French General
Staff; M. Daladier and the government as a whole desired it;
and it appeared to be the only solution capable of averting
the catastrophe.

M. Bonnet did not disguise the fact that negotiations with
Russia were difficult and might take a long time. Therefore
he asked whether he had time enough in which to realize
his policy. The Danzig affair disturbed him; it might very
shortly provoke new clashes. Could Poland avert danger or
at least postpone the conflict? Would Hitler make a further
attempt to gain Britain's consideration? In a word, was it
still possible to gain time for military preparations and get
the U.S.S.R. onto his side? That was the whole question.

The reply to this question was not long to be delayed. It
came while I was still in Paris. At a luncheon at which my
wife and I were present at the Quai d'Orsay on April 28, the
French Foreign Minister received the verbatim reports of
the speech Hitler had made, that morning, to the German
Reichstag. I heard the first observations which Hitler's words
provoked in France.

Drowned in a flood of verbiage, this speech contained
three important new facts. These three new facts were such
as to convince the French Government that time was very
short.

As I read the verbatim reports handed me by M. Bonnet,
I recognized many of the words that Hitler had spoken to me.
The Chancellor recalled the offer he had made to Poland regarding Danzig; this offer seemed to him to be "the proof of
the greatest spirit of conciliation that could be imagined as a
contribution to the cause of European peace." Such an
offer—of which "posterity will judge—can only happen

once." Poland had not taken the opportunity. It had tied itself to Britain. Its pledge was "in contradiction to the declaration of the German-Polish Pact of Nonaggression."

Then came the new pact. "I consider," said Hitler, "that the agreement concluded in his day between me and Marshal Pilsudski has been broken unilaterally by Poland, and consequently has ceased to exist."

Thus "unilaterally" Hitler denounced the agreement which, for five years, had ensured the best possible relations between the Third Reich and Poland and which, in his own words, had "contributed to an extraordinary amelioration of the European situation." No doubt his denunciation of the agreement would contribute to the creation of an equally extraordinary tension in the said situation.

There were amiable words for England in the speech—the same as those I had heard. "During all my political activity, I have never ceased to argue in favor of friendship and close collaboration between Germany and England. If I wish to see this friendship realized, it is not simply because this wish corresponds with my own sentiments but also because I realize the importance of the existence of the British Empire to humanity as a whole. I have never allowed any doubt of the fact that I saw in the existence of this empire a factor of inestimable value to the whole of human civilization and to world economy. If one looks at things from an elevated, human point of view, the idea that anyone might wish to destroy the fruits of this labor appears to me as a sort of madness worthy of an Erostratus." These amiabilities had their counterpart. Hitler outlined the idea of partitioning the world, while giving it historical justification. "The British people govern a vast world empire. They created this empire at a time when the German people had lost something of their vigor. Germany was once a great world empire. It dominated the west. But this empire was lost in a deep sleep. . . . If Germany, constantly attacked, has been unable to hold its possessions and has had to sacrifice many provinces, that is due entirely to the unfortunate development of its state organization. Those days are gone." Hitler emphasized the principle of parity with Britain: "Let all the British understand that we have not the slightest sense of being inferior to the British people. Our glorious past is far too great for that!" Hitler might have added: our future, as we conceive it, is even more so. For he was certainly thinking of the future, and of the possibility of the German people occupying again the imperial scene established by two thousand years of history. Before its "profound sleep," the German Empire "dominated the west." In what direction would it overflow when it awoke? "I have always kept within the limits of claims closely bound up with Germany's vital living space, and therefore with the eternal estate of the German nation." These claims, modest as they may have seemed, included in fact a large part of Europe. Hitler left it at that; it was for the British to speculate. In such conditions, it was possible to establish "a lasting friendship between the German and the British peoples based on mutual respect and the recognition of reciprocal interests."

Since the time Hitler had spoken to me there had been another change. The Chancellor had come to realize that Britain would not be a partner in a scheme of partition: "I have heard the British Prime Minister's declaration, in which he says that he feels that he cannot place any confidence in the assurances given by Germany. In these circumstances, I find it reasonable not to force on him, or on the British people, a situation unimaginable without a feeling of confidence." The British guarantees had impressed Hitler more than Mr. Chamberlain's statements. Above all he had been impressed by the British Government's decision to introduce compulsory military service into the United Kingdom. He wished therefore to offset England's "unfriendly action" by a move tending to demonstrate that he no longer counted on the understanding of the British Government. If he had again been careful to recall his past good intentions, this was not to be interpreted as a new appeal to London but rather as fixing responsibilities of which history would judge. Henceforth, ". . . upheld by the consciousness of our strength and that of our friends, we shall find ways which will ensure our independence and not injure our dignity."

One thing was bound to end the policy of trust which, "despite everything," Hitler had hitherto followed. This was the denunciation of the Naval Agreement of June 18, 1935. The Government of the Reich, in signing this agreement, had "voluntarily recognized the precedence of British maritime interests." It had thought "by this decision, probably unique in the history of the great powers," to facilitate the establishment of friendly relations between the two nations. But "naturally, this act presupposed that the British Government had decided to adopt a benevolent political attitude toward Germany." Was it to be understood that the British Government should recognize the "precedence" of the Reich in some other direction?

On the contrary, far from responding to this suggestion, the British Government opposed any disturbance of the European order. Hitler could not hide his disappointment. "So England unilaterally shatters the basis of the naval agreement of June 18, 1935, and renders this agreement null and void. By its policy of encirclement, it destroys the basis of the naval treaty."

Once more a generous German initiative, "unique in the history of the world," had met with a lack of comprehension on the part of neighboring peoples! In denouncing the naval agreement, as he had denounced the agreement with Poland, Hitler claimed that he only recognized realities. He claimed that he closed doors which others had no wish to leave open. But he definitely closed them, to seek elsewhere "the ways of his independence."

What were these new ways? There was as yet no indication. At first sight the Soviet Union seemed to be hermetically sealed against any attempt by Germany toward closer relations. Had the Soviet not been eliminated at Munich, at

Hitler's express demand? Was it not the object of the intrigues persistently set on foot by the Reich—intrigues to
which the famous Anti-Comintern Pact had just given a
solemn sanction? Was not the U.S.S.R. insulted in almost all
of Hitler's speeches?

However, the simultaneous denunciation of the Polish
agreement and the naval agreement might have roused certain suspicions. Had not the Reich rid itself of the engagements which bound it to Poland and Britain to free its hands,
so that they might be stretched out toward Russia? By giving the Polish guarantee before coming to a precise agreement
with the U.S.S.R., Britain played into the hands of those
who were interested in preventing an entente between London and Moscow. The Soviet Union did not love Poland;
and the British guarantee was not such as to gratify Moscow.
The persistent refusal with which Poland, relying on the
British guarantee, opposed all attempts to draw it closer to
Russia could not fail to estrange the Soviet leaders still more.
If Hitler could exploit the difficulties between Poland and
Russia, which would doubtless increase, he could nullify
Britain's entire policy of "encirclement." This was his only
way of giving play to his will to conquer. In drawing closer
to the U.S.S.R., not to protect Poland but to partition it—
was he not replacing the British plan by a maneuver more
enticing to the Russian leaders, and opening a path which
Berlin had taken more than once in the settlement of eastern
affairs? At a time when the Soviet leaders liked to recall Peter
the Great and Catherine the Great, Hitler might well be
tempted to counter British policy by resorting to the traditions of Frederick the Great.

This strange hypothesis appeared to be corroborated by
the fact that, in his recent speech, Hitler made no attack on
the Soviet Union. No more of his famous diatribes against
Moscow, the Bolsheviks, and Bolshevism! That was the
third new fact. Taken all in all, it was the most important.

A few days later—May 7—M. Bonnet was to receive a

---

report from his Ambassador in Berlin which shed some little light on Hitler's enigmatic attitude. "May I call your Excellency's special attention," wrote M. Coulondre, "to the information contained in the attached report. It was furnished by one particularly well placed to know the intentions of the Führer and his principal lieutenants. These new declarations may be summed up as follows:

"1. The Führer is determined to make sure of the return of Danzig to Germany and join East Prussia to the Reich.

"2. The Führer, patient and deliberate, will not tackle the question directly, realizing that from now on France and England will not give way, and that the coalition against him would be very powerful. He will maneuver until the time is propitious.

"3. *With this in view, the Führer will come to an understanding with Russia.* The day will come when he will thus reach his objectives without the Allies having any reason for, or any intention of, intervening. Perhaps we shall see a fourth partition of Poland. In any case, it will soon be seen that something is afoot in the east." [1]

The attention of the world now turned toward Russia. It seemed that the key to the situation was henceforth to be found at Moscow and that there the issue of war or peace might be decided.

---

1. A résumé of the remarks exchanged on May 6 between a member of the French Embassy and one of Hitler's intimates was attached to M. Coulondre's report. From this source came the following statements:

"Do you think that Hitler will begin to play before he holds all the trumps? That would be contrary to his practice, which has won him all his previous successes—without firing a shot.

"Did it not strike you that in his last speech he made no allusion to Russia? Did you notice the comprehensive manner in which today's press —which, moreover, has had precise instructions in the matter—spoke of M. Molotov and Russia? You must have had wind of certain pending negotiations, and of the journey of the Ambassador and the Military Attaché of the U.S.S.R. to Moscow. They were received on the eve of their departure, the former by Herr von Ribbentrop, the latter by the Oberkommando of the German Army; and they were fully informed of the views of the German Government. I cannot tell you anything more, but

Henceforth the Quai d'Orsay knew the full gravity of the issue. The bridges to Germany had definitely been destroyed. Should negotiations with Russia fail, the policy of aggression would be encouraged, Danzig attacked, and war ensue.

The French Government was equally well aware of the precise relations established among the states concerned since the beginning of the negotiations. The U.S.S.R. was being canvassed—France and England were the canvassers. That Russia would profit by this situation was to be foreseen. It had some long-standing grudges to wipe off—especially after Munich. But this should not be allowed to carry too much weight. Moscow was worth certain sacrifices. No price was too high to stave off war.

The French Minister of Foreign Affairs became the chief negotiator for the western powers. He took not only the initiative in winning Moscow's confidence but also the task of encouraging the patience and good will of the British Government.

M. Bonnet expounded to me in detail the difficulties of his task. In addition to political difficulties, there were innumerable formal complications. The necessity of including in the agreement certain countries which must be aided but not named had landed the Quai d'Orsay in the same difficulty that the British Foreign Office had previously experienced. Here was a diplomatic headache, and the technicians joyfully set about curing it, devising subtle variations on the same theme. Every article of the agreement went through many and strange metamorphoses, passing backward and forward between London and Paris many times, accompanied by long memoranda and verbal notes, before going on its way, in French and English, to Moscow. It was unrecognizable when it came back from Moscow. Everything had to be begun all over again.

---

one day you will learn that something is being arranged in the east" ("dass etwas im Osten im Gange ist").

The formulæ devised in London, which were drafted in a manner acceptable to the Foreign Office, were not always easy to grasp. Those worked out by the Narkomindel, whose subtlety was incomparable, seemed impossible to reconcile with the first. It needed the precision of the French language to clarify this confusion a little. This was one of the best trump cards of French diplomacy. But it could not alter the order of things. The negotiations were to last a long time.

The main problem facing the Quai d'Orsay was that of reconciling the intentional lack of precision in the English formulæ with the manifest wish of the Soviet Government to understand exactly what the western powers were driving at. On April 19 Moscow put forward its counterproposals (in reply to the French proposal of the 14th and the British proposal of the 15th).[1]

The Soviet reply was clear and well thought out. It included:

1. An undertaking on the part of the three great powers to afford each other aid against any aggression in Europe.

2. An undertaking on the part of the three powers to aid the eastern states bordering on Russia: Rumania, Poland, Latvia, and Esthonia.

3. An undertaking on the part of the three powers to study the military means of application of the aid foreseen in paragraphs 1 and 2.

Thus, from the beginning of the negotiations, the Soviet Government adopted an attitude which it was never to abandon. It was ready to undertake the broadest possible engagements, conditional on knowing to what it was committing itself and how, should the need arise, it could fulfil its engagements. Its inclination was not to haggle over the extent of the assistance, provided that the engagements to be undertaken were precise and could be carried out. In this spirit, it offered more than was asked, and insisted that the aid should be as automatic and as strictly regulated as possible from the mili-

1. Cf. Chap. V, pp. 126–127.

tary point of view. This attitude would allow it to direct the negotiations according to its wish, and to interrupt them, though still retaining the advantages of manifest good will.

The British, though they were the initiators in these negotiations, showed themselves infinitely more circumspect. Their traditional fear of committing themselves beyond certain limits, of being bound by formulæ, and of being dependent on the good will of their partners, inspired them with multiple reticences and deprived them of the benefit of their very real good faith. This circumspection on the part of the British Government, in contrast with the assurance displayed by the Soviet counter-proposal, was strikingly evidenced by a note of April 29, in which it was stated:

"The policy pursued by His Majesty's Government in its contacts with the Soviet Government aims at attempting to reconcile the following considerations:

"(*a*) Not to neglect the possibility of receiving aid from the Soviet Government in case of war.

"(*b*) Not to compromise the common front by disregarding the susceptibilities of Poland and Rumania.

"(*c*) Not to alienate the sympathy of the entire world by affording a pretext for Germany's Anti-Comintern propaganda.

"(*d*) Not to compromise the cause of peace by provoking violent action on the part of Germany. . . ."

In return for the slight advance marked by point (*a*), what a wealth of reservations! One step forward, three steps backward! . . . And to think that it was the British Government which was seeking Soviet assistance! It was obvious that the government was uneasy because of the very impetuosity with which the Soviet had accepted. London was chary, perhaps not without reason, of the automatic assistance which Moscow wished to extend to countries not yet in question, such as Latvia and Esthonia. The Soviet proposal revealed a certain "dynamism," which, although contrary to the dynamism of Germany, still ran counter to Great Britain's policy of political equilibrium. Thus the British Government was glad to be able to advance the "susceptibility" of Poland and Rumania, for the purpose of limiting the engagements which the U.S.S.R. would undertake. These susceptibilities, which London did not wish to "disregard," expressed an apprehension shared by the British Government; the fear was that the defensive system of which the western powers dreamed might afford Russia an opportunity to settle the eastern questions to its sole benefit.

M. Bonnet attached less importance to these considerations. The Polish and Rumanian reservations interested him only so far as they might determine the precautions necessary to avoid all risk of war. It seemed logical to him not to provoke Germany needlessly. But he was convinced that an agreement with the U.S.S.R. was the only barrier that could be put in the way of war. Once this barrier was erected, the Rumanian and Polish reservations would automatically disappear. I was inclined to agree with M. Bonnet on this point. From the moment that a *real* agreement was established between the west and Russia, creating an effective guarantee, Rumania would have no further reason to stand aside. It appeared to me less certain that Poland would do likewise. M. Bonnet seemed to hope that, by keeping the Poles informed of the course of the negotiations, they could be prevented from finally withdrawing.

The formula of a unilateral declaration of guarantee on the part of the U.S.S.R.—a formula to which the British Government seemed firmly attached [1]—seemed insufficient to the French Minister. In his opinion, this stood no chance of being accepted by the Moscow government. This latter wished to know exactly to what it was committed, and what

1. In its note of April 29th the British Government had once again suggested that the Soviet Government should, "on its own initiative," make a public statement referring to Stalin's latest pronouncements and engaging Russia to support the western powers if they had to fulfill the obligations they had assumed with regard to "certain countries of Eastern Europe."

was the counterpart of its engagements. Unilateral declarations meant nothing to it whatsoever.[1]

As for the French Government, it considered that a bilateral engagement would correspond much better to the ends to be reached. Only by confronting Hitler with a pact concluded in due form between the western powers and the Soviet could there be hope of halting the approach of war. On April 29 the Quai d'Orsay proposed a new formula for a bilateral accord, which ran as follows:

"In case France and Great Britain should find themselves in a state of war with Germany, as the result of action taken by them with a view to preventing a modification by force of the status quo existing in central or eastern Europe, the U.S.S.R. will immediately lend them aid and assistance. In case the U.S.S.R. should find itself in a state of war with Germany, as a result of action taken by it with a view to preventing a modification by force of the status quo existing in central or eastern Europe, France and Great Britain will immediately lend it aid and assistance."

The British Government found this proposal too wide, and involving too automatic an assistance. But M. Bonnet held his ground. He informed London that, having considered the objections of the British Government, he still believed "that his proposal was better and more simple, and that it also had more chance of being adopted."

He was wrong only on this last point. The Soviet Government was to find the French proposal quite as inadequate as the British proposal. It did not wish simply to lay down principles; it wished to settle the details. The western powers, by asking it to guarantee with them the defense of several countries, had caused it to consider the entire question of

1. The British Government, on its part, had been able to verify how little faith the Soviet had in the unilateral guarantees of the western powers. "I do not understand why the Soviet Government should pretend to believe that His Majesty's Government is not bound by the declarations made to Poland and Rumania," declared the head of the Foreign Office in a note of April 22.

eastern Europe. Henceforth Russia would no longer halt on
this road; it had to solve these problems definitely, with the
cooperation of France and Britain, or, if this were not possible, without, and against, these powers. The constantly
exaggerated terms submitted by the Soviet Government
were all designed to lead toward the double end of giving
normal and free exercise to the projected agreement and of
giving the U.S.S.R. an active and preponderant role in the
east, from the Baltic to the Black Sea. If, for reasons of prudence, the western powers hesitated to come to the required
definition of terms, the responsibility for the failure would
be theirs alone. The U.S.S.R. would retain its liberty of action.

The task which French diplomacy set itself to accomplish
became increasingly arduous. Discussion regarding the formulæ to be employed had revealed serious political divergencies. There was more in the question of balancing the
west with Soviet Russia than a pact of mutual assistance
guaranteeing the status quo: agreement was necessary on
the principles which would allow the U.S.S.R. to become
an integral part of the European order. This was a problem
particularly difficult to solve when Hitler was using his destructive energies. It was to remain open to the outbreak of
war, to create much confusion during the war itself, and to
reappear immediately peace came.[1]

The diplomatic action regarding the Soviet Union had the
full approval of all those who were responsible for French
policy. There was not such perfect unanimity as to the
policy that France ought to follow with regard to Italy.
M. Bonnet believed that Italy might be won over to a policy
of understanding and pacific collaboration. M. Daladier did
not share this hope. The President of the Council was tired
of the equivocal conduct of the Fascist government, which

1. Cf. Epilogue, pp. 201 ff.

LUNCH AT THE HOTEL MEURICE

From left to right: M. Daladier, the Rumanian Ambassador in Paris, Grigore Gafencu,
M. Bonnet, the Polish Ambassador in Paris.
In front (back view): M. Alexis Léger, Admiral Darlan.

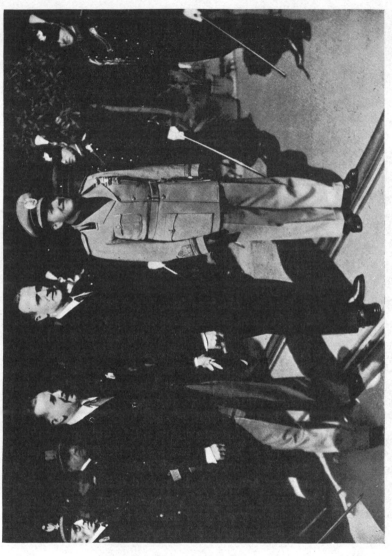

ARRIVAL IN ROME

"I had been apprehensive of the moment when I should find myself in Fascist Italy. . . .
It was evident that I should have to navigate between dangerous reefs."

(See page 156.)

periodically started violent campaigns against France, and at the same time encouraged popular rumors according to which Italy was ready to treat with France on advantageous terms. By a strange coincidence, every time that Germany made a show of drawing closer to France (as at the time of von Ribbentrop's famous journey to Paris, December 6, 1938) Rome echoed with demands for the "return" to Italy of Corsica, Nice, and Savoy. Then these noises quietened; Italy wore a smile again; and—surprising fact—French travelers returning from Italy were unanimous in admitting that they had had a very good reception. Among these travelers were observers and clandestine negotiators (like M. Baudouin, an influential businessman, who was later to play a political role in the Vichy regime). They all returned with the conviction that there existed means of coming to an understanding with the rulers of Italy.

M. Daladier put no trust in these "optimistic" reports. He had no interest in the government at Rome, but thought that Italy, making secret advances to France while proclaiming its adherence to the Axis, was only playing to win on both sides. The bureaus of the Quai d'Orsay, directed by M. Alexis Léger, shared the same distrust of Italian policy. The Secretary-General of the Ministry of Foreign Affairs said to me, with his characteristic subtlety of thought, that he did not regard the situation in Italy as one which would justify any serious effort toward rapprochement. "They will have to be allowed to carry their experiment through. Any external effort made to bring them to our side is doomed to failure: it will strengthen them in their policy of duplicity, cause them to ask the highest price for what they have to offer, and give them a keener appreciation of the benefits which the Axis can bestow. Only when they have thought it through will the idea that only just begins to dawn—the danger to Italy of subservience to Germany—cause them to turn again to us, not so that they can make a deal with us, but to rediscover the state of equilibrium that has always ensured their safety. Only then we shall be able to clasp hands."

M. Bonnet was less patient, because he feared that the crisis would develop more rapidly on the German than the Italian side. The return of Italy to sanity would be of little value if war broke out beforehand. Italy's "good feelings" must be played upon at the earliest opportunity, even though the change of policy needed to be speeded up by some inducement. M. Bonnet had just learned that "secret" meetings had taken place between Count Ciano and M. François-Ponçet, during the course of which the ideas of the two parties had been remarkably similar. Count Ciano had let it be understood that Italy would be satisfied with a free zone at Djibouti, some seats on the Board of Directors of the Suez Canal Company, and, finally, the extension of the Statute of 1896 applicable to the Italians in Tunisia. M. Bonnet believed that to be an acceptable basis for discussion, and that an understanding could be reached if Italy ceased making a fuss over sham territorial claims.

As I was leaving the next day to pursue my journey via Rome, M. Bonnet gave me a message. I was to say to Count Ciano that it seemed to me that the French Government would not refuse to end the tension between France and Italy, and to make it clear to him that, the situation in the Mediterranean being as it was, with the concentration there of an Anglo-French fleet whose numerical superiority was obvious, Italy had every interest in joining the western powers. The latest "suggestions" of the Italian Government, reported by the French Ambassador, strengthened his conviction that an immediate arrangement was possible. It was therefore hoped in Paris that the government of Signor Mussolini would put a damper on the extravagances of the fascist press so that nothing might retard the conclusion of an agreement.

I willingly promised so to speak. The real intentions of the

Italian Government were unknown to me; but I wanted to perform the slight task asked of me. The idea of a rapprochement between the two great Latin countries was pleasing to every European and particularly sympathetic to a Rumanian. In addition, I thought that an accord between France and Italy might ease the situation in the Balkans, where Axis policy was exerting a steadily increasing pressure. France, freed of the intrigues of fascist diplomacy, would regain influence in the east; and the influence would be to the good, for France alone still shed a measure of light in a gloomy Europe.

In taking leave of my French hosts, I again expressed to them the feeling of uneasiness which predominated in my country regarding the spiritual relations between France and the nations of eastern Europe. It was not only in the field of politics that France's withdrawal was to be feared; the influence of France had also maintained there an element of security in matters of the spirit. It was above all in this sphere that the weakening of French influence might bring about the greatest disasters. Because of French thought, many countries, large and small, were attached to the European order—the protector of their patrimony, their rights, and their moral possessions. Britain preserved the balance of the Continent from without; France gave content to the idea of Europe. Now the new influences which were raging tended not only to overthrow the European balance of power but also to undermine the foundations of a civilization. By substituting for real values the commandments of a doctrine founded on violence, they stirred up trouble among individuals and nations. They were striking first at France and weakening its position as a great power. France diminished in the measure that Europe was emptied of its substance. Obscurely, we realized that any danger which threatened France was our danger.[1]

1. Cf. Appendix III, pp. 230 ff.

CHAPTER VII

ITALY SIGNS THE "PACT OF STEEL"

A dinner at Villa Madama. Mussolini and Ciano. Political statement
by the Duce, comments by Ciano. Audience at the Quirinal. King
Victor Emmanuel's "opposition." Visit to the Vatican. Pope Pius
XII. Italy and France.

FROM the beginning of my journey, I had been apprehensive of the moment when I should find myself in
Rome. Fascist Italy and Rumania had but few points in com-
mon.The common Latin origin of the two countries might
be exploited in official speeches and diplomatic conversations. The natural sympathy of the Rumanian people for
the Italian people was such as to lend some truth to such
references. But the positions taken by the two countries
were at the opposite poles of European politics. Rumania
was part of the French system of security which Italy
sought to destroy. Italy struck at the Balkan Entente, while
Rumania tried to strengthen the bonds between the Balkan
countries. Rumania had received the English and French
guarantees with satisfaction. It felt a joint responsibility
with Turkey and Greece. Italy was pursuing the policy of
the Axis and ostensibly protecting Hungary. My task was
hardly easy. It was evident that I should have to navigate
between dangerous reefs.

At least I was not condemned to do so mournfully. The
evening of our arrival in Rome Count and Countess Ciano
gave a brilliant dinner for my wife and myself in the magnificent setting of Villa Madama. Beneath the ceilings
painted by Raphael gathered the gilded youth of Rome,
charming aristocrats and very lovely women. The scene
was beautiful, the atmosphere pleasant, and the next day
the fête was repeated in the bar of a big hotel. It made the
strenuous diplomatic conversations less wearying. In its ambition to retrace the course of ages, so as to reach that Roman

grandeur which the Duce offered as a model, official Italy seemed to have halted on the threshold of the Quattrocento. This stage had certainly not brought it near to the creative spirit of the masters of that age. But, among the works of the masters, it allowed official Italy to live with a renewed audacity the vibrant hours when intrigues of love mingle with those of politics and fortunate men share with their lovely favorites the pleasures, and the dangers, of power. This fantasy of ostentatious life was superimposed on that of an industrious and sober people, which unceasingly made the most strenuous efforts in every sphere of activity. The administration, like an overripe fruit, fell away from the country. Its seizure of power was already far behind; its doctrine had become wiser; its militants had found comfortable berths; and the tension of its violence diminished. Fascism was entering into the most uneasy period of its history just when it hoped for nothing beyond the quiet enjoyment of favor. True, the day when its zealots would abandon their leader was not yet in sight. The party had renounced revolution but not power. But "betrayal" was already there; it wanted only some trick of chance for it to take effect.

Mussolini had tried to guard against the danger by continually changing his team. In vain! He replaced men who had been undeceived by others who wanted nothing more than to accommodate themselves to the requirements of profitable power. The administration could hardly be said to improve. Moreover, by assuring a certain permanence to Count Ciano for family reasons, the Duce seemed himself to have compromised with what was easiest and least heroic in fascism. The little court surrounding the young Minister of Foreign Affairs daily grew in importance and brilliance as Mussolini's son-in-law strengthened his influence in the government and the party. Henceforth it was useless to change the lower ranks, since the same mind continued at the head.

At the time of my journey to Rome Ciano's prestige was

at its height. I was assured that he was the second man in the country. Only Achille Starace, who drove through the streets of the capital in a famous "Topolino," to tighten party discipline (he was Secretary-General), wielded influence approaching that of Ciano. But Starace was not gifted enough to stand up to Ciano. So all the flatterers turned to the Minister of Foreign Affairs, some praising his ability and astonishing "maturity of mind," others his hold on the Duce, and all of them celebrating the unfailing good luck with which he went through life.

In Mussolini's attachment to his son-in-law there was something more than fascist family feeling. Mussolini was compelled to devote much more time to his growing preoccupation with foreign policy. The course of action he had begun did not overplease him. The more he felt compelled to proclaim his faith in the excellence of his policy, the more he felt its disadvantages and risks. The Duce had to fight against doubt all the time. He might have chosen a disciple who kept up his convictions. But he preferred to take a companion who stimulated in him a sense of uneasiness. For Count Ciano, who believed in nothing much, had but little faith in the Axis policy. If compelled he might have accepted it as a means of blackmail; but he had a presentiment of the dangers which military collaboration might entail. In Ciano's disillusioned nature there was something more acute which put him on guard against his German partners' excess of language and brutality of action. He was not, however, of a stature to thwart the established policy, but he could point out its danger by words that carried a certain weight. His obedience kept him in power; his incredulity consolidated him in it.

In brief, there was between the dictator and his minister a relationship similar to that which existed between bygone feudal lords and their attendants, half pages, half jesters, whose jesting aroused a salutary uneasiness and whose advice was the more endurable because it carried hardly any weight.

Ciano's function was to maintain doubt. This assured his permanency. The voice of the young Minister could not be very loud, since it tallied with an inner conviction of the chief of the government. Ciano was only once to dare to speak forcefully, and that was to "betray." But the treason would be only apparent, for he had never believed in the policy he carried out and in keeping with his character he had always said "No."

The peculiar effect of Ciano was to show itself during the conversation I had in Rome with Mussolini and his Foreign Minister. Their pictures are etched in my memory, closely bound together. They make an inconsistent unity, a pair at once disproportionate yet indissoluble. Mussolini spoke, Ciano listened, shaking his head. Sometimes the Duce's words seemed intended to answer questions I did not put. There was a question mark hanging between us. I soon realized that it was the presence of his son-in-law which urged Mussolini to quiet some of his own apprehensions by talking, by making long explanations. Something like a secret dialogue went on between them, the tone of which I did not gather, but which betrayed the hesitations of Italian policy. Sometimes Ciano made me a sign to indicate that later he would comment on what his father-in-law said. Sometimes, also, he gave me an understanding glance, as if to warn me not to take certain statements literally.

I thought of the religious silence in which Hitler had spoken at the Imperial Chancellery, and of Ribbentrop's attitude of concentrated, fanatical conviction. The Führer did not recognize doubt. He allowed it neither in himself nor in those near him. He proceeded by affirmations, "to simplify everything," and his entourage even outdid these affirmations. No voice about him, or within him, was raised to recall the words of Ecclesiastes concerning the vanity of mortal things. Without any hesitation whatsoever he was steering, with all sails set, toward catastrophe.

Mussolini had challenged Fate too long not to feel the

threat of an ever-possible reverse. Like the too happy Poly-
crates, warned by gloomy forebodings, he seemed anxious to
escape destiny. His association with Hitler, who could call
on infinitely greater forces, was not without elements of
uneasiness. He saw himself being dragged along the very
road he had opened, a prisoner of the system he had created
and of the passions which he had unleashed—toward a goal
which seemed to him to be at least uncertain. Having sowed
the wind, he feared the whirlwind—a whirlwind over whose
approach he had no control. He still hoped that his momen-
tum would carry him safely between the rocks. His instinct,
contrary to Hitler's, was not to charge headlong at obstacles;
he wanted to avoid them with profit; but his consciousness
of danger did not free him from the powers which had taken
hold of him: old grudges, violent irritations, and constant
surges of self-esteem. In face of the misfortune which he
somehow perceived, his trouble was daily to become more
emphatic. But he was to tolerate at his side this lucid young
sensualist as a warning that power was already slipping from
his grasp.

Ciano first received me in his sumptuous office in the
Palazzo Chiggi. I endeavored to carry out the mission which
M. Bonnet had entrusted to me. Ciano tried to appear in-
different and incredulous. He accused the French of understanding nothing about Italy's policy. I replied that, in my
opinion, the French were following this policy very closely,
and that in Paris I had noted two trends of thought on the
matter. Certain Frenchmen thought that their country
ought to make a move toward better relations with Italy,
to prove the desire for an understanding. Others thought
that Italy must be left to convince itself of the necessity of
a rapprochement. "It is the first who are right," exclaimed
Ciano, suddenly forgetting his frigidity and indifference.
"If they wait, it will be too late."

The next morning the Minister conducted me to the head

of the government. The long way visitors had to go across the slippery tiles of the reception room of the Palazzo Venezia has been described more than once. The dictator, most amiable, met me halfway between the massive door and his table. So guided, I was able to reach my chair without losing my balance. Contrary to Hitler, Mussolini was not like his photographs. In private life his face was free of the striking expression he assumed to impress the crowd. The man was not without charm. His eyes, when they did not flash lightning, seemed benevolent. He spoke French correctly, using phrases with a tang made keener by his southern accent. Not once in the course of the conversation did he seem to strive for effect. He seemed to enjoy the role of the simple man at rest after scenes played on the famous balcony. Avoiding monologue, he encouraged conversation by asking questions and listening to the replies.

Nevertheless, his first question, which was direct and sudden, almost destroyed the harmony of the interview.

"You come from Berlin," he said to me. "What did they say to you about the policy of the Axis?"

I was greatly embarrassed. In Berlin there had been no mention of the Axis. The German leaders had spoken about the Reich, a little about Rumania, and much about Great Britain.

I tried to frame my reply in the manner least calculated to wound, but my embarrassment did not escape Count Ciano, who gave me a conspiratorial glance.

Without showing any emotion, Mussolini went fully into the problem closest to his heart. He spoke to me with animation and warmth of the Axis and its policy. He clung to Germany's friendship, because he had confidence in Hitler.

"The policy of the Axis is a living reality," he said, "even though up to now it may not have been defined in writing, or by any formal engagement."

The Duce emphasized the words "up to now." His big eyes held me, full of implications. He added:

"The bond uniting us to the National Socialist Reich, though not yet material, is still so firm as to withstand every trial. Those who might be tempted to break it are cherishing dangerous illusions. There is between us an identity of conception of the world [Mussolini used the term *Weltanschauung*] which is stronger than all conventional texts. We are united by the same aim and the same revolutionary ardor. That is why I do not fear the Germans."

This unexpected conclusion, to which he returned later, showed the fears which plagued Mussolini's thought at the time. He no longer affirmed his policy. He defended it. He discounted the objections which he felt rising around him; and he pleaded his cause with warmth, as though he wished to convince himself that he was right and to give himself courage.

"No," he continued. "Italy really has no reason to fear Germany! There is not a single divergent interest separating us. The Germans are exerting their pressure to the east. . . ."

When I looked questioningly at him, he corrected himself:

"I mean, to the northeast, while Italy concentrates its whole attention on the Mediterranean. Since the Mediterranean is still a prison for us, closed at one end by Gibraltar and at the other by Suez, we can at the moment have no other goal save to escape from the prison by breaking the bars of the cage. That is why we fought in Spain. That is why Germany cannot embarrass us. What harm do you think it would do us? Germany will never come down on Italy. Of that Hitler has given us categorical assurances. Besides, he knows his history. Every time the Germans have marched southward, they have paid dearly. The warriors from the north have never dominated our country; some of them were driven out, the others assimilated. That for time immemorial. Do you remember how the legions of Marius cut up the Cimbri and the Teutons? Do you remember the calamities of the Hohenstaufen emperors and how they were defeated by the Italian republics, although they were still separated and divided? Some of the invaders found refuge in the mountains [here the Duce underlined with a dramatic gesture the Nordics' flight to the Alps]; others were absorbed by the lands of Sicily and mingled with our nation. None of them imposed his law on us."

I listened with growing amazement to this recital of the historical conflicts between the Axis partners.

"Today the problem which we and the Germans face has reached precise definitions. Our policy is determined by a line of demarcation. We have no concern with what happens above this line, what happens below it is no concern of the Germans."

Here Ciano glanced at me. He felt that he must reassure me. The Duce continued:

"I am afraid of what is in store for the brave Poles. I know them. They are fiery and courageous, even when they are in the wrong. They are good soldiers and they do not easily abandon the thought of fighting when they think that they are in the right. This time they are undoubtedly wrong. The City of Danzig is German and it should return to Germany. It may be the cause of armed conflict; I realize how serious it is. When a stone starts rolling, it is difficult to stop the avalanche. We have reached the point where violent passions rouse others, and where before long the whole earth may begin to shake. But I cannot oppose Hitler on a point where he is in the right, and which is beyond the line in which I am interested. . . ."

Mussolini's pessimism did not stop his drawing up plans for the future regarding his relations with the countries nearest to Italy and its interests. He spoke sympathetically of Hungary. He emphasized with obvious pleasure Yugoslavia's new policy. The Axis, he said, was not only a link between two great powers but a complete political system destined to reorganize eastern Europe. The Hungarians had been the first to understand this. The Yugoslavs were realizing it in turn. These two peoples looked to Rome. (But were these peoples situated to the south of the famous line? The Duce did not say so expressly; he let it be understood that, if the need arose, he would not refuse them his support, while he would be obliged to refuse it to Poland.)

Mussolini was severe in his judgment on those eastern states "which did not yet understand." What meaning was there in the Anglo-French guarantees? How could France and Britain ever keep their engagements? Rumania was a big country; it needed nobody's protection. For the rest, the western powers were meddling in what was no business of theirs. They were trying to split the Axis and oppose Italian interests to German interests. It was all labor lost. The Axis would never give way.

I replied that the guarantees had no purpose other than to prevent aggression and to consolidate the peace. The best means of taking from them the character which Mussolini ascribed to them was to make them general. If everyone guaranteed his neighbor's security, it would be possible to speak of peace without giving offense to anyone.

As for the Axis, no one dreamed of breaking it or making it give way. What exactly did the Axis mean? Was it not an agreement with a view to the establishment of a certain harmony of strength, and peaceful equilibrium, between two neighboring powers? Such agreements should neither be weakened nor destroyed, but on the contrary extended and multiplied. It was in the general interest that, to the ties existing between London and Paris on the one hand and Berlin and Rome on the other should be added new ties, capable of the peaceful assurance of general harmony.

The Duce did not reject my slightly tendentious definition of the Axis and its policy. It suited him. He saw in it an interpretation of his ideas; it recognized the need he felt of loudly proclaiming his loyalty to the Axis, and it left him a free field for diverse speculations as to new and more extensive agreements.

The moment had come to speak of M. Bonnet's message. The head of the Italian Government, warned by Ciano, expected me to give him my impressions of Franco-Italian relations. I preferred that he should speak of them himself, so that I might estimate the interest he had in the matter. I had not long to wait. The Duce tackled the problem with his customary ardor.

"The difficulties which exist between Italy and France are serious, but they are not grave."

He pronounced these words carefully, looking me straight in the eye. This was evidently the reply he intended me to report to the French Government. Mussolini added the following explanations:

"These difficulties are of a colonial order—they are not of a territorial order. We shall not make war on account of this."

He put heavy stress on the last words of his sentence: *"they are not of a territorial order."* I thought I understood that he desired an agreement and that he thought it possible.

With this declaration our conversation ended. I could hardly ask more of Signor Mussolini.

The last words uttered had a pleasing ring about them. The Italian dictator seemed satisfied at having put the idea of a possible reconciliation with France at the end, as one puts leaders after a sentence.

Later I received from Ciano, who accompanied me, certain valuable explanations.

"Did you notice," said the Minister, "when Mussolini told you that there was no written agreement between Germany and ourselves, he said, *'up to now'?* That means something. What has not existed up to now may exist tomorrow. The Germans do not waste their time. It would be advisable for your friends not to waste theirs."

Ciano said no more on the matter. I was to learn from other sources that a meeting between him and von Ribbentrop at the Villa d'Este had already been fixed for the following week. The "Pact of Steel" was being prepared. Did Ciano want this formal and precise sanction of Axis policy? Nothing in his attitude seemed to indicate it. He allowed himself to be borne along by the current. The forces he would have had to fight were too immense. Ciano knew he was not big enough to withstand them. His role was to execute orders in whose value he did not believe. If it pleased him to doubt, this was never in order to impede an important move but simply to profit by his position of favorite, which permitted him to enjoy power while declining in advance its responsibilities. The compulsion exerted by Berlin on Italian policy evidently displeased him.

"You were quite right," he said to me, "to say that the Germans spoke to you a great deal about the Reich and very little about the Axis. It is useful for the Duce to be told the truth."

Then he returned to his chief's words, as though he would draw all the possible inferences from them.

"The fact that the Duce insisted so strongly on the words '*up to now*' seems to indicate that he himself would like France to intervene before it is too late."

"But what," I asked Ciano, "is the meaning of this 'line' about which so much was said? Must it be understood that you have divided the east into zones of influence?"

"Not exactly," replied the Minister. "Still, it has been agreed that the affairs of the Baltic Sea do not concern Italy and that Mediterranean affairs do not concern the German Reich."

"That puts us in a pretty pickle!" I exclaimed. "Located, as we are, toward the middle, you put us in a fine state!"

"You are not so abandoned as you think, for the Danube flows into the Black Sea, which is only a prolongation of the Mediterranean. . . ."

I understood that the line of demarcation had not been traced precisely, and that there still was room for certain Italian illusions. Ciano revealed Italy's ambition to assure for itself, "if there was still time," certain privileges on the Danube and in the Balkans. His sympathies went to Hungary, Fascist Italy's first customer. The confidence which all the successive Hungarian Governments had shown in the Italian regime deserved some recognition.

"Our road to Bucharest goes by way of Budapest," Ciano declared to me. "When the green light tells us that the way is clear between Hungary and Rumania, we shall come to you, as we should wish."

Another country still claimed his attention: the Yugoslavia of Stoyadinovitch and Prince Paul. Since the assassination of King Alexander, Yugoslavia had inclined toward the Axis and leaned toward Italy. For this the Italian Government was doubly grateful.

"I may say that the ties which bind us to Belgrade are among the most interesting we have made up to now. The Hungarians took the affair very badly at first; they were jealous, and had serious grievances against the Serbs. We patched things up between them: the general interest was at stake."

The "general interest" was that of erecting against the Balkan system, supported by the west, another system of the Axis. To the Balkan Entente, as it then existed between Athens, Ankara, Bucharest, and Belgrade, were to be opposed agreements starting in Central Europe and linking Budapest to Belgrade and Sofia. In Ciano's mind (a secret thought which he however failed to hide), this system had still further interest. It allowed the Italian Government (which the Hungarians and Yugoslavs caused to believe that it had a greater hold on them than the German Government) to play the part of protector of the Balkans. This role the government thought to be its due, after the incorporation of Albania into Victor Emmanuel's empire.

Was the Italian Government's line of thought going to meet Colonel Beck's, which led southward from Warsaw? Ciano did not admit it; but some of his words, and others

I had heard in Warsaw, led me to think that there was a great deal in common in the points of view of Beck and Ciano. Neither seemed hostile to the idea of a two-sided political system which might be offered either to the right or the left, to the western powers or to the Axis. These thoughts óbviously could only remain in the realm of speculation. When the storm broke, Poland was isolated; Hungary, which leaned toward Rome, fell to the side of Berlin; while Yugoslavia, in spite of its policy of maneuver, did not play the Axis game but remained faithful to the Balkan Entente.[1]

"It can't go on like this!" Ciano declared to me at the end of our conversations. "The fever rises; the abscess will burst one day. We shall have war, unless there is a new conference. At all costs, the situation must be cleared up."

"What could a new conference do?" I asked.

He replied: "Bring about at last the four-power pact, or, who knows, perhaps a five-power pact, including Poland."

It was clear that, of these two eventualities, war or a conference, the Italian Government preferred the latter. On this it based its hopes, and was preparing itself in view of a new and supreme European showdown.

This showed the profound dissimilarity between the foreign policies of Rome and Berlin—a dissimilarity of which the Italian leaders, despite their boastings, were perfectly aware, and which created in them an incurable uneasiness as the moment approached for the inevitable written pact. In vain had Mussolini put the emphasis on "force" in his speeches; he was too much of a Mediterranean to ignore the value of "moderation." His concern was always to be on the side of the strongest power, and never to have to face it alone. The company of his opponents was as indispensable to him as the support of his partners. He needed to cultivate

1. In the course of my journey through the Balkans I myself was to make serious efforts to thwart Ciano's machinations, and the fulminations of the fascist press were to accompany me in these peregrinations.

his enmities as carefully as he cultivated his alliances, in the hope that he might always play the part of mediator.

These intentions of Mussolini clearly ran counter to Hitler's plans. The German wanted complete success, and shrank from nothing; war was the simplest way of obtaining the full measure of totalitarian demands. The Italian wanted limited successes—the only ones which could assure him his share of the profits. The battle he wanted to wage ought to be fought out in conferences. Of the two Axis partners, the one wanted to overturn the equilibrium of the world to his profit, while the other hoped to save this same equilibrium to his profit. This clash of interests and wills could not be long continued. The weaker of the two must give way to the arguments of the stronger.

The program of my stay in Rome included a visit to the Quirinal. I was received early in the morning of May 1. The King liked to begin his days early.

They had just put on his frail shoulders the burden of an empire taken by force. He felt its weight and danger, and bore his new and ephemeral title with uneasy resignation.

This man, already aged and astonishingly small, had abandoned actual power to fascism but he had reserved for himself the nominal title. He seemed to expect that, by the equitable turn of events, the principle of continuity which he incarnated would overcome the "revolution"; and that royalty would be restored to him, though he might lose his empire. The day of restoration was, perhaps, not so far distant. . . . A ceremony to which the King attached some importance (for he saw in it a sign of the times) was to take place immediately following my audience. He was awaiting a delegation from the Senate, which was officially to bring him the reply of Parliament to the Speech from the Throne. In view of this event, Victor Emmanuel was in full dress. His chest was studded with decorations. Around his neck was the collar of the Order of the Annunziata.

His state of mind was in keeping with his attire. The King felt himself "sovereign" as he awaited the ceremony which restored him to his powers and position. The first words he addressed to me were to explain that the homage which was to be paid him had a political, not merely a ceremonial, character. In the text of the reply to the Speech from the Throne, one part dealt with the internal affairs of the kingdom and another contained a detailed statement of foreign policy. "It is like a return to normal constitutional life," the King said to me. It pleased Victor Emmanuel to enumerate the advantages of such a "return." Parliament, constituted on corporative principles, seemed inclined to take its role "seriously." It intended to exercise effective control and was already voicing certain criticisms, which certainly were not always to the liking of the rulers of the regime. A spirit of opposition was making itself felt which might increase and serve as a fulcrum for public opinion and the monarchy. Every movement tending to limit the excesses of dictatorship was bound at the same time to restore the liberties of the people and the prerogatives of the Crown. The King went so far as to celebrate the reawakening of the Opposition.

I listened with interest to this strange conversation. It reflected a peculiar constitutional situation. The little King, his breast sparkling with stars, liked to be considered the leader of the Opposition in his kingdom.

Whilst I was taking leave of him, he wanted to show me a heartening sight. I was led to the massive staircase up which the solemn procession of the parliamentary delegation was just mounting.

The Duce marched at the head, clad in his black shirt, on which the collar of the Order making him a relative of the House of Savoy made a bright splash of color. He was no longer the simple man who had received me at the Palazzo Venezia. His glance was imperious, his gait exaggerated. He might have been on the stage, portraying the character he intended to be for the cinema and history. Following him came Count Ciano, sprightly and carefree, who waved joyously to me as he passed. The senators followed in serried ranks.

Thus the elect of fascism mounted toward the Throne Room. Was this the sign of a return to lawfulness, of the re-establishment, as the King seemed to hope, of a certain balance of authority? Or was it the call-up of the last company, already marked by fate, who would only let go of power when faced by catastrophe?

The King himself was to do nothing to encourage any change. His "opposition" did not show itself at any decisive turn in the policy of his kingdom. He would only intervene much later on, at the time of military disaster; early enough to hasten the end of fascism but not early enough to free the person of Victor Emmanuel from the responsibilities which lay heavily on the fallen regime.

Thus, throughout my journey, I had seen those signs which foretold catastrophe. I had seen the principal characters of the drama in action. I had heard their cries and their appeals and had gauged at the same time their weaknesses and the fiery intensity of their passions. But I had not yet gauged how inevitable the catastrophic issue was. In the atmosphere spoiled by so many conflicting interests, certain illusions persisted. Politicians, whatever their leanings, still let so much calculation come between them and the facts of the situation that it created a false idea of the coming conflict. Many believed that, if only they could carry their plans through to the end, they would ward off Fate.

The Vatican had no such illusions. There, where news came into a purified atmosphere free from impassioned commentaries, a profound and painful certitude reigned. Strength was appreciated at its true value. Everything was judged there: causes as well as actors; those who believed themselves strong and those who believed themselves weak.

This truth was made clear to me when I went to the Vatican, where my office obliged me to seek, not spiritual consolations, but indications of a political nature.

Accompanied by M. Nicolas Comnène, Rumanian Ambassador to the Holy See, and guided through the sumptuous labyrinth of the papal apartments by gentlemen of honor, gentlemen of the chamber, and the Papal Guard, I came with some emotion into the dazzling presence of Pope Pius XII. Light and intelligence surrounded the strong personality of the Holy Father like an aura. But the truth which the Pope kept for the man of politics was one entirely of contrition. The picture he drew seemed the darker in the light of his presence.

The news the Vatican received from Poland was bad. The conflict of interests there was such that at any moment it might bring about a collision. The Pope feared that, in the case of Danzig, the world would again be presented with a fait accompli. What seemed to him even graver than the open threats were the backstage maneuvers of which he was informed and the secret measures which were being taken with a view to a sudden outbreak of hostilities. It was no longer possible to place any confidence in the word of certain powerful men who directed the destinies of the peoples; and herein was to be seen a sign that men's actions were tending to get away from the law of God. Deceit had become the last weapon of politics; it was creating an idolatry of the State; it was leading the enthusiasm of the peoples astray, and unleashing in them ungovernable passions. Deceit governed the relations between states. Even before it unleashed war, it had made peace impossible. Security was dead. In these circumstances, was it possible to believe in the reality of an agreement between France and Italy? For the sake of the salvation of Europe and of Christianity, the Holy Father wished to retain the hope that it might be so.

The Pope spoke quietly, without raising his voice or making any gesture. His knowledge of men and affairs, the calmness of his judgment, gave an impressive depth to what he said. The diplomatic language of this aristocratic ascetic was simple: it expressed the truth. Europe was exactly as he saw it with his calmly clear vision; it had engendered destructive forces which no human will could master. Pius XII saw still farther into the future, and his gaze became veiled with an unspeakable sadness. In a world preparing for war, spiritual forces would be inoperative. The realm of the spirit and the realm of action were already divided into watertight compartments, as they had been in the most turbulent periods of history. Men were deserting the Kingdom of God. The task of the good shepherds was to safeguard the values of the soul and of conscience, to preserve them from the cataclysm.

In this hour of trial, the Pope retained an absolute dignity. His attitude, as well as the majesty of his appearance, gave the impression of perfect beauty. I thought once more of the crude gestures and language of certain "great men." I was grateful to the Holy Father for having restored to me the sense of human greatness.

From the Pope's apartments I passed to those of the Cardinal Secretary of State, who at that time held his receptions in the celebrated Borgia Loggias. Cardinal Maglione wished to discuss Franco-Italian relations with me. His informants had told him that I carried a message from M. Bonnet, and that I had spoken to Count Ciano in favor of a rapprochement between France and Italy. The Cardinal wished to express his cordial thanks for my having given support to so just a cause. "The proverb has it that one should never intervene in quarrels between brothers. But, in this case, everybody's interest is involved, and we must do our best to hasten this necessary reconciliation."

So the Cardinal Secretary of State confirmed the fact of which I had been informed, that the diplomacy of the Vatican was making the greatest efforts to bring the negotiations between Paris and Rome to a successful conclusion. It was considered at the Vatican that this was the only point where a well-meaning intervention might still be of some use. Everywhere else the impulse of forces which deliberately thrust toward war was such that the intervention of third parties of good faith was utterly ineffectual. The language of reason could only serve where there was no wish to put a match to the powder. This was the case with "the two Latin sisters." France wanted peace, and Italy did not want war. Unfortunately, unseen influences from one side and the other weighed on the negotiators. The Italian Government was not free to act as it would. It was being closely watched. Cardinal Maglione at least was persuaded that Italy had done everything in its power to reach an entente with France. It was for the French Government to take the negotiations in hand and bring them quickly to a happy issue. Alas! The action of the French ministers seemed also to be hampered by contrary forces. The last news was bad. While Rome avoided, and Paris postponed, decisions, Herr von Ribbentrop was due to arrive in Italy. The Vatican expected no good from this journey. The Cardinal begged me to urge the friends I might have in Paris to make haste: it was essential that France should intervene at the earliest possible moment.

That same evening I transmitted to Paris by special courier what I had heard at Rome regarding the Franco-Italian negotiations. I had no longer any great hope that the desired intervention would come soon enough. How could Mussolini avoid concluding a "pact of steel" if Hitler demanded it? He had talked too much. In order to remain on terms of equality with his partner, he had threatened and defied the world in the same terms as the Führer. Should he now refuse the agreement which the latter offered him, he would stand alone. Hitler could conquer without him, or come to terms

AT THE VATICAN

"From the Pope's apartments I passed to those of Cardinal Maglione, who at that time held his receptions in the celebrated Borgia Loggias."

(See page 174.)

JOURNEY TO TURKEY

". . . I was happy, in Ankara, to shake the hands of friends."
From left to right: Grigore Gafencu, M. Lukasiewicz, Consul-General of Rumania, M. Sarajoglu, Minister of Foreign Affairs in Turkey.

with the west without him. What would become of him, were he no longer able to profit by the fear which Germany inspired in the world? And, alone, how could he face Germany's active wrath?

Prisoner of his own words, his resentments, and the continual excesses of his pride—prisoner, like Hitler, of iniquity—the master of Italy could no longer resist the Germans. An entente with France was possible; the last difficulties had been overcome, and the conditions were acceptable to both sides. But no agreement was to be made with France. France and Italy continued to be adversaries, and tomorrow they would be enemies.

The Pact of Steel was accepted at the Villa d'Este during the first week of May, a few days after my departure from Rome, and solemnly concluded on May 22. From that moment Italy no longer controlled its fate. For a little while longer it tried to keep a trick or two in its hands. The day that Hitler, determined on war, called on his allies to keep their engagements, Ciano (at Salzburg, on August 12, 1939) recalled the fact that Italy was not pledged to military participation for three years. Mussolini made a last attempt to redress his position when the German armies penetrated into Poland. He proposed an immediate armistice and new conversations among the great powers. This was Italy's moment; and on this Mussolini had staked his whole previous policy. The attempt failed, Mussolini remained bound by the Pact of Steel. Hopes which Ciano still had of combining the neutrals with the co-operation of the Balkan States and under the ægis of Italy were also doomed to disappointment. Germany bluntly told Italy to come into line. The course of the war ruined all its secret hopes. The collapse of France finally upset all possibility of a "peace by compromise." Dragged along in the wake of the German victories, Mussolini gave himself to the Axis forces without scruple. He bowed before the German hegemony over the Continent. On June 10, 1940, came the stab in the back at France. But when Mussolini made up his mind to strike at France, he committed a crime against his own country and his defeat was certain.

This outcome could not be foreseen when I left Italy. It was contained in acts which seemed to be a challenge to reason.

CHAPTER VIII

RETURN JOURNEY

Stop in Belgrade. Prince Paul and his ministers. The "prudence" of the Regent of Yugoslavia. Arrival in Bucharest. Visit of M. Potemkin. The Assistant Commissar is optimistic.

M Y journey to the west finished at Rome. On the way home I wanted to visit Belgrade.

The Yugoslav Government, after the great disturbances caused by the assassination of King Alexander, was, of all the Danubian and Balkan governments the most sensitive to the European crisis. Its uneasiness led it to pursue a hesitant policy which was contrary to the traditional valor of the Serb people. Particularly exposed to Axis pressure, Yugoslavia first let itself be steered into the path of absolute neutrality by Stoyadinovitch, President of the Council, as though it hoped that its passive attitude toward the German and Italian maneuvers would appease the animosity of ancient adversaries. After each blow at the existence of the small countries, official Yugoslavia sought assurances in Berlin and Rome and a guarantee of survival. After the disappearance of Czechoslovakia it had succeeded in tightening its bonds with Germany. After the disappearance of Albania it made ready to strengthen its relations with Italy. The situation which it thus assured itself was not wholly illusory. Hitler and his acolytes pretended to esteem the Serb people for their military valor and boasted of their friendship. There was even a certain rivalry between Berlin and Rome; the question was which of them would exercise the greatest influence on Belgrade. In former times, I had heard the wily Stoyadinovitch claim that, by his astuteness, he was maintaining a profitable competition between the Germans and the Italians, to his country's advantage.

Yugoslavia was still a member of the Balkan Entente. It

was an essential part of this entente; and its allies were by no means disposed to give it up. If Yugoslavia gave way, Rumania would be completely cut off from Greece and Turkey, and the Balkan system would crumble. If, on the other hand, Yugoslavia stood fast, it was possible to hope that Bulgaria would join us. The secret struggle in Belgrade between the representatives of the Axis and of the Balkan countries was extremely close.

Under Axis pressure, Hungary intervened, and let Yugoslavia know that it would renounce all territorial claims. By this means, Rome hoped to bind the Yugoslavs to the Hungarians. The Belgrade government appeared to remain faithful to its alliance with its neighbors. But I had gained the impression in Rome that the Italians were not giving up the game. More than once Ciano had let me see his desire to substitute for the Balkan Entente another system based on Budapest and Belgrade. I was determined to thwart this project.

It so happened that the Yugoslav Prince Regent was preparing to leave for Rome. He also intended to pay a visit to Berlin the following month. His Minister of Foreign Affairs had preceded him in these two capitals and had carefully prepared the ground. Neither the Regent nor his Minister dreamed of pushing their diplomatic investigations further to the west.

In following the suggestions which came to him from Berlin and Rome, Prince Paul did everything but pursue a policy of sentiment. The Yugoslav Regent did not love the Third Reich, and he suspected Fascist Italy. Educated in England, liked and spoiled by English society, he had definitely pro-British tendencies. But this nice and uneasy gentleman, a lover of the fine arts, was subjected in politics to the influence of rough and domineering forces. The fear inspired by the violence and excesses of the totalitarian countries determined his actions and his attitude. He smiled at people whom he did not like. By cultivating prudence as an art, he had succeeded in a period agitated by every sort of brutality in gaining the reputation of being the most "neutral" and, in consequence, the most adroit of princes.

Moreover, his prudence was not entirely due to his temperament. At the death of his cousin, he had received a threatened crown on trust, which he was obliged to return intact. The fact that he exercised only a temporary stewardship increased his cares and forced him to take increased precautions. But he was never the dupe of his own policy, and he did not share the optimism of certain of his collaborators. He knew precisely what were the intentions of the Germans and the Italians. When he felt confident of the people to whom he spoke, he delicately expressed his suspicions and his terrible anxiety. He knew that his journey to Rome, coming as it did just after the occupation of Albania, was not popular in Serbia. He felt that the Serb people did not like his policy. He did not like it himself. He followed it because he believed that any other course would drive Yugoslavia into the abyss wherein Czechoslovakia had disappeared and into which Poland was ready to plunge.

The Hungarians did not inspire him with any confidence. In spite of their good words, they lost none of their resentment. The Prince had a special grudge against the King of Bulgaria, who was trying to be even cleverer than he. In speaking of his royal neighbor the Regent used the most cutting language. On the other hand, the Balkan Entente pleased him. To him it appeared the only decent line of policy. Thanks to this entente, an indirect glance could still be risked toward the great countries of the west. The Prince meant to remain faithful to his allies, but he had to calm Axis suspicions. And attention must be paid to the Soviet Union! The Prince spoke to me of Russia with a remarkable insight, which he doubtless owed to his Russian ancestry. Of all the statesmen whom I had met, he alone understood the significance and importance of the change that had just taken place at Moscow, where M. Molotov had replaced

M. Litvinov at the head of the Commissariat of Foreign Affairs.

As I listened to the Regent, I thought of the inconsistencies of politics, which made him force on a brave people the most timorous of attitudes by the most audacious methods. For Paul of Yugoslavia exercised almost personal power. In that strange and dark period excess of prudence, like excess of force, created dictators.

Prince Paul was to show himself as expert as he was tenacious at this game. I recollected having seen him at the beginning of the year, in the presence of Stoyadinovitch. It was at the White Palace near Belgrade, where the Prince and his gracious consort entertained me in a residence of the best English style. In these highly cultured surroundings the broad shoulders of the President of the Council had stood out with a strange and disturbing force. Should a clash occur between the Regent and his chief collaborator (rumors of crises and plots were current at the time), everything was to be feared, I said to myself, for the person of the Prince. I had taken the train that evening, listening all the way to the station to M. Stoyadinovitch's confident peals of laughter. Before arriving back at Bucharest, I learned that the crisis had been reached, but that it was the Prince's plot which had succeeded. The powerful Stoyadinovitch had vanished as if through a trap door; and henceforth nothing prevented the Prince from taking the fullest power into his delicate hands.

It was one of the men trusted by the Prince, M. Cinçar Marcovitch, formerly Yugoslav Minister in Berlin, with whom I was to discuss the problems in which I was interested.

M. Cinçar Marcovitch was dominated by the same fears as was the Prince. The Third Reich seemed to him the more dangerous because he believed that it was already all powerful. Already persuaded to a policy of extreme prudence, he was entirely devoted to his chief. Since he had no nostalgia for England, he gladly executed the orders which the Prince gave him with regret.

He had just returned from a journey (which had taken him into the Axis countries) profoundly thankful to have been able to see that, on the eve of a major crisis, Yugoslavia was not threatened. Count Ciano, whom he had met at Venice, had given him the assurance that Italy, after having occupied "defensive positions" in Albania, intended to respect the territorial integrity of Yugoslavia. In Berlin Herr von Ribbentrop had made most assuring statements to him. M. Cinçar Marcovitch considered that, if Yugoslavia committed no fault and roused no suspicion, it might hope to keep out of the war. Naturally, the Yugoslavs knew how to fight! But the last war had cost them too dear. The Minister thought that at all costs it was necessary to remain outside the conflict, at least in the beginning.

I deduced from his words that the Axis leaders had been more explicit with M. Cinçar Marcovitch than they had been with me. They had spoken to him openly of war; and they had convinced him of the advantages of neutrality. There I met again one of Hitler's ruling principles: if the Führer was so determined on keeping the Serbs outside the theater of war, it was because he did not wish to repeat the "faults" of his predecessors. War must not begin again where it had broken out in 1914.

I tried to convince my Yugoslav colleague of the necessity of maintaining continuous and close relations with the western powers. A policy founded exclusively on the desire to avert threats of war from his country seemed to me bound to favor the worst designs of conquest. M. Cinçar Marcovitch no longer believed in the possibility of saving the peace. Everyone, he thought, should think above all *of his own safety*. There was no question of breaking with the west; Serbia's relations with its former allies were of such a nature that they could never lead to a rupture. Prince Paul could always count on the understanding and sympathy of British political circles. As for the Soviet, nothing was less certain than its attitude with regard to Germany. Like his chief, the Minister saw in the change which had just occurred in Moscow the indication of a possible collusion between the U.S.S.R. and the Third Reich; and it seemed to him all the more difficult openly to take a position contrary to the policy of the Axis. M. Cinçar Marcovitch thought therefore that care must be taken not to be among the first victims, and only the presumed aggressors were in a position to give effective assurances against the danger of aggression. The Minister willingly conceded to me that the Balkan Entente had lost nothing of its usefulness. Yugoslavia would remain faithful to its neighbors. It would not conclude any separate pact with Hungary, however tempting the Hungarian proposals might be. But the Balkan Entente ought to safeguard its "independence" and not meddle at all with the discussions between great powers. The entente should not weaken the international position of any of its members. Now, Yugoslavia's position—M. Cinçar Marcovitch had just confirmed this in Berlin and Rome—was excellent!

My Yugoslav colleague's optimism was soon to be put to the test. He accompanied Prince Paul to Rome, and there he noted "a great change of attitude." Still under a strong emotional stress, he told me at once of his uneasiness.

What had happened? In the meantime, Britain had defined its policy regarding the Balkans. As Lord Halifax had informed me, it had begun active negotiations with Turkey. These negotiations had led on May 12 to an exchange of public declarations. The two governments had undertaken to "conclude a definitive long-term agreement of a reciprocal character" (this agreement was only concluded on October 19), and had agreed that in the meantime "in the event of an act of aggression leading to war in the Mediterranean area they would be prepared to cooperate effectively and to lend each other all the aid and assistance in their power."

Article 6 referred to the Balkans, and said that "The two

Governments recognize that it is also necessary to ensure the establishment of security in the Balkans. They are consulting together with the object of achieving this purpose as speedily as possible." [1]

These texts had given Ciano the opportunity he sought to launch a violent attack against the Balkan Entente. What was the meaning of Turkey's game? How could it assume engagements on behalf of its neighbors? And did this not amount to the adoption of a general position against Rome and Berlin by all the Balkans?

Such language was designed to force the Yugoslav Government to *choose* between the Axis and its Balkan allies. "The situation was very grave," said M. Cinçar Marcovitch.

With the assistance of the Turkish Government I at once tried to find a formula flexible enough to emphasize the "independence" of the Balkan Entente, and to allow the Yugoslavs to repulse the assaults of the Axis. The crisis was averted and the entente stood fast. But it had been a narrow escape! And from that time M. Cinçar Marcovitch was to doubt the "excellence" of his position with respect to Berlin and Rome.

I had been home for two days and had had time to make my report to King Carol and the Rumanian Government, expressing to them my anxiety, when M. Potemkin, Assistant People's Commissar for Foreign Affairs in the Soviet Government, arrived in Bucharest.

In 1939 Soviet Russia was approaching the end of a period of rigorous isolation from Europe. Moscow was preparing a national foreign policy. The disappointments which the U.S.S.R. had suffered, the consciousness it had gained of its strength, and, finally, the hopes it cherished on the eve of a great crisis capable of bringing about many changes, all combined to give the Soviet Government the desire to take an increasingly greater part in international politics.

1. Speech of Mr. Chamberlain to the House of Commons, May 12, 1939.

If the governments of the states bordering on Russia could have grasped a little of what was actually going on beyond their eastern frontiers, they might perhaps have avoided more than one political error and many deadly shocks. Diplomatic incursions into the interior of Russian territory were extremely difficult. In the absence of such contacts, Russia's neighbors had to be content with exchanging pacific assurances and pleasant conversations with the representatives of the Soviet Union abroad. And the carriers of Moscow's official views, once beyond the mysterious frontiers of their country, acquired a turn of mind which often led them to give a wrong impression of the real disposition of their government.

So M. Potemkin, during his journey in the Balkan States, sowed the most reassuring illusions on the way. M. Potemkin's uprightness, as well as his loyalty to the Soviet Government, could not be doubted, but there was something of the old regime in his affable manner, and one was happy to give pleasure to this friendly man in expressing the hopes of an entente. One felt that he in turn was very happy to be able to express, in elegant French, the kindly thoughts which the Soviet Union had for its nearest neighbors.

When M. Potemkin arrived in Bucharest, he had so reassured three quarters of the Balkans. To Ankara, where he had been informed of the policy which the Turks wished to pursue with England and France, he had conveyed the support of the Soviet Union and had left the hope that the structure would soon be completed by a Russo-Turkish pact of assistance. In Sofia, the game the Axis powers were playing had disturbed him. He had been lavish with warnings and good advice; and the cheers with which the mass of the people had welcomed him, and which seemed to him to run counter to the government's views, had impressed him.

I received M. Potemkin at my house and spent the day with him in long and interesting conversations. I told him of my journey and spoke of the danger of war everywhere apparent, and of the efforts being made by certain powers with a view to common resistance. M. Potemkin told me that he had found in the Balkans a desire for union in view of Hitler's threats. In his opinion, "the resistance front was crystallizing everywhere." Through the usual precautions of diplomatic formulas, we soon recognized that we spoke the same language. To us, all the maneuvers of the Axis seemed suspect; all the efforts tending to close the road to the expansion of the Hitlerian Reich we regarded with sympathy. The messenger from Moscow spoke at that moment as people were speaking in London, Paris, and Bucharest.

M. Potemkin believed that there would be a happy outcome of the negotiations between Moscow and the west. "The totalitarian powers are circulating the rumor that the Soviet Union is about to draw closer to Germany and Italy. These are the particular tactics of the government in Berlin to prevent the reunion of Britain, France, and Russia. Hitler himself has made use of this procedure by letting his intimates believe that he had reserved to himself the possibility of renewing close ties with the U.S.S.R. at the opportune moment. None of these tricks will affect Soviet policy. Moscow wishes peace—and intends to defend peace by pacific means."

These declarations encouraged me to expound Rumania's foreign policy in detail to M. Potemkin. I did not hide from him the hope we put in an agreement between the western powers and Russia for the defense of general security. If we did not take a direct part in the negotiations, this was in order not to provoke any unfortunate reactions by Germany, and not to aggravate, by anything we might do, an international situation already strained enough. But the guarantees we had accepted from Britain and France, the mistrust which Axis behavior inspired in our public opinion, the attitude of our government, and, above all, the concentration of our armed forces along our western frontiers, all clearly proved from which direction we felt ourselves menaced and against whom we intended to organize our resistance. This attitude, we knew, was a pledge of security for our eastern neighbors. The military measures we were taking in Transylvania covered indirectly the territories of the Ukraine. The strengthening of our good-neighborly relations with Russia, which we desired, should further increase the value and the possibilities of our resistance. I added that within the Balkan Entente we were striving to group our neighbors into a powerful organism at the service of peace. We were happy to see that, thanks to the assistance of Turkey, we were entering into the system of security that would link Moscow with the western powers.

M. Potemkin seemed very satisfied. He showed a particular interest in our Balkan projects. Nevertheless, he strongly urged us to be watchful of Bulgaria, considering that no concessions should be made to this power unless we were assured of its assistance. As long as Bulgaria did not prove its determination to free itself from the malign influence of the Axis powers, M. Potemkin advised caution.

The Assistant Commissar wished to ask me a more delicate question regarding the Polish-Rumanian alliance. Was this treaty to take effect only in the case of Soviet aggression, or was it established *erga omnes?* I replied truthfully: The text of the treaty was worded in general terms, but the military terms completing it provided for the hypothesis of a Soviet attack only. Nothing, however, prevented other hypotheses from being taken into consideration, and the Rumanian Government was ready to extend the convention to all foreseeable cases.[1]

M. Potemkin took note of this. He assured me that soon the Soviet Union would give manifest proofs of its wish for a general entente. He also told me that the change at the

1. On my way through London, I had given the same reply to Lord Halifax, who also had interrogated me on the subject of the actual bearing of the Polish-Rumanian alliance.

head of the Department of Foreign Affairs in Moscow which had taken place in his absence was simply a matter of personnel: M. Molotov would follow exactly the same policy as M. Litvinov. The instructions which he himself had received from his new chief were identical with those given him before his departure.[1] In Bucharest, as in Ankara, the visit of M. Potemkin had calmed the atmosphere. It seemed that a ray of hope was beginning to shine from Moscow.

It was in Warsaw that the visit of the Assistant Commissar was to have the most surprising effect of all. His persuasive charm worked on the intractable Colonel Beck. The Colonel expressed his happiness to M. Noel, the French Ambassador:

"For the first time since 1932, I have had a conversation free from mistrust with a representative of the Soviet Union. M. Potemkin has perfectly understood Polish foreign policy. He has understood that, if Poland refused to enter with the U.S.S.R. into any system of mutual assurance analogous to the eastern pact, this was essentially for reasons of prudence, which, moreover, are equally valid for Moscow; and that Poland would not associate itself with any combination in the opposite direction."

M. Potemkin put to M. Beck the question he had put to me on the subject of the Polish-Rumanian alliance. The reply was not identical. Beck accepted no military extension of the Polish-Rumanian engagements. He cited his policy of circumspection with regard to Hungary; and flattered himself "on having dispelled all Soviet suspicions on this point also." He believed equally that he was at one with M. Potemkin "in confirming the common interest which Poland and the U.S.S.R. had in conserving to the Baltic States their full independence." M. Beck was convinced that, to be able to give

1. The Soviet Government gave the same assurance to all governments. The Soviet Ambassador in Paris declared to M. Bonnet "that the departure of M. Litvinov was not to be considered as a change in Russian policy." The Soviet chargé d'affaires in Berlin assured M. Coulondre "that the departure of M. Litvinov did not denote any modification of the essential lines of Soviet foreign policy."

such assurances, "M. Potemkin had received precise orders from his new chief."

The general satisfaction occasioned by M. Potemkin's journey was not confined to those who spoke with him. The Assistant People's Commissar seemed to share the joy he spread. Thus it was that he mentioned to M. Payart, French Chargé d'affaires in Moscow, "the favorable impression he had received from his conversation with M. Beck." The latter, it seemed, had ended by recognizing that, in the event of a German attack, "Poland would inevitably be bound to the U.S.S.R., and in such case obliged to rely on it for support."

M. Potemkin's satisfaction spread to M. Molotov, who "expressed himself with sympathy concerning M. Beck's speech and emphasized the interest he took in safeguarding Polish independence."

I heard similar echoes regarding the impressions that M. Potemkin had gathered at Bucharest. The Soviet diplomat informed the Rumanian Minister that his long conversation with me "had entirely satisfied him." He added that, "*everywhere he had gone, he had noted the same desire to work for peace and to organize resistance against a possible aggression.*" M. Potemkin also stated: "It was understood everywhere that, in one form or another, collaboration with the U.S.S.R. was a necessity." And he added: "Even the countries most refractory because of their previous ties with Germany, like Poland, now understand these truths."

What M. Potemkin had ascertained was entirely correct. Of all the border countries which felt increasingly threatened by the terrible menace of Germany, none could have aggressive intentions toward the Soviet Union. Even Poland, in spite of its "previous ties with Germany," would be led to defend itself in the west. The resistance front virtually existed. As M. Potemkin said, it might "crystallize" everywhere.

That depended on the negotiations between the great

powers. These negotiations were to be the framework into which we all would enter.

Was it foreseen in Moscow how the negotiations were going to end? There is no way of knowing. In any case, M. Potemkin's optimism on the subject was colored by no false impressions. After the visit of the Assistant Commissar, the last illusions flourished which the countries to the east were still to cherish—before the Moscow agreement and the war.

CHAPTER IX

BALKAN JOURNEY

Ankara: Turkey, turntable of peaceful diplomacy. A ball at the
Ankara Palace. *Jalova:* Audience with President Ismet Inönu.
Athens: The ruins of the Acropolis. An evening at Cape Sunion. The
heroism of General Metaxas.

I DESIRED to convey in person the result of my reflec-
tions to our friends in Ankara and Athens. The King put
at my disposal one of the white ships of the Rumanian Maritime Service, which have built up an excellent reputation
during more than forty years of service along the eastern
shores of the Mediterranean. I embarked on the *Dacia* with
my wife and a few colleagues during a spell of the most perfect summer weather. This last voyage into a region where
war was soon to penetrate left with us the ineffable memory
of a sea wonderfully calm and blue under a cloudless sky.

Constantinople received us with joyous eagerness, but did
not detain us long. For the official visitor, the magnificent
capital of the ancient empires is no more now than a halting
place—a stage on the way to the high Anatolia tableland
where the leaders of the Turkish Republic had chosen to
live. One may like or dislike the arid district where the new
Turkish capital stands, so distant in space and spirit from the
enchanting shores of the Bosphorus. But it is difficult not to
be impressed by the magnitude of the effort to which all the
works completed or in course of construction bear witness,
designed to incorporate with Europe one of the most for-
bidding regions of ancient Asia. The quiet but indomitable
energy that emerges from these sites is the same as that of the
men whose character I had long appreciated. So I was happy,
in Ankara, to shake the hands of friends.

Ankara seemed to be at the center of the efforts being

made throughout the world to bar the road to war. The Turkish capital lent itself willingly to the role of peaceful diplomacy's "turntable." The Turkish Government had rounded out its security agreements with Britain. On May 12 an exchange of declarations on the matter had taken place; identical declarations were shortly to be exchanged with France. But the agreements with the west were not to be concluded publicly until Turkey had arranged a pact of mutual assistance with Russia. The threads of European security could thus be knitted together in Ankara. Strong in the support it counted on receiving from Moscow, as well as from the western capitals, Turkey intended in turn to support a policy of resistance in the Balkans and hoped to be able to avert the danger of Axis aggression to the south. This resolute policy threatened nobody. Turkey was facing Hitler but not provoking him. Between Turkey and Germany there were long-standing economic relations, which the Berlin government wished to develop and which the Turkish Government had no wish to impede.

The relations between Moscow and Ankara seemed so good and so hopeful that M. Sarajoglu offered me his good offices to assist me in any way that I wished in establishing a closer contact with the Soviet Union. It was agreed that, pending the nomination of a new Soviet minister to Bucharest, Rumania would maintain constant relations in Ankara with the Soviet ambassador. On the other hand, Rumania would act as a link between Poland and Turkey. The Turkish Government thus hoped to bring to its side and bind to its policy of resistance the only country in the east stubbornly averse to the idea of a system of general security.

It is certain that Turkey (where, more than anywhere else, the determining influence which Russia could exert on the development of the European crisis was appreciated) was firmly convinced of Moscow's determination in favor of general peace. This conviction explained M. Sarajoglu's optimism and his confidence in the efforts he was making.

Moreover, the Turkish Minister of Foreign Affairs was not the only one to look on the future with confidence. In spite of the great waves of depression reported in the west, the barometer was at "fair" in Ankara, and the foreign diplomatic corps rivaled the Turkish Government in optimism.

The diplomatic corps had a very peculiar existence in the capital of the Turkish Republic. It was forced by the smallness of the area to meet always in the same places. I was able to appreciate this on the occasion of the reception given in my honor at the Ankara Palace. Since the Turkish Minister of Foreign Affairs favored peaceful agreements, the brilliant heads of delegations of every political hue accredited to the Turkish Government seemed eager to support his views. On the margin of the official transactions, there was an active diplomatic game, in addition to which there were receptions, followed by dances. When, under the friendly glance of President Kemal Atatürk, whose portrait hung alone on the wall, the banqueting hall had been transformed into a ballroom, the coryphées of eastern politics made their solemn entry. Herr von Papen, surrounded by his political and military staff, appeared, and with most ostentatious grandeur performed his evolutions among the first couples who took the floor to the strains of the jazz orchestra. He excelled in the art of playing at peace. He seemed to be the most vigilant guardian of European security. "I congratulate you," he said as he accosted me," on the pacific work you are carrying on here. Minds must be calmed. For my part, that is what I am trying to do here and, above all, in my own country. We don't want war. War is a misfortune I should like to spare the regime which governs Germany at the moment." And Herr von Papen added with a meaning smile: "You doubtless understand my solicitude for the regime. I have more reason than anyone to wish that the little experiment now being tried by my country will not cause too many disappointments." The "little experiment," for which the

Ambassador of the Third Reich had every right to feel himself responsible and which he cited with such pleasant freedom, was the National Socialist regime! If Herr von Papen had taken to himself the task of calming men's minds by those means, it must be admitted that his was a thankless task.

The French Ambasador, M. Massigli, who was by nature little inclined to mingle the cares of his office with the amusements of the dance, spoke more seriously with some of his colleagues. On the other hand, His Britannic Majesty's Ambassador could profit by the happy relaxation afforded by an evening's dancing. After a good dinner and eloquent speeches, over coffee and liqueurs, when the first tango is played—is not that often the propitious moment for great decisions? Sir Hugh Knatchbull-Hugessen sought to unite in a solid bloc the countries of the southeast. Like his illustrious compatriot, Mr. Winston Churchill, he was convinced that only the question of Southern Dobruja prevented Bulgaria from joining the Balkan Entente. Consequently, it was necessary to profit by a good gesture from me to win Bulgaria to the common cause—at the cost of Rumania.

By him, and by my friend Sarajoglu, I was invited to come away from the place where attentive young secretaries were inviting the wives of ambassadors to dance, so that I might meet, in a less noticeable corner of the room, a pale, sad man with a feverish look, M. Christoff, the Bulgarian Minister.[1]

M. Christoff had prepared for this conversation. He expounded to me with warmth and eloquence all the benefits which might accrue to the Balkans from a Rumanian-Bulgarian agreement. A generous gesture by Rumania—the cession of Southern Dobruja—could, in his opinion, seal the peace forever. I replied very plainly that I had always desired an entente between my country and Bulgaria; and, so that I might sound the real intentions of M. Christoff, I added

1. Monsieur Christoff died shortly afterward, in Moscow, of a disease of the lungs.

that no act seemed to me excessive if it would really assure peace in the Balkans. But would Bulgaria be satisfied with Southern Dobruja?

Surprised at this unexpected success, the Bulgarian Minister showed his mind. Obviously Bulgaria could not be satisfied with so little. But it was not right that Rumania alone should defray the cost of the reconciliation. As I seemed to encourage him with a look, M. Christoff outlined his entire program. Yugoslavia was to cede Tzaribrod and part of Macedonia, Greece must give up western Thrace. . . . I was enlightened; nothing remained to prevent me from rejoining the dancers.

"Well," the British Ambassador, who had followed the conversation from afar, asked me, "did you come to an understanding?"

"Beyond all your expectations," I replied gaily.

"You have allowed him to hope for the return of Southern Dobruja?"

"If only that were all! I have given up everything: Tzaribrod, Macedonia, western Thrace. . . ."

"What?" exclaimed Sir Hugh in consternation. "He has again asked for everything?"

"Everything. That is only a beginning. Appetite grows with what it feeds on."

I drew the Ambassador toward the buffet, where M. Sarajoglu already awaited us. It was agreed that I should not carry my conversations with the Bulgarian Minister any further. M. Christoff had outrageously disappointed the hopes that had been put in him. He had laid claim to territories which neither England nor Turkey wished to see change hands.

The diplomatic corps resumed the conversations so well begun in another place propitious to the discussion of world problems—namely, Ankara railway station on the day of our departure. The number of ambassadors who had come there

PRESIDENT ISMET INÖNU

". . . expounded, in a firm and quiet voice, his views on the
political situation."

(See page 195.)

ATHENS

From left to right: Prime Minister General Metaxas, Grigore Gafencu, the Permanent Undersecretary for Foreign Affairs, and the Rumanian Ambassador in Athens.

to bid us farewell, some presenting bonbons, and others bouquets of flowers, might have turned the head of a traveler from abroad, had he not known that, in the Near East, nothing encourages the exchange of diplomatic views more than the platform of a railway station. Our departure was superb; and, as M. Sarajoglu accompanied us on our journey, we shared with him the honors of the warmest of ovations.

We were escorted to Jalova, a charming summer resort on the Asiatic shore of the Sea of Marmora, where the President of the Republic, M. Ismet Inönu, awaited us. This man, who, under the name of Ismet Pasha, had taken so great a part in the liberation of Turkish territory, had just inherited from his great predecessor, Kemal Atatürk, a national state whose "revolutionary" principles he faithfully respected, while still trying to reconcile them with certain ancestral traditions which he cultivated with distinction. It was a singular favor to share a meal with him and his intimates, and to hear him expound, in a firm and quiet voice, his views on the political situation.

The President hoped that peace could be saved. But he hoped so as a soldier, taking precautionary measures and studying the political problem "on the ground." Spreading out a map, he explained to me where the Axis could attack and where the Balkan countries, united, should establish their defenses. The study of the map of the Balkans, at the side of Ismet Pasha, awoke me to certain military considerations which I had not had any occasion to fathom up to then. Better than some diplomatic statements had done, it made it possible for me to grasp the political views of the President of the Turkish Republic. My host believed in only one possible aggression, that of the Axis. Against that it was necessary to be forearmed, by organizing general resistance. The President was convinced that this resistance could rely on the Soviet. With his finger he indicated the point where the Russians would land in order to bring their assistance into conjunction with that of the Turkish armies. Calculating the chances of success of the two enemy camps, the President stated that he was certain of an Allied victory.

A month after my visit to Jalova, on August 11, 1939, King Carol's yacht, cruising in Turkish waters, moored in front of the Palace of Dolmah Bagtché. President Inönu, receiving the King, repeated to him with some insistence what he had said to me. The German danger was increasingly menacing. The President considered that "the interests of Turkey, Rumania, and the other Balkan States were so closely linked together that any penetration into this zone by Germany or Italy would be fatally dangerous to all." It was urgently necessary to erect a "barrier of border states" firmly relying on Soviet Russia for support. When King Carol expressed doubts with regard to Russia, Ismet Inönu promised to use his good offices to bring about better relations between Russia and Rumania. This, let me repeat, took place on August 11, 1939, twenty days before the outbreak of war.

It is rather curious to compare the positions which the Turkish leaders consistently maintained up to the last moment with those which the Polish rulers at the same moment were obstinately fighting for. We have shown that the Poles were mistrustful first of all of the Russians. They believed that if Poland never drew close to Russia war would not break out. The Turks, on the other hand, refused no alliances and believed in collective security. According to them, Russia could bring, and wanted to bring, aid which would be decisive. The two policies were brought to nothing by the same event. On August 23, 1939, the German-Soviet Agreement put an end, at the same time, to the calculations of Colonel Beck and the hopes of President Inönu.

As far as the neighboring states were concerned, this agreement at one stroke swept away the good as well as the bad policies. Under the sudden pressure of events, "independent" Poland was to be the first to founder in war. Turkey, which had lent itself to the scheme of assistance and had compromised its neutrality in a thousand ways, was to preserve its neutrality beyond all expectations.

When we took leave of our hosts at Jalova, we had little idea that, as we shook hands in confident farewell, it was to be the last for a long time to come. The *Dacia* set course for Athens. We entered the port of Peiraeus to the sound of deafening noise. Everything was beflagged and festive. The ships' sirens whistled. Sailors, lining the decks of the ships, waved their caps, and a boisterous crowd had swarmed onto the quays. Under a brilliant sky, the pile of the Parthenon stood out even more brightly, as though lifted on invisible wings. In this setting, the most beautiful in the world, where so much joie de vivre and such an overflow of happiness welcomed us, I felt the approach of disaster on the rebound. Has not the sense of tragedy always been near to the emotion stirred by the sight of beauty, in this region where the Gods dwelt? Forsaking the traditional formulæ of diplomacy, I tried to express my forebodings in my reply to President Metaxas' speech of welcome.

"Doubtless you know that, since our last meeting, I have made a long journey to the capitals of Europe, as the envoy of my country. When today, under the blue sky of Athens, I saw the sacred hill and the white columns of the Temple of the Goddess of Reason, I realized that I neared the end of my journey. Does not this temple, by its perfect proportions, express the idea of the unity of Europe, inheritor of the most brilliant civilization ever known; and does it not give, with its magnificent but mournful ruins, a solemn warning to all those who would again blight our common heritage?"

The Greek Government gave us a particularly warm welcome. In regard to foreign policy, there was no possible conflict between President Metaxas and myself. We were in agreement on all the points of our common action. Since the creation of the Balkan Entente, Rumania and Greece had shared the same opinions and taken the same decisions. The European crisis had brought our two countries still closer together. Greeks and Rumanians grasped events in the same way, with the same swift intuition.

So that, removed from official ceremonies, we could discuss the latest news of the "crisis," the President took me to Cape Sunion to see the sunset. A few yards from the ruins of the temple where Byron had inscribed his name there was a little inn where dinner had been prepared. Alas! I could not do honor to M. Metaxas' hospitality. A sudden attack of the indisposition which I had simulated when with Herr von Ribbentrop's messengers this time really gripped me. I had to lie flat on a camp bed, in a small room in the inn, where through an open window rose the sweet-smelling air of the Greek countryside mingled with the odor of fish on the grill. The old President seated himself paternally at my bedside; and, to take my mind off my indisposition, quietly spoke of the many phases of his political life.

General Metaxas had seen a great deal during his restless life: parliamentary quarrels, party strife, conspiracies, revolutions. In the course of his relentless opposition to a very great adversary, he had suffered imprisonment, exile, persecution, and had been condemned to death more than once; afterward, he had "governed," freely dealing out exile and imprisonment in turn and maintaining public order with an iron hand. The voice of the redoubtable General became surprisingly gentle in tone, to spare the ear of a sick friend, and also the better to convey the intensity of his passionate love for his native land. This love filled him completely, since the passion of the partisan had died down. The only end which Metaxas still wished to serve was that of arming Greece so that it might be in a condition to defend itself. If he had been led to thwart the savage appetite of his people for freedom, it was, he said, the better to assure the preservation of the national freedom. Times were at hand no longer favorable to the small countries. Everywhere the "new order" was attacking our most cherished conceptions. In face of the tendency toward unification by force, our native countries were constantly in danger. Henceforth, it seemed, nations were unnecessary. But what in the world could be greater than our small native lands? The President extended his arm in the direction of the spot where the ruins of the Temple of Minerva had been lost in the darkness.

"It is there, there that Europe began," he said with a simple pride. "And there it may end if we are not constantly on the alert." Then, turning toward me, he asked suddenly: "If they come at you, are you determined to fight?"

"I certainly think so. Does not our whole line of action show it?"

"I hope," he replied, "that it will be possible for you to do so. As for us, the sea ensures our freedom of action. We shall fight, even if we have again to cover our country with ruins."

President Metaxas kept his word. On the night of October 27–28, 1940, when the Italian Minister entered his villa at Kiphissia and handed him the peremptory note, Metaxas, without a moment's hesitation, rejected the enemy's injunction. At a time when almost all the European nations had given way to the Axis, this was a very great gesture. Its echo, and the echoes of the first successes of the Greek Army, reached me in Moscow, where I was thenceforward to represent my country's interests, and filled me with fear and pride at the same time. Greece was avenging the honor of the Balkan Entente. The newspapers reproduced Metaxas' magnificent words to the Greek people:

"A few days ago, a treacherous enemy attacked us without any cause. His sole aim was to rob us of what we held most dear: our independence, our freedom, our honor. Greece has risen as one man; it has taken up arms; after desperate battles, victory smiles on us; from Macedonia to Epirus the enemy is in flight along the entire front. I have only one thing to add: Greece forgets neither Santarosa, nor Fratti, nor Garibaldi, nor the many other Italians who shed their blood for our liberty. Were they alive today they would be oppressed, for the fascist regime cannot tolerate free men. Mussolini has warned us that Greece will be annihilated. We reply that we are determined not to let ourselves be annihilated. Greece will continue to be independent and free. As for the Italian people, it will have to weigh the consequences of its defeat when it settles its accounts with Mussolini.

"Until then, Hellenes, let us clench our fists and lift up our hearts. Let us fight with the ferocity aroused in us by a treacherous aggression. We are not fighting simply for our own cause. We are fighting for the freedom of the Balkan peoples. We are fighting for an ideal which goes far beyond the frontiers of our country and extends to the whole human race."

When, a few months later, the German armies broke the heroic resistance of the Greek people, General Metaxas died of heart failure.

I cherish the recollection of the words I heard one evening at Cape Sunion. The old Europe would end when the swastika flew above the Acropolis.

EPILOGUE

THE diplomatic efforts—noted in the course of the journey which has been the subject of this book—became more intense at the end of the spring of 1939. Europe, having been warned, tried quickly to organize its defense. From June onward the decisive issue was joined. The crisis was not spectacular, a swift succession of sensational events. The battle between the foreign ministries went on *sotto voce*, unseen by the world, and sometimes with unbearable slowness. The balance of power was at stake. Some wished to strengthen it to ensure peace; others wished to overturn it so that they might be able to make war. The powerful pressure exerted by both sides, which might suddenly start a conflict, did not reach the ordinary people. Few even of the initiated knew its full importance.

The disorder in men's minds was such, and such was the uncertainty of their judgments, that many asked themselves whether the German preparations really corresponded with the somber premeditation of a crime, or simply hid yet another bluff. Anxiety alternated with "optimism."

In reality, Hitler, having openly defied the European order and having turned away from the west, was already pledged to a decisive trial of strength. If Europe could raise a common resistance against him, he would stand alone; and his ambition, judged and condemned, was doomed to impotence. If, on the other hand, Europe failed in its effort, the explosive forces accumulated in Germany would be freed; and Hitler's success would then be so great that nothing could check his will to conquer.

The Moscow negotiations—where the west and the U.S.S.R. confronted each other in a search for means of saving the peace—were in the last analysis to decide everything.

While the affairs of Danzig and Poland were played out in the foreground of politics—quarrels between neighbors, minority risings, the exchange of notes, and shots fired—the fate of the world was being decided in the secrecy of the chancelleries. There, over certain formulæ and a few points of procedure, the most important diplomatic contest in history was being decided.

On June 2 the negotiations between the cabinets of London, Paris, and Moscow entered into a new phase.[1] On that day the Soviet Government put forward a basis of agreement which had roused certain hopes in the western capitals. In London, opinion was "happy to note that a substantial measure of agreement was now achieved." This agreement— still according to London—comprised the following points:

1. A treaty should be concluded among the three great powers, on terms of equality, each one of the three accepting similar obligations toward the other two.

2. The three powers would render each other immediate aid:

(*a*) should one of them be the object of a direct attack by a European power.

(*b*) should one of the three powers go to the help of certain states which it had engaged itself to assist against aggression.

The progress achieved during the month of May, as a result of a continual exchange of notes among the three capitals, was, in fact, "substantial." The British had accepted the principle of a tripartite agreement instead of the unilateral declarations envisaged at the beginning of the negotiations. They had equally agreed to provide for the case of a "direct attack," as the Russians wanted. On its side, the Soviet Government had consented to take part in the protection of the border states.

In order to speed the conclusion of the negotiations, the British Government sent Mr. Strang of the Foreign Office

1. Cf. Chap. V, pp. 124 ff.; and Chap. VI, pp. 146 ff.

to Moscow. Negotiations by means of notes and counter-proposals were to be replaced by direct contact and "a procedure of negotiation, article by article." The western powers were in a hurry. On June 6 the French Council of Ministers unanimously decided that "it was of extreme importance to end matters quickly."

Unfortunately, in the Soviet proposal of June 2 certain points raised "essential difficulties." The Foreign Office noted that these points were "extremely embarrassing to His Majesty's Government."

The first difficulty related to the Soviet wish to add Finland, Latvia, and Esthonia to the list of states which it was agreed to aid. The Russian point of view seemed logical: since it was a question of consolidating the situation of two border states (Poland and Rumania), why should not protection be extended to the whole eastern region between the Baltic and the Black Sea? But this counterproposition had aroused suspicions in London. The question was asked as to what was meant by the Soviet insistence in favor of the Baltic States, which until then had refused to accept the guarantee of the great powers. The Quai d'Orsay was no less uneasy. It was said there that "the pact, as conceived, was intended to ensure the security and independence of the peaceful states, but that the U.S.S.R. must not be allowed to derive from it a special right to intervene militarily in the Baltic States."

The opposition of the western powers aroused Moscow's suspicions. Why were England and France limiting their protection to Poland and Rumania, while leaving an open road to Russia via the Baltic States? Was this not equivalent to confessing that the western powers wanted a tripartite agreement only if it concerned those countries of the east in which they were directly interested?

From the moment of his arrival at Moscow Mr. Strang was to encounter this mistrust on the part of the Soviet. M. Molotov informed him that he was disappointed by the refusal to include the Baltic States in the agreement. He "expected something better from the western powers." The direct negotiations began in an atmosphere devoid of mutual confidence. The words employed did not have the same meaning for both parties. Intentions guessed at were feared, and those not discerned were feared even more.

The western powers tried to explain in good faith. M. Bonnet instructed his Ambassador to recall to the Soviet Government, "in order to dispel mistrust," that the British and French Governments put the greatest value on the effective collaboration of the U.S.S.R. This they had amply proved "by seeking this collaboration and by constantly striving for the last two months to draw closer to the Soviet point of view. Nothing justified M. Molotov's supposition that the two governments wished to reserve any loopholes for escape."

These reassuring explanations called for others of the same nature, but the Soviet was silent. To facilitate a compromise on the question of the Baltic States, the British and French negotiators proposed a general formula, which was to include all the "border" states—those to the east as well as those to the west. As soon as this idea became known it raised a chain of protests. No small country wished to figure on a list which would make it the subject of German anger. Certain of these countries feared Russian interference. The Netherlands Government made it known that "it was not involved in any way in the negotiations between the great powers." The Esthonian Minister of Foreign Affairs declared that the Baltic States did not intend to submit themselves to the protection of a great power which in its own interest wished to "act the part of defender."

Paying no heed to these reactions, the Soviet Government went on its way. It would not accord its aid to either the Netherlands or Switzerland, because it had no diplomatic relations with these countries. On the other hand, the Baltic States must at all costs figure in the tripartite agreement.

Far from dreaming of any compromise on this point, Moscow on the contrary demanded new precisions. The western powers gave way. On July 6 the Soviet point of view was accepted in full.

Meanwhile the Soviet Government had still further increased its claims. Thus the famous question of *indirect aggression* was raised. In the scheme put forward by M. Molotov on July 4 the text of Article 1 read:

"England, France, and the U.S.S.R. undertake to lend each other all immediate and effectual aid, if one of the three countries is engaged in hostilities with any European state, as a result either of an aggression by this power against one of the three countries; or of aggression, direct or *indirect*, by this power against any European state, in the event that one of the three interested countries considers that it is obliged to defend the independence and the neutrality of this state."

In an annexed letter, it was to be specified that the treaty would apply "in the case of direct, or *indirect*, aggression; that is to say, an *internal coup d'état or a political change favorable to the aggressor.*" By this proposal Molotov seemed to wish to make matters as difficult as possible. The pact of assistance began to look like an international document authorizing intervention in the affairs of small countries. To justify its demands, the U.S.S.R. cited the precedent of Czechoslovakia, where the Hacha regime had been correlative to the German conquest. Ought not the great powers to be forearmed against such proceedings? But the right to control "political changes" among its neighbors, which the U.S.S.R. wished to arrogate to itself, opened up disturbing prospects and justified the apprehensions of the western powers. The claims put forward by the U.S.S.R. regarding the Baltic States were known. To recognize the right of the U.S.S.R. to supervise the internal affairs of this region meant, in fact, abandoning these states to the Soviet's will to power.

On receiving the new Soviet proposal, London and Paris

were disturbed. "The Foreign Office appears to be very discouraged," the French Ambassador reported to his chief. M. Bonnet was also discouraged. The words "indirect aggression," which for the first time appeared in a Soviet text, seemed to him to contain "dangerous equivocations." The Minister thought "that it was impossible that an internal political change in a state should automatically be able to bring about a general conflict."

But neither in London nor in Paris was there any thought of rejecting out of hand Molotov's "suggestion." The desire to reach agreement increased as the fever in Europe rose. M. Bonnet, while resigning himself to the use of the new terms proposed by the People's Commissar, tried to define their limits: indirect aggression should be regarded as any event "which might be intended to bring about an internal coup d'état obviously involving alienation or alteration of sovereignty for the benefit of the aggressor."

On its side the British Foreign Office also sought a definition, "with a view to allaying the worst suspicions of the Baltic peoples." It proposed the following formula: "It is agreed that the term 'aggression' should be extended to cover also action accepted by a state, under the threat of force, and involving the abandonment of its independence or its neutrality."

For his part M. Molotov, to gild the pill, offered to specify to the British and French Ambassadors that the indirect aggression in question was one "whose purpose was to make use of the territory of one of the states indicated to carry out an aggression against this latter, or against one of the contracting powers."

This definition, the best of the three, crossed the proposals of the western governments. M. Bonnet hastened to accept it by telegraph. He was too late. M. Molotov had seized upon the British "suggestions" and already "combined" them with his own project. The formula to which he was to adhere was the following: ". . . in the case of an indirect aggression, the aim of which would be, *under the menace of force or without such menace*, to make use of the territory of one of the states indicated, in order to carry out an aggression against this latter, or against one of the contracting powers."

The labor spent by both sides to combine complex formulas while war was at the gates might seem stupid. In reality, it revealed the full gravity of the problem. The U.S.S.R. wished to ensure itself complete freedom of action with respect to its neighbors; it wanted to solve the "problem" of the Baltic States. That was the price of its collaboration. The western powers did not believe that they ought to pay such a price, when they opened negotiations with the east. Were they not offering to Russia—the first country to be threatened by the Reich—assistance at least of equal value to that which Russia could furnish? But, as the U.S.S.R. increased its claims and seemed in less of a hurry to conclude an agreement, a vague uneasiness spread through the foreign offices. If Moscow could enjoy dragging out the discussions, then the U.S.S.R. must have less to fear from Hitler's behavior. So where could this assurance come from? The possibility of German-Soviet collusion made a prompt conclusion of the negotiations absolutely necessary.[1] The British and the French seemed to be resigned to giving way all along the line. The strife over formulas no longer meant anything save a desire to save appearances. The Soviet definition of indirect aggression, with all that it involved, was still to be the subject of a few more exchanges of views. In reality, it had been accepted ever since the first half of July.

A further condition put forward by the Soviets caused still greater uneasiness. From the beginning of the negotiations

1. The last information received did not, however, furnish any ground for envisaging such a collusion. Thus M. Coulondre reported from Berlin on July 8: "The chargé d'affaires of the U.S.S.R., whom I saw yesterday evening, stated to me most categorically that there were no political negotiations going on between Berlin and Moscow. . . . *I can affirm to you,*" he said to me, "*that no political conversations of even a nonofficial character have been entered into with Berlin.*"

the Russians had shown the desire to see the political agreement completed by a military and naval agreement. In his note of June 2 M. Molotov had expressed the idea that the tripartite pact should be considered concluded only after military arrangements had been signed. The Foreign Office had at once stated its reservations. It feared "the effect that postponing the operation of the tripartite pact until the conclusion of a military convention would have on the European situation." Such a convention seemed to it desirable, but it did not believe it could be concluded "in a sufficiently short space of time."

This question was to crop up again as soon as the repercussions caused by the idea of "indirect aggression" had died down a little. It was to demonstrate the extent of the mutual mistrust. M. Bonnet, who had not ceased to exert a conciliatory influence, informed London, on July 9, that the condition put forward by M. Molotov seemed to him to be unacceptable. "The Soviet formula," said the Minister, "by making the operation of the political agreement depend on the conclusion of the military arrangement, risks deferring the psychological effect and the practical application of this agreement during a period which shows signs of being particularly critical. The Soviet Government must understand that the French and British Governments would not have given their best efforts to conciliation for many months past with a view to reaching an understanding, if they were not determined to ensure the full efficiency of this entente with the least possible delay. . . . To enter on this path is to risk finding ourselves, in August, that is to say, when the gravity of the international situation may be at its greatest, faced with the following alternative: either to submit to all the Soviet Government's demands from the military point of view, that is, to give it a total cooperation in the west in exchange for a limited cooperation in the east; or else to accept a rupture of military negotiations, which would destroy simultaneously both the military and the political agreement. To play this game against us would be the easier because the military agreement, to become effective in the east, requires the consent of Poland and Rumania, which is by no means certain." Such were M. Bonnet's suspicions on the matter. Moscow replied by displaying an equally great mistrust. M. Molotov thought that, "as long as the military convention was not signed, it could not be held that there was a treaty." Speaking of the Soviet statesman, the French Ambassador said: "What haunts him seems to be that we might content ourselves with the moral exploitation of the conclusion of a solemn treaty, which would still be void of all significance and all practical bearing because of the absence of a military convention. A two hours' discussion has not succeeded in making him abandon this position." M. Naggiar added the very significant comment: "I fear that a discussion carried to the limit in order to reject the Soviet proposal may accentuate the mistrust of those members of the Politburo who charge us with seeking a common declaration rather than a concrete engagement. German propaganda is being used in this direction and seeks to prove that Britain and France will not go through with their engagements."

It was quite evident that the western powers were seeking for a psychological effect (they did not hide this fact). They wished to create a solidarity between the west and the east which would prevent Hitler from starting his war. This plan was perfectly justified; and it was natural that any delay in its realization seemed insupportable. The Soviet point of view was equally tenable; Moscow did not want to engage itself lightly. If, despite agreement in principle, war broke out, the greatest German effort might be made against the U.S.S.R. In demanding increasingly precise engagements the U.S.S.R. was defending its cause; but it was wrong in making a show of its suspicions. Britain, which up to then had accepted everything, then felt how offensive the Soviet's mistrust was. The Soviet procedure seemed to it "altogether unusual." "The fact that M. Molotov puts forward such a request," it was said in London, "reveals the most offensive suspicions regarding our sincerity and good faith, suspicions which are the more unjustified since we are ready to open military negotiations immediately the treaty is signed. In the matter of an agreement of mutual assistance, the natural procedure is for the political agreement to precede military arrangements. The insistence with which the Government of the U.S.S.R. demands that the political agreement shall depend on the military agreement suggests the disagreeable suspicion that the Government of the U.S.S.R. thereby hopes to force us to accept military conditions which might be contrary to our views." The numerous concessions which England had already made to win the confidence of Moscow were recalled:

"1. We have accepted the proposal of the Government of the U.S.S.R., tending to incorporate the case of the Baltic States in the treaty.

"2. We have abandoned the request that the Low Countries, Switzerland, and Luxemburg should be included in the countries which the agreement is to cover.

"3. We have agreed to take action in the case of an indirect aggression.

"4. We have in self-defense agreed to define this matter.

"5. We are ready to insert this definition in the agreement itself . . . but we are approaching the point where we can no longer follow a method which consists in accepting each new demand brought forward by the Soviet Government."

It was allowed to transpire that England's patience was "almost" exhausted, and that His Majesty's Government "might have to re-examine its whole position." On the same date Paris was informed that, if the Soviet Government refused all concessions on the sole point on which the British Government had reservations, the latter was of the opinion that "the continuation of the negotiations would become impossible."

The French Government realized how well founded the British reaction was. It understood the danger arising from it. The stoppage of the negotiations would be a triumph for Hitler. Discarding the reservations which he himself had put forward, M. Bonnet addressed himself directly to Lord Halifax: "I am aware of the very important concessions to which we have already consented. But we are coming to a decisive moment, where it appears to us necessary to neglect nothing in order to reach a conclusion. It is impossible to conceal the disastrous effect the failure of the pending negotiations would have not only for our two countries but also for the preservation of peace. I even fear this might be the signal for a move by Germany against Danzig. These negotiations have lasted for more than four months. Public opinion in every country attaches the greatest importance to them. For this reason they have acquired a symbolic character. The President of the Council and I are of opinion that, in such circumstances, it is of capital importance to carry through negotiations whose success today appears to us to be one of the essential conditions of the maintenance of peace."

For some days the Quai d'Orsay lived in a state of alarm. The irritation of the British Government did not abate. London considered that the Soviet negotiators had never been sincere, and that they were using the Allied concessions to extort something else. New tactics, it was thought, must be tried. The French Government tried again. It demonstrated that a rupture of the conversations might weaken the entire structure of European security. "The conclusion or the failure of the negotiations," it said, "will exercise a decisive influence on the actions of the Axis during the coming months." And it exhorted the British Government to make one final concession: "In view of the gravity of the hour, and taking into consideration the incalculable consequences which the conclusion or the failure of the agreement involves, the French Government is of the opinion that, whatever damage the actual substance of this agreement has suffered, its preventive and political value still remains sufficiently effective to compel us to sacrifice the reservations, serious though they may be, which certain of its provisions have required of us. . . ."

Finally, toward July 24, the British Foreign Office gave way. As a London dispatch announced, it consented "to make its instructions more elastic." Following a restricted Cabinet meeting, the British Government decided once more to yield. The news, which was immediately communicated to Moscow, had an excellent effect. M. Molotov expressed his entire satisfaction. His policy had scored a new point. The negotiators considered the political agreement as being "virtually concluded." The examination of the military problems must be expedited. The Soviet Government declared itself ready to begin conversations at once. The Allied ambassadors, fearful of new mishaps, were of the opinion that the matter should be taken in hand as quickly as possible. They comforted themselves with the hope that the negotiations had at last taken a favorable turn. M. Naggiar considered that "the Soviet Government, by asking for the opening of the technical conversations without further delay, while still taking care to recall the fact that the political and military clauses are inseparable, is now coming into the open enough for us henceforward to be able to derive from this public attitude the psychological advantage we hope for."

The western governments accepted this argument. While the diplomats sought to express in a communiqué the "provisional" agreement established on the political clauses (such a communiquè, having failed to win the approval of the three partners, was never to be published), the military delegations left for Russia.

Moscow gave the Allied officers an extremely warm welcome. From the moment of the first banquets the new negotiators appreciated the magnificence of Soviet hospitality.

It plainly affected the relations between the delegates. Optimism was the order of the day, and the conversations seemed to have begun under the best auspices.

But, during the night of August 14–15, the French and British Foreign Offices were warned that a *coup de théâtre* had just taken place. In the course of a "technical" conversation Marshal Voroshilov had raised the following question; "In case of an aggression directed against France and England, would Soviet troops be authorized to penetrate into Polish territory, across the Vilna Corridor and Galicia, and also into Rumanian territory?" This question seemed to the Marshal all the more natural, "since France already had a treaty with Poland and Great Britain had guaranteed the integrity of that country."

When the Allied missions had mentioned the political character of the problem, the Marshal had immediately declared that "the Soviet delegation considered that, in the absence of a solution of this question, further discussions were doomed to certain failure, and that it could not recommend to its government to undertake an enterprise so manifestly destined to fail."

This unexpected turn of events brought the negotiations back to their point of departure, after four months of laborious efforts. A great deal of trouble had been taken to build up a system which would protect the border countries without asking for their consent. The problem to which a political solution seemed to have been found now arose anew on military grounds.

It is hardly probable that the Soviet Government, in raising Voroshilov's question, was not aware of the trouble it would provoke. It is equally true that the necessities of the discussion demanded that such a question should be settled. How were precise military engagements to be undertaken without providing a plan of operations and without clarifying the position of the intermediary countries? That the question rebounded onto the political plane was another matter, which no longer concerned Marshal Voroshilov. He confined himself to asking whether the military treaty which he was supposed to sign could be executed, and in what way. The reply to his question, in the form in which he had put it, could no longer be escaped. It must be either "Yes" or "No." On this "Yes" or "No" the fate of the negotiation directly depended, and with it the peace of the world.

It was necessary to obtain the consent of the border countries with the utmost speed. The western governments addressed themselves to Poland.

The Quai d'Orsay was of the opinion that the reply of the Polish Government could not fail to be favorable. Had not M. Beck recently stated, regarding the Moscow negotiations, of which he was aware, "that he would be satisfied if they succeeded, and that he would regret their failure? The French Foreign Minister summoned the Polish Ambassador, M. Lukasiewicz, and asked him to transmit the Soviet question to his chief. Would Poland agree, in the event of an enemy aggression, to Russian troops crossing Polish territory via the Vilna Corridor and Galicia? "To say 'No,' " observed M. Bonnet, "is to lead to a rupture of the negotiations with all its consequences. Catastrophe would be the result." M. Lukasiewicz replied that he would transmit the message without comment. He believed that he could state in advance that M. Beck would refuse to accept the proposal. The Ambassador added, "What would you say if you were asked to have Alsace-Lorraine guarded by the Germans?"

M. Bonnet was forewarned. He immediately urged M. Noel, the French Ambassador in Warsaw, to put pressure on the Polish Government. "It is urgent that you yourself see M. Beck and insist on the necessity, for the Polish Government, of accepting Russian aid under the clearly defined conditions under which it is proposed. You will not fail strongly to emphasize the fact that Russo-Polish collaboration, if needed, in the eastern field of operations is an *indispensable condition* for the efficacy of our common resistance to the Axis plan of aggression. . . . We cannot suppose that, by refusing to allow the strategic conditions of Russian intervention to be discussed, Poland would accept the responsibility for the failure of the military conversations at Moscow and for all the ensuing consequences."

Warned by M. Lukasiewicz, Colonel Beck was ready to hold his ground with the French Ambassador. "Upon entering his office," M. Noel telegraphed, "I immediately had the impression that, in spite of his habitual courtesy, he had become again the person whom in the course of the last few months I have had to ask to explain his position—sometimes with a certain liveliness—on matters in which Polish policy was opposed to ours."

Beck reserved his final reply for the next few days; but he immediately raised the following objections: It seemed evident to him that the Soviet Government was maneuvering, so as to make the responsibility for the failure of the negotiations fall on Poland. If Poland lent itself to the proposed scheme, Germany would immediately be informed (the Russians themselves would take care to advise them) and war would become inevitable. If Poland accepted what was proposed, the U.S.S.R. would not keep its military engagements (it was materially incapable of keeping them) but it would obtain political pledges.

All Beck's old arguments, all his old bias, reappeared: fear of German brutality, profound mistrust regarding Russia. If the U.S.S.R. was militarily weak, what was the use of joining up with it? And if it were strong, it would never evacuate the Polish regions which it occupied. Against these apprehensions the best arguments were of no avail. In vain M. Noel argued that, in order to foil the Soviet maneuvers—if maneuvers they were—the most proper reply for Poland to make would be to accept what was proposed. M. Beck showed himself intractable.

Time was running short. "The next meeting," announced M. Naggiar from Moscow, "has been fixed for the 21, to give us time before this date to receive information regarding the Polish problem. I confirm that, in the absence of a favorable solution, official, unofficial or even tacit, permitting us to reply affirmatively, the military conversations will be interrupted."

M. Bonnet sent a new message to Warsaw. "However unsatisfactory Colonel Beck's first reaction may have been, it seems too obviously of a political and psychological nature for us to accept as final on an essentially technical question."

The Minister ordered M. Noel to be indefatigable in bringing the discussion back to the military plane. "It is from the technical point of view that the Polish Government should be led to consider the Russian problem as an essential part of the general problem of the organization of the defensive front in eastern Europe. The matter cannot be limited to a question of Polish-Russian relations. The military action in course of preparation equally engages Turkey, Rumania, and perhaps other countries. Its coordination must be total." And M. Bonnet added: "If the Polish Government is determined to refuse all practical aid from the U.S.S.R., it is inadmissible that it should have let us undertake political conversations without advising us of its point of view, and that M. Beck should several times have said to you that he sincerely hoped for a favorable conclusion." He finished: "We are entering on a decisive period. Next Sunday Herr Hitler is to make his Tannenberg speech. *The success or failure of the Anglo-Franco-Russian negotiations depends on the Polish reply.* It is for the Polish Government to measure the full extent of its responsibilities, should its attitude lead to the rupture of our negotiations with the U.S.S.R."

Before receiving this last message M. Beck had made up his mind. It was decidedly—and resolutely—"No!" "For us," he said to M. Noel on the evening of August 19, *"it is a question of principle.* We have no military agreement with the U.S.S.R., and we want none. We do not admit that, in any form whatever, the use of a part of our territory by foreign troops should be discussed. Besides, this is nothing new; this has always been our doctrine, and we have often explained it to you." Thus, even before having taken cognizance of M. Bonnet's last arguments, Beck replied to them. The question which the western powers looked at from a technical angle was, for Poland, eminently political; more than this, it was *an affair of princple*. Colonel Beck seemed to be saying to the French Foreign Minister: "Why did you let yourself be misled into negotiations which must necessarily lead up to this, when we have never hidden our 'doctrine' from you?"

General Stakiewicz, Chief of the Polish General Staff, supported Beck's refusal. "Poland cannot agree that foreign troops should penetrate into its territory."

The French Government thereupon decided to take extreme action. In face of the imminence of the peril, M. Naggiar and General Doumenc (chief of the French military delegation) had suggested, on August 20, "that M. Beck's suggestions should not be taken absolutely literally, since perhaps he desires only one thing—namely, to remain ignorant of the whole affair"; and that the negotiators should be authorized to give *in principle* an affirmative reply. This reply should specify that the envisaged right of passage would be accorded only after the commencement of hostilities.

On August 21 General Doumenc received by telegram M. Daladier's instructions, which gave him full power to sign the military agreement under the best obtainable conditions. The French Government agreed to disregard Colonel Beck's refusal.

Too late! On that same day it was learned that von Ribbentrop was leaving for Moscow. Two days later, on August 23, 1939, the German-Russian Agreement was signed.

So failed Europe's last effort to escape its destiny, which was to face the Hitlerian menace. Can the responsibility for this fatal outcome be defined?

Britain had acted with rectitude, without excessive eagerness, but with the manifest determination to see things through. It might be reproached for its hesitations, its vague proposals, and its complicated formulas; even its resolution to intervene by arms could be doubted. This doubt was entirely unfounded. Britain was the first to declare war. It had the courage to open hostilities—and this in order to keep its word.

France had exerted itself far more during the negotiations. In its desire to reach the goal it had not ceased to discard differences. Foreseeing the catastrophic consequences of failure, it had striven obstinately. Finally, France, too, had the courage to declare war, to keep its word.

Nevertheless, France's action, like England's, was hampered by a heavy load: the Munich Agreement. In the course of the negotiations the U.S.S.R. had not brought it up, but the mistrust attached to this matter had certainly persisted, and had run through the negotiations themselves. To compensate for this, it would have been necessary for the negotiators to have a new factor to their credit: the formal support of Poland. This support they did not get.

The Poles threw the blame on the Russians. Beck was not the least troubled when he learned of von Ribbentrop's journey. He assured those with whom he spoke that, "materially speaking, nothing much would be changed." Beck saw in the event "a supplementary justification" of his mistrust of the U.S.S.R. Russia had never been loyal; it was now "Herr von Ribbentrop's turn to estimate Soviet good faith."

The Russians accused Poland. Marshal Voroshilov, announcing on August 24 to the military delegations that the "technical" negotiations no longer had any point, laid the entire responsibility for the failure at the door of the Polish Government. M. Molotov was equally categorical. On the 25th he received the French Ambassador in order to declare to him: "Having noted that, in spite of the efforts of the three governments, *the obstinate refusal of Poland rendered im-*

possible a tripartite pact of mutual assistance, the Soviet Government had had to solve the problem, so far as it was concerned, by the signature of a pact of nonaggression with Germany." M. Molotov added that the responsibility for the profound upheavals which the German-Soviet treaty might entail *would fall exclusively on the Warsaw Government.* "A great country like the U.S.S.R. could not go to the extent of supplicating Poland to accept an assistance which it did not want at any price."

The Soviet Government had every advantage in accusing the others. It had played its hand with infinite skill and seemed to have made no mistake. From the beginning its sole care had been to define the nature of the engagements. It had never haggled over its share in the common work; and if it had been obliged to register the impossibility of an entente, this was because it had been given no practical means of fulfilling its obligations. A stoppage of the negotiations might certainly provoke war, and this war might first of all turn toward the east. Therefore the U.S.S.R. took its precautions in time. There was no flaw in this compact argument.

Among other things, the Russians might be reproached for being too devoted to logic. The lack of precision by the western states which they encountered did not change the nature of the agreement put forward. It was still an agreement to maintain peace. This lack of definition did not expose the U.S.S.R. to imminent danger, since France and England, in any case, had guaranteed the border countries covering the Soviet frontiers. In preferring the proposals of the Third Reich, which certainly were much more "precise," Russia chose Hitler, who wanted war. Had Soviet mistrust expressed itself more judiciously, it might have "solved the problem," as M. Molotov said, in such a fashion as to save the world—perhaps—as well as Russia, from disaster.

On Poland, then, the real responsibility fell. M. Beck had done everything to provoke general irritation; and his diplomatic acts had been deliberately of a negative significance. His rigidity, his emphasis, and above all his pride, had led him with culpable obstinacy to play Germany's game. Nevertheless, behind this unpleasant self-sufficiency there was a deeper feeling: almost an anguish, which reflected the mind of the Polish people in face of the darkest possibilities. The fear of Germany, and the mistrust of Russia, confronted Colonel Beck with an alternative determined by the tragic and dangerous forces which might decide the fate of Poland. This recalled the eastern story which tells of a servant, who, fearing death, escapes from his master's house in the country and hides in the city. Death, meeting the master, says that she is hastening to the city to claim the servant. Colonel Beck might try his best, with moves that he thought subtle, to thwart Hitler's intentions, but war loomed over him and would ultimately overwhelm him.

Poland's "fault" can only be assessed when considered in connection with the total framework of the relations as they existed at this period between the west and the Soviet east. Situated on the line of demarcation between two worlds fundamentally alien to each other, Poland had learned by sad experience how difficult it is to bring them together. Was Poland mistaken regarding the misunderstanding that separated the west and Russia? On this very misunderstanding Hitler framed his policy. He insinuated himself between disunited peoples, who were still equally desirous of avoiding the misfortune of conflict, and he forced a war, which ended by encompassing them all.[1]

As to Rumania, it was not involved in the last phase of the drama. The western powers had not informed it of the final negotiations. The question put by Marshal Voroshilov was not communicated to it. The Rumanian Government was not aware of any requests, and it was not called on to make any decision. Did London and Paris think—as a result of my conversations in those two capitals—that they could count

1. Cf. Appendix II, p. 226.

on an affirmative reply from Rumania at the decisive moment? However that might have been, *no responsibility rested on Rumania for the failure of the negotiations.*

No one in Europe could be deceived as to the meaning of the Moscow treaty. The great preventive coalition was dead. Thereafter the smaller associations were bound to disappear. The policy of the Balkan Entente and of Turkey was paralyzed. Eastern Europe was separated from the west.

Hitler's war began. Out of the vast cataclysm into which countless peoples were to be plunged emerged two men who were to challenge fate for the dirction of affairs.

One was the winner of the diplomatic battle. Hitler had been uniformly successful. He had separated and divided the world, to reduce it to his mercy. "In one way or another," according to his formula, everything had given way to him. Hitler chose the war he wanted, and as he wanted it. He thought to limit in advance the number of his enemies. He would crush Poland first. His disdain for men and nations was so great that he was sure of the immobility of the western powers. In his speech of September 1, 1939, proclaiming the aggression he minimized the problem: "Here are our aims. I am determined first to solve the question of Danzig; second, to liquidate the question of the Corridor; third, to take the measures necessary to effect such a change in the relations between Germany and Poland as will guarantee a peaceful life in common. I want to free the German frontiers from the element of insecurity and the atmosphere of a situation of unending civil war. I want the same peace to reign on our eastern frontiers as on our other frontiers."

It is known now that Hitler could not arrange the war as he had arranged the bad peace. From the beginning, war broke the bounds he had laid down: and because in making war on Poland he was making war on the world, the whole world was to make war on him.

The other was Winston Churchill. It was to the noise of

the first British reverses and during the military collapse of France that Mr. Churchill became Prime Minister. Twice he had seen the collapse of the whole structure of security which he had worked so hard to create. One by one the states on which he had counted had fallen away from the western powers. Russia had vanished into the mists of the Moscow agreement; and these same mists shrouded the border countries. No longer could Mr. Churchill find a friendly Europe to the east. The first battles completed the disintegration of Europe. Even the allies of Britain were torn from it by force. Great Britain seemed doomed to isolation and defeat. Mr. Churchill, who had spent so much energy in trying to unite the whole world against war was to have to fight alone. But he did not lose faith. This fierce defender of collective security found words of superlative nobility in which to exalt his country as it stood alone:

"We have become the sole champions now in arms to defend the world cause. We shall do our best to be worthy of this high honor. We shall defend our Island home, and with the British Empire we shall fight on unconquerable until the curse of Hitler is lifted from the brows of mankind. We are sure that in the end all will come right." [1]

War succeeded where diplomacy had failed. It isolated the conqueror, and gave reality to Winston Churchill's thought, by compelling the nations to unite for victory.

But this unity between Allies, the outcome of necessity, not of agreement, calls for a consecration more precisely defined. Agreement cannot be put off. Negotiations interrupted by Hitler begin again now that he is gone; and it is on their happy conclusion that the sense and the value of the common victory depends.

The vanquished have surrendered unconditionally. To make peace possible, the victors must agree between themselves on the conditions.

1. Broadcast, June 17, 1940.

APPENDICES

I

The Russo-German Negotiations

IN coming to a final judgment on the events of the summer
of 1939, it is not enough to know the tenor of the negotiations between the French, the British, and the Russians. It
is equally necessary to know how the conversations between
the Moscow and the Berlin governments began. The official
texts are silent on the point, and there is no available source
of exact information. It is permissible to suppose that Hitler's
silence regarding the U.S.S.R. in his speech of April 28, 1939,
had a secret significance. Facing the failure of his western
policy, the Führer already contemplated an about-face in
his eastern policy. Such a change (which Hitler's "intimates"
had long predicted) would obviously find support among
the German General Staff, which had always tried to maintain contact with the Red Army, as well as in German economic circles, who wished to develop the commercial exchanges between the two empires.

But the question that arises is: When and how was the
collusion effected between the policy of the Reich and that
of the Soviet Union? According to a version current in the
entourage of Count Schulenburg, German Ambassador to
Moscow, the political rapprochement leading to the agreement of August 23, 1939, was the result of a move ordered
by Hitler, and not the outcome of sustained, secret talks.

According to the German version, things came about in
this way:

The day after Marshal Voroshilov had put to the military
delegations of the Allies the question of the right of passage
through Poland (a question which was to cause the last and

fatal crisis between the western powers and the Russians), a German economic commission signed a *commercial agreement* in Moscow. This German-Soviet agreement did not go beyond the margin of 200 million marks, established by the previous agreements of 1935 and 1937. Its conclusion at such a critical moment, nevertheless, had a special significance. In the course of the customary banquet given by M. Mikoyan, People's Commissar for Foreign Commerce, to the members of the German mission, the possibility was considered—in an unrestrained atmosphere—of coming to agreement "on still other questions." That same evening a long telegram was dispatched by the German Embassy to Berlin, and at once put before the Führer.

Hitler jumped at the chance. The military negotiations at Moscow hampered his schemes and caused him the greatest irritation. At last he had the means of putting an end to these negotiations, breaking British "encirclement" and making *his* war against Poland. Count Schulenburg was instructed to offer Russia a pact of friendship and nonaggression at once.

When the Ambassador brought this offer to the Kremlin, he received from M. Molotov a friendly but procrastinating reply. The Soviet Government did not reject the German proposition, which seemed worthy of attention; it could not, however, take it into consideration while negotiations with the Allies continued. It was necessary to wait for these negotiations to end.

But Hitler was not disposed to wait. He charged Count Schulenburg to follow up his move, and to warn M. Molotov that such an offer "was only made once"; it would be withdrawn were it not immediately accepted. Count Schulenburg was to add that the airplane of the Reich's Foreign Minister was ready to start. If the Soviet Government so wished, Herr von Ribbentrop as plenipotentiary could be in Moscow in a few hours.

The Führer's impetuosity overcame the Kremlin's hesitations. Tired of the interminable negotiations which failed quite to meet their desire for security, the Soviet leaders were pleased by the German dictator's speed of decision. Hitler's wish to send his Foreign Minister in person made a good impression. The Russians understood the advantage accruing to them from an agreement concluded in haste with a rushed partner. Hitler's offer contained a guarantee of security, ephemeral perhaps, but categorical and immediate.

What the U.S.S.R. wanted in those days, above everything else, was the solution of the problem of its security.

M. Molotov no longer tried to postpone his decision. He told Count Schulenburg that the German offer was under consideration. Herr von Ribbentrop could start.

This occurred on Sunday, August 20, 1939. The next day, August 21, was the date when the time allowed to the Allied military delegations to reply concerning Poland expired.

The Germans' first thought was meticulously to keep all knowledge of these steps from the western powers. Later, the Reich diplomats were pleased to recall that, on that famous Sunday, Count Schulenburg had invited the members of the foreign diplomatic corps to a "garden party."

A tennis tournament was held in the gardens of the German Embassy, and it is said that Mr. Strang, the head of the British mission, won the first prize.

On the following day, August 21, Hitler's private airplane, flying the flag of the Minister of Foreign Affairs, landed in Moscow. Herr von Ribbentrop, solemn and obviously moved, was at pains to shake every hand extended to him. He was conducted at once to the Kremlin. Forty-eight hours later the Moscow agreement was signed.

This event sent Hitler into a delirium of pleasure. Receiving the news at Berchtesgaden, as he was about to dine with a few of his devotees, the Führer waved the telegram above his head, exclaiming: "I hold victory in my hand—a hundred per cent victory!" That very night he made preparations to attack Poland.

As for Herr von Ribbentrop, that evening he paid the price of his success. Seated next to Stalin, at a table groaning with good things, he was obliged to drink glass after glass of vodka and Crimean wine, now to the prosperity of the Reich, now to that of Soviet Russia. In vain the Minister pleaded violent dyspepsia so that he might avoid acknowledging this mark of respect. Stalin, implacable, allowed neither grace nor respite. "Drink!" he said, "drink now! It is for your country!" How could such an injunction be denied? Ribbentrop drank and suffered. That was the first shadow cast on the Moscow agreement.

II [1]

THAT the partition of Europe must inevitably lead to war was shown in the following article (published in the *Journal de Genève*, July 25, 1945):

The Silence of Potsdam. Two Principles in Conflict

Before going to war, Hitler denied that he wished to destroy the British Empire. "During the whole of my political activity," he said in his speech of April 28, 1939, "I have not ceased to speak in favor of friendship and collaboration between Germany and England."

This idea of "collaboration," which, he asserted, was his most earnest desire, was one that Hitler had often made known to the British, in asking them: "Will you partition the world with us?" And the British had replied: "No."

This obstinate and implacable "No" roused Hitler to fury. In the course of an official visit to the Imperial Chancellery (at the end of April, 1939), I was a witness of one of those famous scenes when Hitler was carried away by his emotion. Underlying Hitler's imprecations against "the incomprehension and blind obduracy of the British leaders" there seemed to be a secret hope

1. See p. 10.

that this much-desired partition would ultimately come about in spite of everything.

Three days after this interview I was in London, and had the honor of being presented to Mr. Churchill at a dinner given by the Rumanian Legation.

When I told him what the German Chancellor had said to me about Great Britain, Mr. Churchill exclaimed:

"I know well enough that they are ready to come to an understanding with us! But at what a price? And against whom?"

Mr. Churchill referred me to a speech he had made twelve months earlier, on May 9, 1938:

"There is another foreign policy which you are urged to pursue. It is not to worry about all these countries of Central Europe, not to trouble yourself with preserving the Covenant of the League, to recognise that all that is foolish and vain and can never be restored, and to make a special pact of friendship with Nazi Germany. . . . But . . . I want to know what that pact is going to be, and at whose expense it is to be made. Undoubtedly our Government could make an agreement with Germany. All they have to do is . . . to give Herr Hitler a free hand to spread the Nazi system and dominance far and wide through Central Europe. That is the alternative foreign policy. It is one which, in my view, would be disgraceful and disastrous. In the first place it leads us straight to war. The Nazi regime, elated by this triumph, with every restraint removed, would proceed unchecked upon its path of ambition and aggression. We should be the helpless, silent, gagged, apparently consenting, spectators of the horrors which would spread through Central Europe."

Mr. Churchill repeated this argument to me. "What can we share with Germany?" he exclaimed. "The world? But the world is not ours. And if, in a mistaken moment, we were to cede to Hitler everything that does not belong to us, tomorrow we should be unable to protect what does belong to us against him. Herr Hitler is angry with us for believing what he wrote in his own book. Why should we not take him at his word, when it is the security and very existence of our empire that are in question?"

There was no possible compromise between the principles of partition and equilibrium.

These two principles were in such violent and irreducible opposition that war must inevitably follow. The country which Hitler needed to share the world equally with him simply did not exist—its only existence was in the imagination of the German Chancellor. Britain as it really was must inevitably oppose ambitions tending to overthrow European equilibrium and order, and thereby weaken the bases of the greatness, security, and very existence of the British people. The impossible partition of which Hitler dreamed could only acerbate his passions and drive him further along the road to catastrophe.

The war raged for six years. Europe and the world have been completely overturned. A guilty empire has crumbled. But the two contradictory principles still stand; and their unshaken antagonism, the cause of the disaster, today shadows the advent of peace.

Certainly this opposition is not so flagrant and its political character is less pronounced. The three great powers which now determine what sort of peace it is to be are unanimous in rejecting, in principle, the partitioning of the world into zones of influence. The Soviet Union, particularly, is severe in its condemnation of the ideas of partition. *L'Humanité*, inspired by Moscow's policy, said last November (when it was a question of forming a Western bloc): "Such a bloc would be only the first engagement of the gears of a terrific machinery entailing a third world war, far more frightful than this. The world would be divided into sealed zones, necessarily antagonistic. This cannot be, and will not be. The blocs will be killed, so that the peaceful union of the free and democratic peoples may abide."

The Communist newspaper expressed basically the European idea for which Britain had gone to war. But situations still exist which seem as though they will defeat the theories. The sealed zones exist. This should not be; but it is. And, so long as this holds, the peoples of the world will be neither democratic nor free, and their union will be only a dream.

This situation may be only a consequence of the war; nevertheless its continuation would be dangerous, for the principle of partition comes up again; it is gaining ground even in Britain. Some circles there dream of forming blocs, not with the idea of giving effect to a policy of justice, but in the hope of successfully countering both faits accomplis and a system that is making considerable headway, by a protective limit and effective equilibrium.

To us, nothing seems vainer than such a hope. Partition is war, whatever motive inspires it. Mr. Churchill said so in 1938. *L'Humanité* says it today. And these repeated statements are, and will remain, true; the division of the world into zones of influence rouses jealousies, stimulates ambitions, maintains antagonistic interests, and leads to conflict. Of this, the history of Europe provides constant proof.

It certainly is not easy to make peace. The great powers have different ideas of order; and this idea is everywhere subject to political and social influences. Each of these different conceptions naturally seeks to ensure the domination of as extensive an area as possible. It covers a territory which it links to itself. One is tempted in these circumstances to draw a line of demarcation between the different ideological spaces. But let us make no mistake: such a line, wrapped in mystery and silence, is not a peaceful frontier; it is a battle front.

Real peace demands great intellectual effort. There must be the courage to think through to the end and not to be checked by seemingly convenient compromises. Care must be taken to avoid drawing a curtain between two worlds content to remain strangers one to another; and common principles which can create a general political order must be discovered. In brief, the generous inclinations which the "Big Three" have openly announced must be translated into facts. That is why the silences of Potsdam are of burning interest to all those peoples who want to see the specter of war banished forever.

In Europe, especially, the people are anxious to know whether, at the meeting of the "Big Three," order will defeat partition as a solution. If Europe is still partitioned, it will be the lists wherein battle is constantly waged between antagonistic ideologies and great hostile forces. If, by the honest application of an all-embracing regulation, Europe in its entirety comes under the protection of the law, the old Continent will be the link, and a real factor of reconciliation, between those powers that now dominate the world.

Now, when decisions are being reached which will determine

the meaning and worth of the victory, it is well to recall the causes which provoked the conflict.

The world has fought a long war to kill the idea of partition. To make a good peace, it must be killed for the second time.

G. G.

III [1]

ON the subject of France's role in the work of re-establishing an order of law, the *Journal de Genève* published the following article on February 5, 1945:

Justice or Convenience

At the Congress of Vienna the Emperor Alexander once said to Talleyrand that he intended the affairs of Europe to be settled in such a way that "each would find it suitable to his convenience." "And each to his rights," replied the French plenipotentiary.

"Yes, surely," returned the Emperor. "But if you do not want each one to suit his convenience, what are you aiming at?"

"I put rights first, and convenience afterward," replied Talleyrand.

In putting the principle of rights before every other consideration, the great French diplomat had a double object. He thought that this was the best—and the simplest—way of solving the problems that disturbed Europe after the Napoleonic Wars. It was in this sense that he said to Castlereagh (who was trying to convince him that certain affairs concerning the Court of France could be arranged to his satisfaction): "It is not now a question of this or that particular object, but of law, which should regulate them all. Once the thread is snapped, how shall we pick it up again? We are answerable for the wishes of Europe. What shall we have done for it, if we have not given honor to those maxims whose neglect has caused so many evils? The present

1. See p. 155.

epoch is such as happens only once in hundreds of years. No finer occasion could be offered to us. Why not adopt a position in keeping with it?"

"The fact is," said Castlereagh, "that there are difficulties of which you do not know."

"No, I do not know of them," exclaimed Talleyrand, in the tone of a man who was not interested to know.

But the representative of France had still another purpose when he praised the virtue of law at a time when, as Benjamin Constant said, "men, having been the playthings of folly, had conceived an enthusiasm for good sense and justice."

He wished to serve his country and to restore France—which certain powers wanted to keep out of the council chamber—to the front rank of the great powers. France had been vanquished, occupied and disarmed. It was not strong enough to force the doors of the meetings of the great powers. The victors wanted to be undisturbed, to make the final decisions among themselves. True, they did not scorn the right in whose name they had waged a long and difficult war; and their avowed desire was to end forever the arbitrary regime which had troubled Europe for so many years. But scarcely any arbitrary regime falls without bequeathing some of its passion to the power that defeats it, however moved that power may be by the highest intentions. Conquerors are rare who can so rise above victory that at the decisive hour they do not dream of that convenience to which Alexander I alluded. To speak of the rule of law at this precise moment—not in vague formulas but with an exact sense of the value of terms and their importance—to dare to define the general interest, and put the idea of Europe above particular convenience; was that not to discharge an indispensable mission whose contribution to the structure of peace no exclusive interest could either thwart or circumvent?

Talleyrand understood that France could, and should, fulfill this mission. He strove to impress upon the council of the victors both the principle of law and an entire system of political philosophy, and he went so far as to demand that it should be expressly stated that the Congress was to hold its sessions in conformity with the principles of international law. This did not go through without vociferous opposition, the record of which was left to posterity in the Unpublished Correspondence of the French diplomat:

"Herr von Hardenberg, rising to his feet, his fists on the table, almost threateningly stammered the words, 'No, sir! Public law? That is useless. Why say that we shall act according to public law? That goes without saying.'" Talleyrand explained that, if it went without saying, it would go still better if it were said. Herr von Humboldt cried out: "What has public law to do here?" To which Talleyrand replied: "It brought you here."

International law forced itself on the Congress in the end, as France did also. Due in great part to France's predominant influence—to its influence and its method—the Treaty of Vienna remained, despite its imperfections, the charter of Europe for almost a century.

That status of a great power which France had thus regained compelled it thereafter to make constant, often extremely arduous, efforts to maintain its position and defend its interests. But never in all the decisive circumstances did it fail to play the part it had taken to itself. It fought for an order based on law with unswerving disinterest and with generous ardor. It disseminated the ideas of justice that were to liberate and unite the nations. The constant support it gave to weaker peoples was based on no selfish calculation; its aid was given spontaneously—without previous engagements or written conventions—because, in its conception of order and civilization, justice had a value of its own, and because its character impelled France ceaselessly to affirm the idea of human solidarity.

So France gained not only the affection of the peoples but, what is more, their confidence. Everywhere, and especially in eastern Europe, in Latin America, and in the countries of the Orient, its voice was heard, its counsel followed, and its judgment accepted. The greatness of its power was determined by the diffusion of its genius even more than by the extent of its power. Thus the place it occupied in the human community was secure, even at the height of its misfortune. France was as universal in its distress as it had been in its glory.

One example, among many others, made me realize the significance of the fall of France.

It was at Moscow, in May, 1941. The German Embassy had been instructed to give a private showing of the famous film, "Victory in the West." Among the distinguished guests were certain high officials of the Soviet and members of the different foreign missions of all the countries not at war with the Reich. There were many ambassadors and ministers, soldiers and economists, Europeans and Asiatics. The film was remarkable in many ways. It gave an impressive picture of the Blitzkrieg as conceived and executed by the German General Staff. The shattering advance of the German armies, the exploits of the artillery and the pioneers, the attacks by Stukas, and the wave of tanks surging across the smoking ruins and the encumbered highways of France on the way to Paris could all be followed. . . .

It should have been a great success. It was a disaster. I have never felt a heavier, more agonized or painful silence than that which enveloped the audience while "Victory in the West" was being shown. From the moment the lights were dimmed, neutrals no longer existed in the room. A latent hostility to the invaders spread from row to row, from the seats of the representatives of the Danubian and Balkan countries to those of the Turks, the Persians, and the Afghans. The disaster that struck France awoke in each of them anxiety for his own physical and moral security. Each one of them felt that a blow had been dealt against his heritage, his mind, his heart, his rights. The icy, reproving silence continued after the end of the show. It expressed the fundamental thoughts of diplomats who were used to hiding their feelings but who could not help regarding the triumph of the conqueror, at the peak of his power, as an accidental, a "local" phenomenon, whereas the defeat of France appeared to them as a general and unbounded misfortune. . . .

These lines are not written to plead a cause already won. If the problem of France's participation in the work of the councils of the great powers arises afresh, it is certainly only to lead to a more perfect accord regarding the meaning of peace and the importance of the mission which now falls to France. For whatever be the merit of the powers whose heroic resistance, whose efforts and sacrifices have contributed most of all to the common success—a merit which no one would wish to dispute—it would be difficult today to refuse France, the ally, what was not refused it, for the salvation of Europe, after its defeat in 1814.

If peace is to be just, in accordance with admitted facts and principles which cannot suddenly be invented, if it is to be accepted with confidence by the many peoples who should benefit by it; if Europe is again to find the values necessary to its order and its concord, it is not only equitable but supremely advantageous to let France speak. France will do its best, as its leader said—"to cause to flourish again among the peoples of the earth that human and universal influence that has always marked the character of France."

So, it is not to be doubted, France will find the proper arguments, for herself and for others, to put justice before convenience in the supreme councils.

G. G.

IV [1]

The Way of Peace

MR. CHURCHILL was the last to forget the cause he had so eloquently defended during the years 1938 and 1939. Speaking over the wireless on May 13, 1945—five days after the collapse of the Hitlerian Reich—the British Prime Minister declared:

". . . I wish I, could tell you to-night that all our toils and troubles were over. Then indeed I could end my five years' service happily, and if you thought that you had had enough of me and that I ought to be put out to grass, I tell you I would take it with the best of grace. But, on the contrary, I must warn you, as I did when I began this five years' task—and no one knew then that it would last so long—that there is still a lot to do, and that you must be prepared for further efforts of mind and body and further sacrifices to great causes if you are not to fall back into the rut of inertia, the confusion of aim, and the craven fear of being great.

1. See p. 99.

You must not weaken in any way in your alert and vigilant frame of mind. . . .

"On the continent of Europe we have yet to make sure that the simple and honourable purposes for which we entered the war are not brushed aside or overlooked in the months following our success, and that the words 'freedom,' 'democracy,' and 'liberation' are not distorted from their true meaning as we have understood them. There would be little use in punishing the Hitlerites for their crimes if law and justice did not rule, and if totalitarian or police governments were to take the place of the German invaders. We seek nothing for ourselves. But we must make sure that those causes which we fought for find recognition at the peace table in facts as well as words, and above all we must labour that the world organization which the United Nations are creating at San Francisco does not become an idle name, does not become a shield for the strong and a mockery for the weak. . . ."

These declarations indicate that the struggle for peace may very likely be as arduous, and perhaps as long, as were the war effort and the struggle for victory. The question will be not only to come to agreement on principles but still more to come to agreement on the value and the meaning of words. Above all, it will be a question of setting against totalitarian, police methods, which always show a tendency to hegemony and universal domination, the policy of the free countries which seeks to create a higher authority in the domain of international order on a foundation of law.

Mr. Churchill was to return to these ideas to give them precision, and to denounce once more the dangers which menaced the liberty of the world. Having become the Leader of the Opposition, he proceeded to ask the British Government (in his speech of August 16, 1945, in the House of Commons) to make its attitude clear "in these affairs of the Balkans and of Eastern Europe." It was necessary, he said, always to strike the note of freedom. The countries of

Europe were too close to one another for an iniquity which struck one of them not to rebound against all the others. Above all, it was necessary to create, at the earliest possible opportunity, "international bodies of supreme authority [which] may give peace on earth and decree justice among men," so that men might no longer "wish or dare to fall upon each other." Of all the "simple," "honourable" aims which the British people had to pursue, this was the supreme goal which Mr. Churchill assigned to his country and the world.

INDEX